HOW TO WIN NO-LIMIT HOLD'EM TOURNAMENTS

HOW TO WIN
NO-LIMIT
HOLD'EM
TOURNAMENTS

Make Millions of Dollars at the
World's Most Exciting Poker Game

TOM McEVOY & DON VINES

Cardoza Publishing is the foremost gaming publisher in the world, with a library of over 175 up-to-date and easy-to-read books and strategies. These authoritative works are written by the top experts in their fields and, with more than 8,500,000 books in print, represent the best-selling and most popular gaming books anywhere.

FIRST CARDOZA EDITION

Front cover image ©www.pokerimages.com/Bill Burlington

Library of Congress Catalog Card No: 2004111649
ISBN: 1-58042-160-1

Visit www.cardozapub.com
or write us for a full list of books and computer strategies.

CARDOZA PUBLISHING
P.O. Box 1500, Cooper Station, New York, NY 10276
Phone (800)577-WINS
email: cardozapub@aol.com
www.cardozapub.com

About the Authors

Tom McEvoy, the 1983 World Champion of Poker, has won four World Series titles. He is the author of the acclaimed *Championship Tournament Poker*, "one of the most important poker books of all time" according to Gamblers Book Club in Las Vegas. He is also the co-author of eleven other titles, including: *Championship No-Limit & Pot-Limit Hold'em, Championship Stud, Championship Omaha, Championship Satellite Strategy, The Championship Table, Beat Texas Hold'Em, No-Limit Texas Hold'Em,* and *Championship Hold'em Tournament Hands.* In 2005, McEvoy scored a major triumph when he won Professional Poker Tour making him the only player in the world to win both a PPT and WSOP title.

Don Vines is a professional tournament poker player specializing in no-limit hold'em medium buy-in events. He has won more than 40 championship titles including the World Poker Open and the Orleans Open. He has a gold bracelet as the best limit hold'em tournament player at the Peppermill in Reno in 2002 and has cashed in no-limit tournaments at the World Series of Poker. He can be found playing with the greatest players in the game in big tournaments and has faced off against more than a dozen World Champions. Vines is a columnist on no-limit tournament hold'em for *Avery Cardoza's Player* magazine.

Table of Contents

1. The Basics of Playing No-Limit Hold'Em   19

INTRODUCTION   19
    The Sequence of Play
    Different Forms of Texas Hold'Em

THE BASICS   24
    The Deal
    Posting the Blinds
    The Types of Hands to Play
    The Four Betting Rounds
    Betting Structure
    How Much Should You Bet in No-Limit Hold'Em?
    Reading the Boardcards
    The Goal
    The Set-Up of a No-Limit Hold'Em Game

2: Key Concepts in No-Limit Texas Hold'Em   33

INTRODUCTION
YOUR POSITION AFFECTS WHICH HANDS YOU CAN
–PLAY PROFITABLY   34

GOOD STARTING HANDS ARE THE KEYS TO THE KINGDOM   38
Starting Hands in Late Position
Starting Hands in Middle Position

THE TEXTURE OF THE FLOP AFFECTS HOW YOU PLAY YOUR HAND   42
YOU CAN WIN WITHOUT THE BEST HAND   45
BLUFFING IS A POWERFUL TOOL IN BIG-BET POKER   47
KNOWING HOW YOUR OPPONENTS PLAY IS THE MASTER
–KEY TO SUCCESS   48
PATIENCE IS A VIRTUE   50

3: The Basics of Tournament Play   55

INTRODUCTION   55
THE STRUCTURE OF TOURNAMENTS   56
The Buy-In
Your Starting Table and Starting Stack
A Round or Level of Play
Freezeout Tournaments
Rebuy Tournaments
    The Add-On
Things to Find Out Before You Enter a Tournament
The Tournament Buy-In vs. Your Expectations

THE TOURNAMENT PAYOUT   63
WHAT MAKES A TOURNAMENT GOOD?   65

4: Key Concepts in Tournament Poker   71

SKILL AND LUCK   71
WHEN YOU LOSE YOUR STACK, YOU CAN'T COME BACK   72
TOURNAMENT CHIPS ARE LIKE MONOPOLY MONEY   74
AGGRESSIVE AL BEATS MEEK MARVIN IN NO LIMIT HOLD'EM   75
THE TOURNAMENT STRUCTURE IS IMPORTANT TO YOUR SUCCESS   76
THE CLOCK: YOUR ENEMY OR YOUR FRIEND   78

THE CURVE: YOUR ALLY   79
KEY HANDS OFTEN TURN THE TIDE   80
TOURNAMENTS USUALLY PROGRESS IN FIVE STAGES   82
GOOD DECISIONS ARE THE DIFFERENCE   83

5: How to Win No-Limit Hold'em Tournaments   87

INTRODUCTION   87
GET TO KNOW YOUR OPPONENTS   88
    Learn How Your Opponents Play the Blinds
PLAY GOOD STARTING HANDS IN POSITION   95
    Superior Position, Outstanding Results

Early Position
    Starting Hands
    Trouble Hands
Middle Position
    Starting Hands
Late Position
    Starting Hands

DISCIPLINE PAYS DIVIDENDS   103
BET THE RIGHT AMOUNT   105
    Factoring in Your Opponents' Betting Patterns
    Making a Double Bet
    Under-Betting the Pot
    Betting into a Dry Pot

BUILD YOUR STACK   113
    Weathering a Drought of Cards

KEEP AN EYE ON THE TOURNAMENT CLOCK   117
PLAY A BIG STACK WISELY   119
    Beware Forcing An Opponent to Play a Hand
    A Weapon of Mass Destruction

PLAY A MEDIUM STACK WITH DISCRETION   124

PLAY A SHORT STACK CAREFULLY 126
PLAY AGGRESSIVE POKER 128
   Buying Pots That Are Up for Sale
   Watch Out for Early Limpers

BLUFF WHEN THE TIME IS RIGHT 131
   When Not to Bluff
   When to Bluff
   Four Types of Bluffs
      The Semi-Bluff
      The Stone Bluff
      The Positional Bluff
      The Situational Bluff

MIX UP YOUR PLAYING STYLE 140
   The Value of Deception
   Changing Gears

USE SURVIVAL TACTICS TO STAY IN THE CHASE 144
LET THE ODDS HELP YOU MAKE TRICKY DECISIONS 145
TRUST YOUR INSTINCTS 147
Online Instincts

KEEP FIT PHYSICALLY AND MENTALLY 149

6: The Five Stages of Tournaments 151

INTRODUCTION 151
STAGE ONE: THE EARLY STAGE 152
   Stage One Starting Hands

STAGE TWO: THE MIDDLE STAGE 155
STAGE THREE: THE LATE STAGE 157
STAGE FOUR: IN THE MONEY! 158
   The Second Table

STAGE FIVE: THE FINAL TABLE   161
Heads-Up for the Championship

7: Winning Strategies for Low-Stakes Events   165

INTRODUCTION   165
HOW TO WIN SMALL BUY-IN TOURNAMENTS   168
How Much Should You Invest in a Rebuy Event?
Playing after the Rebuy Period Is Over
Playing the Later Rounds
Playing the Final Table

8: Winning Strategies for Medium- and High-Stakes Tournaments   179

INTRODUCTION   179
Building Your Bankroll
What If You Lose?
Moving Up Another Notch
Taking a Step Backward When You Need To
Pros vs. Novices

TOP TIPS FOR WINNING HIGHER-STAKES TOURNAMENTS   189
The Player Mix Is Different in the Big Ones
Playing against Celebrities
Playing against Well-Off Recreational Players
Playing against Seasoned Professionals
Playing against Satellite Players
Play Straightforward Poker Early in the Tournament
Play a Solid-Aggressive Game
Take Your Time and Play Your Game
Adjust Your Play When the Antes Kick In
Manage Your Stack Size With Proven Strategies
You Need Less Strength In Short-Handed Play

Play a Strategically Sound Game at the Final Table
Three- and Four-Handed Play
Heads-Up Play
Keep the Big Picture in Mind

9: The No-Limit Hold'em Playbook   213

INTRODUCTION   213
THE POWER PLAY   213
  A Power Play with Pocket Aces
  A Power Play with Pocket Kings
  When and How to Use the Power Play

THE CHECK-RAISE   219
  Using the Check-Raise as a Semi-Bluff
  Check-Raising against Aggressive Players behind You
  Check-Raising with A-A and K-K
  Check-Raising with A-10 Suited

THE BLUFF   225
  "The Best Bluff That Didn't Work"

THE INTUITIVE PLAY   228
  An Example of an Intuitive Play

THE SLOW PLAY   229
  Slow-Playing from the Blind
  Slow-Playing vs. Check-Raising
  Slow-Playing the Nuts from the Big Blind
  Slow-Playing the Nuts from Late Position

THE DECEPTIVE PLAY   234
THE FINESSE PLAY   235
  Second-Hand Low

THE BUTTON PLAY   237
THE POWERLESS PLAY YOU DON'T WANT TO MAKE!   239

10: Tournament Hands in Action By Don Vines   247

INTRODUCTION	247
POT-COMMITTED AT THE BELLAGIO	247
FEAR FREEZES A WEAK ACE	251
WRONG PLAY – RIGHT RESULT	252
PLAYING A DRAWING HAND OUT OF POSITION	254
POCKET QUEENS PUT MONEY IN MY POCKET	256
PLAYING A SMALL HAND IN THE SMALL BLIND	
–LEADS TO BIG TROUBLE	258

11: Adjusting Your Tournament Strategy   263

INTRODUCTION   263

ADJUSTING BASED UPON THE LENGTH OF THE ROUNDS   264
Fast-Action Tournaments (Rounds of Twenty Minutes)
Medium-Action Tournaments
– (Rounds of Thirty to Forty-Five Minutes)
Slow-Action Tournaments (Rounds of 60 to 90 Minutes or More)

ADJUSTING BASED UPON THE SIZE OF THE FIELD   274
Small-Field Tournaments (Fewer than One Hundred Entries)
Big-Field Tournaments (Four Hundred to Six Hundred Entrants)
Huge-Field Tournament (One Thousand or More Players)

MAKING A DEAL AT THE FINAL TABLE   280

12: Tips for Winning Online Tournaments   287

INTRODUCTION   287

TOM'S TIPS FOR WINNING ONLINE TOURNAMENTS   290
Schedule Your Tournament Play
Determine the Size of Tournament Field You Want to Play
Play Small Buy-in Tournaments First
Avoid Playing Too Loose in Online Tournaments

Concentrate on Playing Strong Starting Hands in Position
Adjust to the Speed of the Game
Take Notes While You're Playing
Look for Online Tells

13: Fatal Flaws and How to Fix Them   299

INTRODUCTION   299
BLUFFING AT THE WRONG TIME   300
BETTING THE WRONG AMOUNT   301
Betting More Than Your Opponents Will Call
Betting Too Little

PLAYING TOO MANY HANDS   305
Pocket Pairs and Suited Connectors
Early Rounds vs. Late Rounds

NOT PLAYING ENOUGH HANDS   307
Don't Let Fear Freeze Your Play
Don't Get Caught Up in a Betting Frenzy

PLAYING MARGINAL HANDS OUT OF POSITION   312
INCORRECTLY EVALUATING YOUR OPPONENTS   314
MISREADING OPPONENTS   316
PLAYING TOO AGGRESSIVELY   317
RAISING WHEN YOU SHOULDN'T   318
NOT RAISING WHEN YOU SHOULD   320
TRYING TO OUTFOX THE FOX   322
ACTING ON REFLEX RATHER THAN REFLECTION   323

14: Managing Your Tournament Bankroll   327

INTRODUCTION   327
BANKROLLING SMALL BUY-IN EVENTS   328
BANKROLLING MEDIUM BUY-IN EVENTS   330

BANKROLLING BIG BUY-IN TOURNAMENTS   **332**
Taking Advantage of Satellites
Scheduling

15: Successful Playing Styles   341

INTRODUCTION   **341**
AGGRESSIVE STYLE OF PLAY   **342**
INITIALLY AGGRESSIVE STYLE OF PLAY   **344**
SUPER-AGGRESSIVE STYLE OF PLAY   **344**
SOLID-AGGRESSIVE STYLE OF PLAY   **346**
PROGRESSIVELY AGGRESSIVE STYLE OF PLAY   **348**
UNPREDICTABLE STYLE OF PLAY   **350**
CONSERVATIVE STYLE OF PLAY   **352**
CHARACTERISTICS OF GREAT NO LIMIT HOLD'EM PLAYERS   **353**
Hand Reading Ability
Knowledge of Big-Bet Poker Mathematics
A Feel for Betting
Discipline
Ability to Adjust and Maneuver
Constant Self-Evaluation
Class

Introduction

Anybody can plunk down a wad of cash and enter a no-limit Texas hold'em tournament. But if you want to win big money—and do it consistently—in poker's most exciting game, you need to do more than pony up an entry fee. It takes skill, an understanding of tournament poker and your opponents, a bit of luck at the right time, and a whole lot of guts.

While no book can give you luck or guts, in *How to Win No-Limit Texas Hold'em Tournaments*, we'll provide you all the information, tips, and tools you need to become a no-limit hold'em tournament champion. The strategies and insider knowledge you'll find in these pages have helped us win countless trophies and millions of dollars. Now it's your turn!

From honing your skills in low buy-in tournaments to butting heads with the stars of poker in the world's foremost events, this book will guide you step-by-step to the winner's circle. Every tournament is unique, and to win, you've got to understand a lot more than the rules of hold'em. You need to know how the tournament structure affects your strategy, what are the major differences between no-limit tournaments and cash games, how the tournament's payout structure influences your decision of whether or not to enter, when and if to make rebuys and add-ons, how to play against small, medium, and large fields of opponents—and that's just the beginning!

These concepts and more can be found in here, including the No-Limit Hold'em Playbook, an exclusive look at special plays the pros use to win big tournaments. To help you sharpen your skills, we've provided practice hands taken from real tournaments. And if you've got your sights set on internet tournaments, you'll find tons of web-specific advice in the Winning Online Tournaments section. Finally, we've created a unique and valuable troubleshooting section entitled Fatal Flaws and How to Fix 'Em to help you identify and eliminate the weakness in your game.

This is the most complete and up-to-date guide to winning no-limit hold'em tournaments in today's marketplace. Armed with the knowledge and strategies in the following pages, you'll be able to climb to climb the ladder of success in no-limit hold'em tournaments—all the way to the very top, where we hope to see you one day soon!

The Basics of Playing
No-Limit Hold'em

INTRODUCTION

Before you read this chapter, take this quiz:

1. Do you play no-limit Texas hold'em in a home game, casino or online cardroom?
2. Have you ever played a no-limit hold'em tournament in a casino or on the Internet?
3. Have you watched a lot of no-limit hold'em tournaments on television?

If you answered yes to any of these questions, you've passed the quiz—and now you can pass over this chapter. You don't need to read it because you already know the mechanics of the game.

But if you've never played poker's most exciting game, this chapter is for you. It lays out the mechanics of the game, starting with the deal and ending at the river. We have adapted this explanation of how to play the game from *Beat Texas Hold'em*, a nifty little primer written by Tom McEvoy and Shane Smith especially for people who have never experienced the thrill of victory and the agony of defeat playing big-bet no-limit hold'em.

No poker game has captured the imagination of the public like Texas hold'em—just ask the millions of viewers who watch the World Series of Poker, the World Poker Tour, or Celebrity Poker no-limit hold'em tournaments on television every week. But as thrilling as it is to watch players push mountains of chips into the center of the table with megabucks at stake, it's even more exciting when you're in the middle of the action yourself. Just stack up some chips, grab a deck of cards, shuffle up, and deal! It's time to learn how to play poker's hottest game.

The Sequence of Play

Texas hold'em is a form of high poker in which the player with the highest-ranking five-card combination at the end of the deal wins the money that everyone has wagered, known as the **pot**. Each player is dealt two personal cards facedown—these are known as his **hole cards**—which will be combined with five community cards to make each player's final five-card hand. The community cards, know collectively as the **board**, are dealt face up in the middle of the table.

The best hand in high poker is a royal flush, A-K-Q-J-10 in the same suit. The second-best hand is a straight flush, any five cards of the same suit in sequence. Next are four of a kind (four cards of the same rank), a full house (three cards of the same rank plus two cards of a second rank), a flush (any five cards in the same suit), a straight (any five cards in sequence), three of a kind, two pair, and one pair. In rare cases when nobody has a pair, the player with the highest card in his hand wins the pot.

To start a round of betting, the dealer gives you and every other player in the game two hole cards facedown When it's your turn to act, you can do one of three things: fold, call, or raise. If you don't like your hole cards, you can **fold** your hand by sliding the cards facedown to the dealer. Or you can **call** by matching the size of the required bet and placing that exact amount of chips in front of you. If you really like your hand, you can **raise** by announcing, "I raise!" and increasing the size of the minimum bet at least twofold.

After every player has acted, the dealer places the first three community cards, called the **flop**, faceup in the center of the table. Every player who didn't fold before the flop can check, fold, call, or raise.

When you **check**, you are staying active without making a bet, and passing play on to the next active player. However, once any player has made a bet, all opponents must match that amount or they must fold. Checking is no longer a viable option for that betting round.

Then the dealer puts a fourth community card, known as the **turn**, in the middle of the table, followed by another round of betting. Finally, the dealer turns up the fifth and final community card, known as the **river**, followed by one last round of betting. If at any point, all but one player folds, the remaining player wins the pot. But if two or more players remain in the pot after all the betting is completed, they turn over their hole cards to see who has the best hand. This is known as the **showdown**.

Different Forms of Texas Hold'em

Hold'em is played with three different betting structures. If you are playing **limit hold'em**, the amount of money you can bet at any one time cannot exceed a predetermined amount. But if you are playing **no-limit hold'em**, your bet is limited only by the amount of money you have in front of you—and you can bet it all at one time if you want to. This is known as going **all-in**.

Limit hold'em and no-limit hold'em are the two most popular versions of the game, but there is a third, **pot-limit hold'em**. Although it has a closer resemblance to no-limit than to limit hold'em, pot-limit is a very different game overall. The biggest difference is that you can't usually put an opponent all-in before the flop like you can in no-limit.

You can never bet any more than the current size of the pot, so the pot has to be built more slowly.

Texas hold'em also is played in two different formats: **tournament games** and **cash games** (when played at the site of an ongoing tournament, cash games are known as **side games**). If you are playing in a cash game and lose all your money, you can buy more chips to stay in action. But if you lose all your money in a tournament, you cannot buy any more chips—you're done for the day. The focus of this book is to teach you how to play and win the no-limit version of hold'em, specifically how to win no-limit hold'em tournaments.

According to an old poker adage, Texas hold'em takes just a few hours to learn and a lifetime to master. That might have been true in the early days of poker, when you had to learn the game strictly by the seat of your pants. But these days, modern instructional poker books, DVDs, videotapes, and televised programs have sped up the learning process.

Nowadays even novice players with a minimum of knowledge and some poker savvy are winning money at no-limit hold'em in casinos and on the internet. Now let's take a closer look at the basics of no-limit hold'em, the game of choice for millions of players worldwide. After all, you can't win it if you're not in it!

THE BASICS

The Deal

Each player is dealt two cards facedown, beginning with the player sitting to the left of the **button**, which is a small disc that indicates the dealer position. In a casino, the dealer uses the button so that he can keep track of who the dealer would be if players dealt the cards themselves, like they used to do in the old days of casino poker and still do in home games. At the start of every new deal, the casino dealer moves the button one seat to the left. When the button has traveled all the way around the table, one round of play has been completed.

Posting the Blinds

The person seated immediately to the left of the button must place in front of him a bet of predetermined size before the deal. The bet and the player who posts it are known as the **small blind**. The person seated to the immediate left of the small blind is called the **big blind**. Like the small blind, this player must post a bet before the deal. The big blind is normally double the amount of the small blind.

The purpose of posting blind bets is to stimulate action. The blinds get the pot started so that there will be some money in the pot to compete for. Sometimes the blinds force people to play hands that they might not have played if they didn't have money committed to the pot.

In cash games, the amount of money that you must post when it's your turn to be the big blind or the small blind remains the same throughout the game. In tournaments, the sizes of the blinds increase at set intervals. When the blinds increase, the tournament has moved to a new level. In some tournaments, levels can change every 20 minutes, while in others, they can last for one hour or more. But one thing's for sure: If you never play a hand, you will eventually go broke just from posting the blinds.

The Types of Hands to Play

In no-limit hold'em, big pairs and high cards rule the roost. Two aces, two kings, two queens, two jacks, and A-K are premium hands. You would like to have a pair in your hand and then see one of your rank come on the flop. You can play other types of hands in certain circumstances, but these premium hands are the best ones to play. In limit hold'em, you can play more types of hands than you can in no-limit hold'em. For example, suited connecting cards, such as Q♠-J♠ and 10♦-9♦, are more valuable hands in limit hold'em games than they are in no-limit hold'em games.

The Four Betting Rounds

Betting begins after all players have been dealt their two hole cards. The player sitting immediately to the left of the big blind must act first, and the action continues clockwise with everyone acting in turn. The big blind is the last player to act before the flop. When he has completed his action, the first round of betting is over—unless someone has raised the pot, in which case the round continues until all players have either called or folded.

Then the dealer puts the flop faceup in the center of the table and the second round of betting begins. This time, the first active player to the left of the button must act first. Then each player who did not fold before the flop can fold, check, bet, call a bet, raise, or reraise when it is his turn to act.

After the betting on the flop is finished, the dealer places a fourth community card faceup in the center of the table, followed by another round of betting. Then he deals the final community card faceup in the center and the final round of betting takes place.

Betting Structure

In no-limit hold'em, you can bet your entire stack of chips in any round, by announcing, "I'm going all in!" and pushing all your chips into the center of the table. For example, suppose the size of the small blind is $1,000 and the big blind is $2,000 at the championship table of a World

Series of Poker tournament. The dealer has just dealt two cards to each player. He has not dealt any community cards yet. The player sitting to the immediate left of the big blind is the first person to act. He has to match the size of the big blind—call—if he wants to play his cards. In this example, $2,000 is the least that he can bet in order to play the hand.

If he wants to raise, he must bet at least double the amount of the big blind, or $4,000. He also can raise any amount up to the number of chips he has in his stack. For example, if he has $80,000 in front of him, he can raise, say, to $30,000 or bet his entire $80,000 by announcing, "All-in."

If this happens, a player who does not have enough chips to call the minimum bet can still play the hand by putting in all the chips he has left in his stack. For instance, if a player only has $3,000 in chips, he can call with all his chips by announcing that he is all-in. At the end of the fourth betting round, the player with the best hand wins all the chips in the middle of the table—unless the player with the smaller stack wins. If that happens, he is only entitled to an amount that is equal to his original wager. Therefore the player with the larger stack will get a refund of $77,000 in chips because the smaller stacked opponent could only call $3,000 of the original wager.

Here's the amazing part of playing no-limit hold'em—you can win more than double or triple the amount of chips you started the hand with, or you can lose all your money on a single bet. It takes a different breed of cat to be willing to take that big a risk, but it sure makes the game exciting! If you lose all your chips in a cash game, you can reach into your pocket and put more money on the table. But you can't do that in tournaments. If you lose all your chips in a tournament game, you're out of action and must head for the rail with the rest of the spectators. And believe us when we say that nobody who plays serious poker likes being on the rail!

How Much Should You Bet in No-Limit Hold'em?

The tricky part of betting in no-limit hold'em is deciding how much to bet. If you've been playing limit hold'em, in which the amount you can bet is set in stone, you will need to move outside your comfort zone and learn new betting skills when you start playing no-limit hold'em.

Most no-limit hold'em players follow a few simple guidelines that help them determine how much to bet. As a general rule, when you are the first person to enter the pot, you should come in with a raise that is three to four times the size of the big blind. Sometimes you might just call the minimum bet, and sometimes you might bet five or six times the size of the big blind. In special circumstances you should move all-in. In later chapters we'll explain all this in more detail.

Reading the Boardcards

You must be able to read the cards the dealer places in the center of the table in order to determine what is the best possible hand. As each new boardcard is turned faceup, ask yourself what is the best possible hand, known as the **nuts**, someone could have based upon the community cards. For example, if you start with two aces in your hand, you have the nuts before the flop. But if three connecting cards such as J-10-9 come on the flop, the best possible hand is K-Q because it will complete the nut straight.

You can use any combination of your hole cards and the community cards to form the best five-card poker hand. Your best hand might make use of none, one, or both of your cards combined with the cards in the middle. Look at it as having a seven-card hand, from which you choose the best five-card combination. If a royal flush is dealt in the community cards, everybody playing the hand has a royal flush because that is the best hand possible. But if the boardcards are K♠-Q♠-J♠-10♠ and you have the A♠ in your hand, you have a royal flush and nobody else does.

If you have two queens in your hand and a queen comes on the board, you have made a set of queens. If you have the A♣-K♣ and the J♣-4♣-8♥ come on the flop, you have the nut flush draw, meaning that you will make the nut flush if another card of your suit comes on the river—in this case, a club. Suppose the flop comes K♥-6♣-4♣ and you are holding the A♣-K♣. You have top pair—two kings with an ace kicker—and the nut flush draw. You are a happy camper.

Depending on the cards that are dealt on the flop, the value of your hand may change. If you have two cards of the same suit in your hand and three cards in your suit come on the flop, you have made a flush, which probably is the best possible hand at the moment—unless someone else has two higher cards in your suit. But if the board pairs on the turn, your flush may no longer be the best hand because it is possible that someone else has made a full house. If the flop comes K♣-Q♦-2♣ and you have the K♠-K♥ in your hand, you have the nuts on the flop. But what if another club comes on the turn? If one of your opponents has two clubs in his hand, he has made a flush to beat your trips. Or if a 10 comes on the turn or river, an opponent who has an A-J in his hand has made a straight. Either way, your three kings may no longer be the best hand. You are not a happy camper.

The Goal

Enjoy yourself! Win money! Of course winning money always adds to how much you enjoy playing the game. In hold'em games, you win the hand if all your opponents fold when you make a bet, or if you have the best hand at the showdown. In no-limit hold'em, few hands are played to the showdown—unlike limit hold'em, in which more people play their cards all the way to the river.

You might also win by bluffing. That is, you might lead your opponents to believe that you have the best hand when you actually may not even have a pair. If you push a big chunk of chips into the pot on a bluff and nobody is daring enough to call your big bet, you can win with any two cards. You'll see a lot of players bluffing at the final table in high-stakes televised no-limit hold'em tournaments, but bluffing isn't nearly as common in the everyday games that most of us play.

When you have mastered the basics—selecting the best hands to play, reading the board correctly, understanding the value of your hand, and determining when to hold'em and when to fold'em—you'll be on your way to becoming a winner. Hopefully, after studying the rest of this book, you'll be ready to take on the challenge of no-limit Texas hold'em tournaments—and win. And that translates into winning megabucks at the most exciting poker game in the world!

The Set-Up of a No-Limit Hold'em Game

2

Key Concepts in No-Limit Texas Hold'em

INTRODUCTION

> "Limit poker is a science, but no-limit is an art. In limit hold'em you're shooting at a target. In no-limit hold'em the target comes alive and shoots back at you."
>
> –Crandell Addington, quoted in *The Championship Table*

No-limit Texas hold'em is a game of skill combined with luck. In all games of skill and luck, there is a basic strategy that will improve your chances of winning. In blackjack, for example, if you have a count of thirteen and the dealer's upcard is a 4, basic strategy dictates that if you stay, you will have a better chance of winning than if you hit. But if your count is thirteen and the dealer's upcard is a 10, you will have a better chance of winning if you hit. All serious blackjack players know the game's basic concepts and strategy and use them as the foundation for how they play at the tables.

All winning no-limit hold'em players understand the basic concepts and strategies of big-bet poker and use them as the cornerstones of their game. Sophisticated no-limit hold'em players customize basic no-limit hold'em strategy to fit their personal profiles, and all of this makes up their "game." They also modify basic strategy to fit table conditions, including the playing styles of their opponents. Top players consciously develop a personal style of play that gets them to the cashier's cage more often than to the rail. You can too.

This chapter spells out the basic strategy of no-limit Texas hold'em. Once you have the basics down pat, you can begin to develop your own personal style of play that will lead you to the winner's circle.

YOUR POSITION AFFECTS WHICH HANDS YOU CAN PLAY PROFITABLY

No-limit hold'em is a game of position—and people.

–Doyle Brunson in *Super System*

The first rule of no-limit hold'em is position, position, position. Your position at the table is where you sit in relation to the blinds or the button, and the other players in the hand, and in big-bet poker games like no-limit hold'em, position is far more important than it is in limit varieties of the game. When you are sitting in one of the first two or three seats after the big blind, you are in **early position.** When you are sitting on the button or two seats in front of it, you are in **late position.** The seats in between early and late position are referred to as **middle position.**

The earlier your position, the stronger your starting hand needs to be. The later your position, the wider variety of starting hands you can play. The closer you are to the big blind, the weaker your position. The closer you are to the button, the stronger your position. When we say that you played a hand "out of position," we mean that you played a less than premium hand from an early position. When players get into trouble in no-limit hold'em, it usually happens because they have played a hand out of position. In fact, if you never played a hand except when you are sitting in the last three positions, you would find yourself winning much more frequently than not.

When you play starting hands out of position, you're at the mercy of everybody behind you. There are other players still to act after you, and they can do major damage to your chip stack by forcing you to put all your chips in on a draw. Sometimes you can play a hand for profit from a late position that you wouldn't play at all from an early position, simply because you have more information about your opponents when you're last to act.

For example, in the right situations, you can expect to make a profit with drawing hands such as K-Q, Q-J, and J-10 from late position. With drawing hands, such as high connecting cards, you have to hit the flop or hit a draw to the best hand. But new players often make the mistake of playing these types of hands from an early position. Then they compound their misery by staying in the hand rather than folding against significant action. We have a solution to this type of problem: If you don't flop to it, drop it. Otherwise, you can make a small bet and still lose all your chips. If someone comes over the top of you and you decide to draw to the hand, you can get broke in a hurry if you don't make your hand.

Even if you hit a draw to the best straight or the nut flush, you still haven't made anything because you only have a drawing hand. New players don't always make this important distinction. Let's look at J-10 as an example. Perhaps you're accustomed to playing a hand like J-10 suited in limit hold'em games from up front, from the middle, and from the backside. And maybe you've shown a profit with the hand. But in no-limit hold'em, these types of hands are chip burners that you should avoid playing from an early position. Here's why: If you have J-10 suited in early position in a limit hold'em game and you flop a straight or a flush possibility, your opponents can't put a lot of pressure on you, just one more bet. In no-limit hold'em, however, they can put you to the test for all your chips and make it very unprofitable to try to draw to the hand.

If anybody puts in a raise before the flop, you're going to have to fold the hand and lose the chips you've already put into the pot. Even if you do get to see a cheap flop for the minimum bet, you will have to act first after the flop, which always puts you at a disadvantage. In other words, a big bet by an opponent can make the pot more expensive than you're willing to play for.

Now suppose only one or two players have entered the pot for the minimum bet and you are on the button with J-10 suited. Now you can come in for a small raise with that same J-10, since most players will normally check to the raiser on the flop. With superior position, you have the opportunity to either fire at the pot, or just sit back and take a free card to see if you make your hand on the turn. Your late position in the betting sequence allows you the luxury of deciding how to best play the hand, rather than having to fold it because an opponent has put in a big raise behind you. Position, position, position!

GOOD STARTING HANDS ARE THE KEYS TO THE KINGDOM

"The value of a hand is affected by your cards, your position at the table, how many opponents you have, and the playing style of your opponents."

–Brad Daugherty and Tom McEvoy in
No-Limit Texas Hold'em

Carefully select the hands you play in no-limit Texas hold'em—and play them in position. If you don't, you're bound to run into trouble. When you are sitting in an early position, we suggest that you play only a few select hands, including pocket aces, kings, queens, and jacks, plus A-K and A-Q, preferably suited. You're going to raise when you come into the pot with these hands, but almost no other hands can be played for profit from the first three seats in either tournaments or cash games.

"I raised the pot with an A-K in a tournament and a guy called from the backside, figuring that I probably didn't have a big pocket pair," Don says. "The flop came 9-5-2. I checked, he bet, and he took the pot away from me."

This is a perfect example of a caller using the power of late position to steal the pot. He knew that if Don didn't have a big pocket pair, he could take the pot away from him with any two cards simply by putting in a bet. Such is the power of position in no-limit hold'em.

You can make an exception to this rule when you're playing at a weak table with very passive players who usually just call the minimum bet without raising, which is known as "limping" into the pot. In that case you might be able to slip into the pot from up front with any pocket pair—tens, sevens, even pocket deuces—in the hope of getting to see the flop cheaply and then flopping a set. Medium and low pocket pairs are easy to play after the flop: If you don't flop a set, you simply fold against a bet. Remember, the only time that playing lesser pairs from an early position makes sense is when the game is passive. If you're in a game with aggressive players, lesser pairs or suited connects are chip burners if you play them from up front.

Starting Hands in Late Position

When you're sitting in a late position, you can play a much wider range of starting hands because you have superior position over your opponents. You get to act after them, so you have the advantage having seen how they're going to play their hands. If you're sitting on the button or in the cutoff seat—one seat to the right of the button—and are the first player in the pot, you can bring it in for a raise with the early and middle position hands plus K-J, K-10, Q-J, Q-10, J-10, the suited connectors 10-9, 9-8, and 8-7, and any pair sevens through deuces. You're looking to win the hand right then and there, and you don't want to get called or reraised.

What if you are not the first player in the pot? If a couple of players have already entered the pot, you don't want to be super-aggressive with hands like Q-10. As a matter of fact, you probably would not play a Q-10 on the backside in an aggressive game because you can run into trouble if you flop a pair. If you flop a pair of queens, for example, you have only a 10 for a kicker, and anyone with an A-Q, K-Q, or Q-J will beat your hand. If you flop a 10, you are in the same sad situation. Making two pair or a lucky straight would be ideal, but it's tough to hit that kind of hand on the flop. It happens, but the chances are slim.

When you are the first person to enter the pot, you can raise with a lot less strength in your hand from a late position than you can when you're sitting in early or middle position. This is especially true if the players in the blinds are passive and do not usually defend their blinds. In that case, you have an excellent chance of picking up the pot before the flop. And even if one of the blinds calls you, you still have superior position, since he'll have to act before you in every other round of betting. You also might have a better starting hand and even out-flop your opponent.

Remember that flops usually miss most people. If you don't start with a big pair, you're only going to flop a pair three times out of ten, and you're only going to flop a flush draw about 11 percent of the time. Of course, the more players in the pot, the more likely it is that someone will hit the flop because more cards are in play.

Starting Hands in Middle Position

We've talked about hands you can play up front and hands you can play from around back. Now let's talk about the tricky middle position starting hands. If you're in a middle position, the way you play your hand depends on whether someone has entered the pot before you and how aggressive the players sitting behind you are.

Suppose you are the first person in the pot from a middle position and at least three players have passed in front of you. You can enter the pot by raising with all the premium early position hands, plus hands such as A-J, A-10, and K-Q. You can also play middle pairs such as tens, nines and eights.

If limpers are already in the pot, you want to have one of the top six hands—again, those hands being pocket aces, kings, queens, and jacks, plus A-K and A-Q, preferably suited—in order to raise. Furthermore, if aggressive players are sitting to your left, you cannot make these kinds of plays for profit. You want just the right mix of players sitting behind you, preferably players who are somewhat conservative or tight.

"I often talk about my two-limper rule," Tom says. "This simply means that if two people have entered the pot for the minimum bet, the pot figures to become a multiway pot."

This is certainly true of limit hold'em, though in no-limit hold'em, things can change quickly if someone puts in a big raise in order to limit the field. It holds true more often in no-limit hold'em when you're playing in a somewhat passive game. In such a game, if two people have already limped in, you might want to also limp in with some of the suited connectors and small pairs. If you hit the flop in an unraised multiway pot such as this, you are in for a nice payday.

THE TEXTURE OF THE FLOP AFFECTS HOW YOU PLAY YOUR HAND

The right way to play a hand is not set in stone—there is more than one way to play every hand. No-limit hold'em is a game that requires judgment.

–from *No-Limit Texas Hold'em* by Daugherty & McEvoy

When the flop hits the felt, take your time to study the boardcards in relation to your hand and your opponents' possible hands. Is it a safe flop for your hand, or a dangerous one? Studying the texture of the flop will help you decide how to best play your cards.

Flops that contain connecting cards such as J-10-8 of different suits offer many drawing possibilities. In addition to draws, coordinated flops might contain cards that make one or two pair hands. For example, with a J-10-8 flop, a player with an A-J has made top pair with top kicker, while someone else holding J-10 has flopped top two pair. And if someone has a Q-9 or 9-7, he has flopped a straight. Another player may have K-Q, giving him two overcards and an open-end straight draw. As you can see, with that many possibilities out on the flop, any hand that is in the lead is very vulnerable to being out-drawn by other hands. And if two of the flop cards are suited, flush draws could also be out. For example, if you are holding pocket tens to this flop, you do not want to slow-play your set. The same goes with any other strong hand such as two pair or a straight.

Now suppose the flop comes Q-J-8. Flops that contain two or more face cards can help many players' hands. Players play face cards for good reasons, and when two or more show up on the flop, you can bet it has helped someone. If you think you have the best hand on this type of flop, you must protect it with a big bet or a raise.

Players often play middle suited connectors, hoping for a coordinated flop that fits their connectors, but these types of flops can be dangerous if you're playing a big pair. For example, suppose the flop comes down with 8-7-6, you are holding Q-Q, and you make a pot-sized bet. If an opponent comes over the top of you, watch out. You're probably in bad shape. The lesson here is be wary of connecting cards, especially face cards, if you have a one-pair hand—even if you have an overpair to the flop.

Some flops are safe enough that you can consider slow-playing a big hand. For example, suppose a player in early position makes a small raise before the flop. Two other players call and you decide to call on the button with 2-2. The flop comes K-7-2 of mixed suits. Unless one of your opponents has K-K or 7-7 in the hole, you are in great shape. Not only do you have a hand that is very difficult to draw out on, you have superior position. This gives you lots of options on how to get the most value out of your hand. If the original raiser leads out with a bet, you can smooth-call, even if another player has already called in front of you. If a non-threatening card such as a 5 hits on the turn and one of your opponents bets, you can call again and wait until the river to either bet if it's checked to you, or raise if an opponent bets.

Here's another example of a good flop. Suppose you have A♠-K♦. You make a standard raise and get two callers. The flop comes K♠-5♣-3♥. You like the texture of this flop because it is unlikely that there are any straight draws or two-pair hands out against you. You can make a bet and expect to get called by an opponent who holds a king and a weaker kicker in his hand. Although there is a small possibility that you'll run into a set, your chances of winning with top pair and top kicker are good.

44

YOU CAN WIN WITHOUT THE BEST HAND

"Funny thing about hold'em—any two cards can win."
–Chuck Thompson in *Card Player* magazine

Being able to bet all your chips at one time is the feature that distinguishes no-limit poker from all other types of limit poker games. The size of a single bet in no-limit hold'em is restricted only by the amount of chips in your possession. You can bet enough chips to force your opponents out of the pot even if you don't have a hand.

You can win a pot at any time by having the best hand. One of the beauties of no-limit hold'em is that you do not need a strong hand to win. World-class players such as T.J. Cloutier have won tournaments when the best hands they were dealt during the entire event were pocket nines and A-Q offsuit. How do they do it? With magic and mirrors? No, they win because they make aggressive, timely plays.

The art of no-limit hold'em is winning pots when you have no cards whatsoever by simply evaluating your opponents correctly and making the right plays from the right position. Ninety-nine percent of the time, the right position is a late position, one that allows you to win a pot with a bet. You can also win by making the best move. Always be prepared to make what you believe to be the best move given the situation. Have the guts to raise or reraise when you sense weakness in your opponent, whether or not you have a hand. You cannot be successful at no-limit hold'em if fear has you in its grip. Sometimes a timid player realizes what the best move is, but he cannot bring himself to execute it. He knows that a bet probably will win the pot because his opponents have shown weakness, yet he can't force himself to commit his chips because he has a nagging fear that someone will look him up and call his bluff.

Anybody can play aces or kings. Winning with hands such as Q-J, knowing when you have the best hand and when to push with it—those are the things that separate winning no-limit hold'em players from the rest. Winning with marginal hands also involves sensing that your opponent doesn't have a hand and knowing when he has the best hand and is trying to trap you into betting by checking.

Sometimes, of course, we make the right move at the wrong time. This doesn't mean that we have made the wrong play. It simply means that we got the wrong result. As you play more and more no-limit hold'em, you will find that making the best move at the right time will become much easier for you to do.

BLUFFING IS A POWERFUL TOOL IN BIG-BET POKER

"Bluffing is like walking a tightrope over a river full of hungry sharks. One mistake and you're shark bait!"

–Tex Sheahan in *Secrets of Winning Poker*

The bluff is an extremely important play in no-limit hold'em. Bluffing is more effective in no-limit hold'em than it is in limit hold'em because, as we said earlier, you can bet enough chips to make your opponents fold. When you can force your opponent to fold a hand that is possibly better than yours, you have succeeded in taking chips away from him that you would not have been able to get in a limit hold'em game.

That's why we say that if the bluff is executed correctly, it is a lethal weapon. If you don't do it correctly, it can be a lethal dose of poison instead. The weapon can be turned on you and made to destroy you. Like so many things in hold'em, timing is everything. We discuss how to time your all-in bets and bluffs in the tournament strategy chapter of this book.

KNOWING HOW YOUR OPPONENTS PLAY IS THE MASTER KEY TO SUCCESS

"I don't worry about everybody in the tournament, I just play the people at my table. I figure all I have to do is beat 'em nine at a time."

–Byron "Cowboy" Wolford in
Cowboys, Gamblers & Hustlers

Observing how your opponents play is one of the most important elements in no-limit hold'em. Great players such as T.J. Cloutier say that within 20 minutes of sitting down at a table, they know how everybody plays. Of course, T.J. happens to be a genius at observation. For the rest of us mortals, it takes a little longer than that.

Because so few hands go to the showdown in no-limit hold'em, you cannot depend entirely on the hands you've seen your opponents turn over at the river for clues as to how they play. Therefore you must constantly watch the action and how they bet their hands, looking for patterns in the way they bet in various situations. On the rare occasions that you see a hand played to the river, take note of what types of hands your opponents have been playing and the positions from which they've been playing them.

"A lot of times I talk to my opponents after the play of a hand," Don adds. "I might say, 'Gee that was a good hand. What did you have, pocket nines?' And many times they will tell me what they had. This is one way I learn how my opponents play."

Of course every time your authors are asked that question, they always have the same answer, "Pocket aces!" That's not entirely true, of course, but the point is that you don't owe your opponents an honest answer if they ask you what you have but didn't pay to see it.

We suggest that you never ever show your hand after you've won a non-showdown hand, whether you have four of a kind or 7-2 offsuit. Do not give free information to any of your opponents because when you do, you are helping them and hurting yourself. You don't want to give your opponents a chance to observe you and your hands for free— that's what you want to do to them.

When you first sit down at your tournament table, try to find out two things: Which players are limit players and which ones are online players. You learn this simply by asking the players directly, but casually, of course. You want this information because it will help you determine the best strategy to use against them. For example, limit players value hands quite differently from no-limit players, and online players are prone to making a lot of marginal bets. Players who are just changing over from playing limit hold'em often play a wider variety of hands than they should. And online players often bet an amount that is double the size of the big blind when they enter the pot, instead of raising three or four times the size of the big blind. One of the reasons they make only a double bet is that they are accustomed to clicking an "advance" button on the computer screen that automatically raises the minimum amount. Following this pattern in live tournaments, online players aren't really thinking about the proper betting strategy, they are concentrating instead on speeding up the game.

PATIENCE IS A VIRTUE

"There are only three basic things to being a good gambler. Knowing when you've got the best of it, money management, and managing yourself. That third thing is the hard one."

–Puggy Pearson, 1973 World Champion of Poker

No-limit hold'em is a game in which you do not need to play very many hands to post a winning session. You simply need to win the few hands you play. You want to get action with your good hands, but you must be patient while waiting for them. And you must constantly observe how your opponents play so that you will know who the action players are and be able to seize the best opportunity to play against them. When you have established a table image as a patient player, your opponents will give you respect when you play a hand. You'll be paid off on your good hands, especially if you play them on the backside, when all the aggressive, eager players are putting money in the pot with less than premium hands.

Be disciplined. Force yourself to think things through carefully before you act, even if you seem to be slowing down the action. One thing you can do in order to avoid making decisions too quickly is to slowly count to ten while you're thinking. And if you decide to pass, remember that there is no shame in folding. In fact, the fold is one of the most powerful and profitable plays in no-limit hold'em. It is one way to hang on to your hard-earned chips.

Patience coupled with an unflappable temperament at the tournament table will lead you to the winner's circle, where we hope to meet you one day soon. But before you can get there, you will need to know the basics of tournament play, which is the topic of our next chapter.

Early Position Hands

Hand One

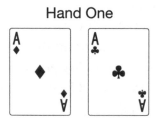

Hand Two

Hand Three

Hand Four

Hand Five

Hand Six

Middle Position Hands

Hand One

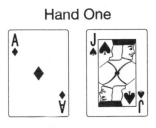

Hand Two

Hand Three

Hand Four

Hand Five

Hand Six

Late Position Hands

Hand One

Hand Two

Hand Three

Hand Four

Hand Five

Hand Six

Hand Seven — Any Low Pair

  through

Hand Eight — Suited Connectors

  through

3

The Basics of Tournament Play

"No matter what the game is, when you hit the final table, the real game is still tournament poker."

–T.J. Cloutier

INTRODUCTION

Before you read this chapter, answer a few simple questions:

1. Do you regularly play a lot of tournaments?
2. Do you support yourself from your tournament wins?
3. Have you ever won a World Series of Poker bracelet?

If you answered yes to any of these three questions, you already know the basics of how tournaments work, so skip this chapter and proceed to Chapter 4.

This chapter is for people who have been playing cash games in casinos or on the internet and have decided to give tournament play a shot. This section has been adapted from *Poker Tournament Tips from the Pros* by Shane Smith, with the author's permission.

The authors' comments come from decades of experience and, in Tom McEvoy's case, the dozen or so poker books he has written over the years either single-handedly or in conjunction with T.J. Cloutier, Shane Smith, or Brad Daugherty.

THE STRUCTURE OF TOURNAMENTS

In tournaments, the playing field is even. Everyone pays the same entry price and begins with the same number of chips, regardless of knowledge or experience. As players run out of chips, they are eliminated from action, and the field of competitors gradually shrinks in size. The tournament ends when all combatants have fallen, leaving but one soldier standing. Actually, the victor is sitting while happily counting his prize money.

Of course experienced tournament players have an advantage over novice players: They know tournament strategy and how it differs from cash-game play. Pros use their knowledge and experience to navigate the tournament's minefields and climb the money ladder to make it to the final table, their favorite place in the volatile world of tournament poker. Sometimes a novice sneaks past the pros and gets to butt heads with top players for the championship. And occasionally that novice wins the whole ball of wax. The purpose of this book is to show you how to cut yourself a slice of the money pie at the championship table, no matter how high the stakes or how good the competition.

But before you take a seat at your first tournament table, here are some fundamentals that you need to know, starting with the basic vocabulary of tournament poker.

The Buy-In

About an hour before the tournament starts, players begin signing up for a seat with the tournament official and paying for a buy-in, which is the basic fee that the casino charges for participation in the event. If the buy-in is $20, the house usually keeps $5 (25 percent of the buy-in) to cover its expenses, and puts the remaining $15 into the prize pool. The amount the house keeps is known as the vig. In big buy-in events, the house keeps a much smaller percentage of the entry fee and adds it to the amount of the tournament buy-in. For example, if a major tournament is listed in a poker magazine as a $1,000 + $60 event, the buy-in is $1,000 and the entry fee is $60 (6 percent of the buy-in). Therefore you pay $1,060 to play the tournament; the house puts the $1,000 into the prize pool and keeps the $60. Quite often, the house also subtracts 3 percent from the total prize pool to distribute to tournament personnel as a gratuity.

Your Starting Table and Starting Stack

When you buy in, you will receive an entry card with your assigned table and seat number on it. When the event begins, report to your battle station and give your entry card to the dealer. You will find a stack of chips stacked on the felt in front of your seat. If the buy-in for the tournament is $100, you usually will receive around $500 in starting chips. Each of your opponents will receive the same number of chips, though most players count them to be sure they are correct.

A Round or Level of Play

Tournaments are divided into segments called **rounds** or **levels**. A tournament round is the length of time during which the blinds remain the same. Many low-limit tournaments feature 20-minute rounds, during which time, the blinds will be, say, $10/$20. At the end of the first 20-minute round, the blinds will increase, often to double the amount of the starting round. Every 20 minutes thereafter, the blinds will rise again. Most tournaments with buy-ins of

$100 or more have rounds that last at least 30 minutes or longer. Big buy-in tournaments have the longest rounds of all, ranging from 45 minutes to two hours in length.

When smaller denomination chips are no longer needed at the beginning of a higher betting level, they are removed from the table in a race-off. The dealer deals each player one card for each of his odd chips and the highest cards dealt receive larger chips equal to the value of the smaller chips.

Freezeout Tournaments

A **freezeout tournament** does not allow players to buy more chips when they lose their stacks. If you begin with 500 tournament chips, for example, you must leave the tournament when you lose all of them. Most of the chapters in this book are devoted to strategies for freezeout tournaments.

Rebuy Tournaments

A **rebuy tournament** allows players who have lost their stacks or have fallen below a designated amount to buy more chips during a limited time known as the **rebuy period**. Most low-limit tournaments are rebuy events, and they usually only allow players to rebuy during the first three rounds, not throughout the entire tournament.

If the tournament buy-in of $20 gets you 300 chips, a rebuy usually will cost $10, and will get you another 300. During the rebuy period of most tournaments that allow them, you can rebuy anytime that you have fewer than your starting number of chips. For example, if you lose the first pot you enter and are left with 70 chips, you can rebuy and add 300 chips to your stack.

If you decide not to rebuy when you run out of chips, your tournament is a done deal. You are out of action and either out the door or into a cash game where you can reach into your pocket any time you go broke.

The Add-On

At the end of the rebuy period in tournaments, you usually can make one final rebuy, called an **add-on**. The two most common add-ons are made under the following conditions:

> 1. If you have more chips than your initial buy-in, you may add on the same amount of chips that you began with, usually for the same price as a rebuy.
> 2. If you have fewer chips than your initial buy-in, you may add on double the amount of chips that you began with, usually for double the price of a rebuy. For example, if you began with 300 chips on a tournament buy-in of $20, and you have 170 chips at the end of the rebuy period, you are allowed to make a rebuy for $10, plus you can buy

> an add-on for an additional $10. So for $20, you receive 600 chips.

After all the add-ons have been completed, the tournament usually schedules a short break in play, at which time the officials count up all the buy-ins, rebuys, and add-ons to determine the size of the prize pool. When the tournament resumes you have only the chips left in front of you with which to fight the good fight. This is why so many rebuy tournament players say that the real tournament begins after the rebuys and add-ons are over. When the tournament recommences, play continues round by round with the limits ever increasing.

Things to Find Out Before You Enter a Tournament

Not all tournaments are created equal. Some are freezeouts in which you cannot buy more chips when you get broke. Others have low entry fees with rebuys and add-ons. Some tournaments have hundreds of players while others have small fields. A few have highly trained, efficient dealers. They all have predetermined formats and rules that you need to know before you enter them.

Here are the things you need to know before you plunk your money on the tournament buy-in table:

1. How early should I be there to sign up?
2. What is the entry fee?
3. What is the usual payout?
4. How many places are paid?
5. Are rebuys allowed?
6. How long are the betting rounds?
7. Which side games does the casino spread?

Many casino tournaments fill their seats quickly, so plan to be there early. Seats are often assigned by the luck of the draw. In many cases, plastic cards for each seat in the event are spread facedown on the sign-in table, and you draw your seat from the pile. Big tournaments use computer programs to assign seats randomly and distribute to each entrant a computer printout with his table and seat number on it. You must take your seat card or printout sheet to the table and give it to the dealer in order to claim your seat.

The Tournament Buy-In vs. Your Expectations

If you enter a tournament solely to win money, it's important to consider the relationship between the cost of the tournament buy-in, including rebuys and add-ons if available, and its expected payout. T.J. Cloutier, who has won more money at tournament poker than any other player, wrote, "You want to get a good overlay on your money. If the winning end of the tournament isn't 50 times the amount of money that you have put in it, it really isn't a good tournament for you. So if you pay $1,000 to enter a tournament, you want to be able to win $50,000."

Your monetary expectations may vary, but always ask yourself, "Will it be worth my time and money to enter this event?" Or, "How much is a shot at this prize money worth to me?" Several other considerations may also affect whether you decide to play, including how much cash you can afford to invest if the event is a rebuy tournament. Another is your state of mind. Do you sincerely believe that you can win the event?

And when deciding whether or not to enter a tournament, keep in mind that the prize money is not the only reward that tournaments offer. Experience is another type of payoff, especially if you are rising through the ranks, honing your skills on your way to winning a World Series of Poker bracelet.

THE TOURNAMENT PAYOUT

Tournaments pay on a percentage basis, approximately 35 percent to first place, 20 percent to second, 12 percent to third and so on. The number of players who receive a payday depends upon the number of entrants. In small events, only the final table is paid, but in big tournaments, several tables finish in the money. Knowing how much money will be paid for each place could affect your strategy at the last table, so find out in advance.

The modern trend is to spread the prize pool among more players, and thus pay a lesser percentage to the top three spots. Many players seem to like this format because it makes the payouts less top heavy. In a groundbreaking experiment, the directors of the inaugural Tournament of Champions in 1999 asked players to vote on how they wanted the prize pool to be distributed. A large majority voted to spread the money to more players, so that that the top few spots would receive a lesser percentage and the middle to bottom spots would receive a larger share than was customary.

When a tournament spreads ten tables, it takes around five or six hours to complete the action. The major reason casino card rooms offer tournaments is because they want your action in their casino, and when players wash out early, they usually want to enter a ring game. These side games can be very worthwhile, especially if several disappointed tournament dropouts are in your game. Here's your chance to recoup not only your entry fee, but some "tilt" chips that loose losers so often fling around like birdseed.

WHAT MAKES A TOURNAMENT GOOD?

Good tournaments give players a generous number of starting chips and provide betting rounds that are adequate in length. The more chips you receive and the longer the rounds, the better the tournament. We discuss this important concept in more detail in a later chapter.

Dealer competence and the quality of the floor personnel are major factors in whether a tournament is enjoyable. In our experience, good dealers do not converse with players and they deal the maximum number of hands possible during each round. Dealer expertise often determines the amount of the tip that winners give them. In low-limit tournaments, you might expect to toke the dealers about 5 percent of your win, while in bigger tournaments the usual amount is around 2 percent. However, many tournaments reserve 3 percent from the prize pool for tournament personnel. If this is the practice in the tournament you're playing, you may want to adjust the amount of your toke accordingly.

Good tournaments are well managed, start on time, pre-announce betting increment increases either vocally or with a tournament clock, and employ good floor personnel and dealers. And of course, the best tournaments are the ones you win! You can expect to crash and burn as much as 90 percent of the time, but the beauty of tournament play is that when you win, you win enough money to reward you for all the times you bombed out.

Tournament Talk

S.K.I.L.L. By Shane Smith

You're watching a rerun of the 2003 World Series of Poker on ESPN. A burly dude with the outrageous moniker of Moneymaker has just called a raise by a slick cardsmith named Farha, who looks like a vintage riverboat gambler. The gambler hits a pair of jacks on the flop and pushes $175,000 in chips to the center. The dude check-raises him for $275,000 more with two low pair. Gambler shoves in the balance of his chips, Dude calls. Dude beats Gambler, wins the championship, stuffs $2.5 million into his jeans, and heads home to Tennessee to his life as an accountant. You're thinking to yourself, "If he can do it, why can't I?" You're hooked.

Chris Moneymaker's dramatic win at the WSOP triggered an avalanche of wannabes—amateurs and professional poker players alike flooded into the formerly unheralded world of tournament poker. Casinos and internet poker sites are sponsoring more tournaments than ever, and the fields have increased dramatically. The first few World Series of Poker championship events attracted fewer than 10 entrants, all of whom were professional players. Thirty years later, in 2000, the Series hit the 500 mark and former Texas road gambler T.J. Cloutier finished second to game theorist Chris Ferguson. A scant four years later, the field exploded to 2,500 when patent attorney Greg Raymer won the title and $5 million.

If you want to make your mark in the world of big league poker, all it takes is skill—or does it? Think of the five letters in the word skill as an acronym for what it really takes to win big bucks in poker tournaments.

Stamina

Big buy-in poker tournaments—those that charge an entry fee between $5,000 and $25,000—last for days on end, literally. Imagine maintaining your concentration for as many as 12 to 14 hours a day, five to seven days straight, on just one decision: Hold'em or fold'em? Hanging in there, making do-or-die decisions on hand after hand, requires more than just staying on your toes, mentally. Good physical condition is a big advantage. Though most poker tournaments are nonsmoking these days, casinos cannot boast the healthiest air on the planet, and sitting in a straight-back chair for hours on end isn't good for your back. That may be why many of the top "athletes" in poker these days are eating a healthy breakfast and hitting the treadmill in the casino's fitness center each morning of the tournament.

Knowledge

Maybe you've heard the axiom, "Poker is not a card game you play with people. Poker is a people game you play with cards." There's a lot of truth to that, as evidenced by a conversation I overheard in the elevator of the Palms Casino in Las Vegas, home to some of Sin City's best low-stakes, no-limit hold'em action:

"You're right, I don't know exactly how to play no-limit, but I'll pick it up as I go along," a young yuppie said to his bud. "So what if I'm sitting next to some famous player? I don't know one from the other, so that's not a factor."

Good luck, I thought to myself. Knowledge not only involves knowing the how-to of the game, but also the when-to and the why-to. But there is one element of poker knowledge—one the elevator guy totally overlooked—that stands to win you more money in the long run than mastering the basics of the game, and that's knowing your opponents.

"Knowing your opponents in no-limit hold'em—how they usually play, and how they play in specific situations—is the most important thing in the game," says T.J. Cloutier. "You've gotta be able to sit down at a table with people you've never played with in your life and after fifteen minutes, know how each one of them plays."

Intuition

The Loser's Lament: "Something told me I should fold, but I decided to call anyway. Losing that pot cost me the tournament. Guess I shoulda followed my first instinct."

Poker professionals define intuition as a "feel for the game" or "good instincts." They often advise new players to follow their first instincts in the play of their hands. I think of intuition as your P.C. No, not personal computer—poker conscience. It's that quiet and ever-present voice that whispers in your ear, "Wait! Think it out," or "Go for it, he's bluffing." Every great no-limit tournament player has learned to listen to this voice, and as a result they have highly developed instincts that guide them through difficult decisions.

Labor

How did Tiger Woods develop the best swing in golf? How do bowling champions learn to make the 10-7 split? Practice, practice, practice. Here's how Roy West put it in his classic *7-Card Stud: The Complete Course in Learning:*

"When you are not practicing, someone somewhere is practicing. And when you meet, he will beat you."

In days gone by, the only way to learn how to play poker was BSOP, by the seat of your pants. Today, you can learn by playing simulated computer games on poker software programs or playing free games at internet poker sites. Of course it's a lot more fun to just jump into a live tournament than to put in long hours on the computer, but if you're willing to labor before you launch, you'll become a winner far quicker than you imagined. You've gotta sweat it before you get it.

Luck

They were playing for the title, the gold bracelet, and a million bucks. T.J. Cloutier pushed it all in with A-Q. Chris Ferguson pushed back for all his chips with A-9. The clear favorite at the championship table of the 2000 World Series of Poker, Cloutier was one card away from fulfilling a lifelong dream. Ooops! A nine slid off the deck on the final card of the tournament. After congratulating Ferguson for the win, Cloutier remarked to a reporter, "That's poker!"

You don't need to be lucky on every hand you play in a no-limit game, you just have to get lucky on a few key hands, the ones that turn the tides of fortune. And then accept whatever Lady Luck deals you as just a part of the game.

Key Concepts of Tournament Poker

"I had four steady days of luck, which is what you need to win this one."

Jack Keller, 1984 World Champion of Poker

SKILL AND LUCK

Poker is a game of skill combined with luck. In order to win a no-limit hold'em tournament, two things must fall into place during your climb to the top. First, you must employ skillful tournament strategy. Second, you have to get lucky at the right times. You need both to win. The best tournament players achieve consistently better results over the long run than their less-skilled opponents. And how do they become so skillful? In addition to having a natural talent for poker, they hone their craft through practice, by playing a lot of tournaments on the internet and in casinos.

They study how great champions play the game. They read books and watch instructional videos and DVDs. And it pays off in the heat of battle.

But as important as skill is in winning no-limit hold'em tournaments, even the best players have to get lucky sometimes. In fact every tournament winner got lucky on a key hand somewhere along the way. Key hands often come down to coin-flip situations, where neither hand has a statistical advantage over the other, such as when one player has a pocket pair and his opponent has two overcards. You have to win pots when you have A-K and are up against a pair of queens, and you have to win when you're playing the pocket queens and your opponent has the A-K. You're always going to play some coin-flip hands such as these in tournament competition—and you need to get lucky to win them.

WHEN YOU LOSE YOUR STACK, YOU CAN'T COME BACK

Not being able to buy more chips when you go broke is what separates tournament play from cash-game play. If you lose your all-in bet in a cash game, you can purchase more chips and stay in the game. In tournaments, if you bet all your chips and lose, you're out of action. Therefore when you bet all-in, you are putting your entire tournament on the line. That's what makes the all-in bet so risky—and so exciting. It's what brings the gallery to its feet. Will the driver crash and burn, or will he steer the dangerous curve perfectly and win the race?

Your tournament is almost always going to be on the line pointing a particular hand—sometimes it happens early, sometimes in the middle rounds, sometimes late. Every time you push all your chips into the middle, you are in jeopardy of losing everything. No matter how pretty your starting hand, even if you have two aces against a 7-2 offsuit, there are no guaranteed winners before the flop. Sometimes that 7-2 is going to beat those bullets.

In today's tournaments, you find more and more players going all-in with their chips. A lot of new players see people going all-in at the final table of televised tournaments, and they mistakenly think that's the right way to play no-limit hold'em. What they overlook is the fact that in the World Poker Tour televised tournaments, you see only the last six players in action. What you don't see is how those six people got to the last table—and believe us, they didn't get there by going all-in very often. At the final table, however, when the blinds are big and the play is shorthanded, you'll see people make all sorts of moves on the pot with weak hands because that's how no-limit hold'em is played under these circumstances. Aggressive players might even reraise or move in with a hand as bad as 4-3 offsuit on a stone bluff.

What so many players new to the game don't realize is that this is not the way you need to play in the earlier stages of the tournament, when you are trying to just survive long enough to make it to the final table. In this book, we will show you when and how to move your chips so that you can cash and earn instead of crash and burn.

TOURNAMENT CHIPS ARE LIKE MONOPOLY MONEY

In cash games, chips equal real money. A $100 chip is worth $100 in greenbacks. In tournaments, chips do not equal a set amount of money. They are simply a way of keeping score. When you're playing a poker tournament, chips are like Monopoly money. They have no value until the tournament is finished.

In a no-limit tournament, always remember that the only money at risk is the amount of the tournament buy-in. If the tournament cost you $100 to enter, $100 is the total amount of your financial commitment, no matter whether you have $50,000 or $100,000 in chips in front of you. Therefore don't let the value of the chips influence your play of the hand. Keep in mind that when an opponent bets $10,000 into you during the play of a hand, that $10,000 bet does not equate to real money. The most you can lose if you lose in a hand when you're all-in is still only $100.

Think of tournament chips as units. "He just bet me $40,000!" in a tournament simply means that he bet forty units. The point is that you should think of tournament chips differently than you think of chips in cash games. As a side note, if big bets scare you in cash games, don't sit down at a table where you see players constantly making big bets or going all-in. If you're not willing to risk all the money you've put on the table in one hand in a live game, don't play no-limit hold'em. Play limit hold'em where you know exactly how much money you can lose in one hand.

AGGRESSIVE AL BEATS MEEK MARVIN IN NO-LIMIT HOLD'EM

No one has ever called his way to victory in no-limit hold'em, neither in a cash game or a tournament. No-limit hold'em is a bettor's game, not a caller's game. It is not for the timid, the passive, the fearful. "He has no fear" are words that tournament reporters often use to describe the winner's play the final table of major events. They might also add, "He shows no mercy." Fear holds you back from playing your A-game. Courage takes you to the top.

The advantage of playing courageously and aggressively is that you force your opponents to react to you, rather than you having to react to them. By playing aggressively, you take command of your table. You inspire fear in your opponents by constantly putting them on the defensive. You can even "train" them to check marginal hands to you on the flop. When they check, you have the advantage. You can seize the opportunity to take a free card if you choose, or you might make a big enough bet to get them to fold some of their weaker holdings. And if they play back at you, the situation is still in your control. You can decide to back off if your hand doesn't warrant further action, or when you really have the goods and get played with, you have the power to create a thing of beauty. By constantly hammering at your opponents and taking control, you will force them into making numerous mistakes against you, mistakes that can catapult you to the winner's circle.

THE TOURNAMENT STRUCTURE IS IMPORTANT TO YOUR SUCCESS

One of the most important features of a no-limit hold'em tournament is the structure of the event. The tournament's structure should be a major factor when deciding whether or not to play it. Every tournament venue should provide players with a structure sheet in advance that lists the number of starting chips, the length of the rounds, and the amount of the increases in the blinds. Let's examine each one of these parts of a tournament's structure.

First, consider the number of starting chips in relation to the blinds. Most no-limit tournaments with buy-ins of $500 and higher give you at least 40 times the big blind, which is what you're looking for. So if the blinds start at $25/$25, you want to receive at least $1,000 in tournament chips.

Next, check out the length of the rounds. Most no-limit hold'em tournaments with buy-ins of $500 and higher have 40-minute or 60-minute rounds. This is quite fair because you have the right amount of chips and enough time to work with them. If the rounds last for 30 minutes or less, we suggest not playing the tournament, since you'll feel pressured to play marginal hands.

The size of the incremental blind increases at the start of each new round is very important. The slower the blinds and the antes increase, the more player-friendly the tournament is. Some tournaments double the size of the blinds for the first three levels and move the blinds up at the rate of approximately 50 percent per round thereafter. This is a little fast, but the average tournament makes up for it by slowing the increase in blinds after the third limit, and slowing it even more in the later rounds. As long as you are able to build your chip stack each round and maintain your chip count at 20 or more times the size of the big blind, you will be okay.

THE CLOCK: YOUR ENEMY OR YOUR FRIEND

As in football, the clock can be your friend or your enemy. If you are way ahead in the chip count, the clock is your friend. When you are ahead, you look for ways to continue to put pressure on your opponents. This doesn't mean you should go after them with weak hands when they are so short-chipped they are almost forced to call. It means you should attack with reasonable hands and force your short-stacked opponents to commit all or most of their chips to play against you. The clock is running in your favor whenever your desperate opponents are close to having to commit their remaining chips with a much weaker hand than normal.

If you are one of the short stacks, the clock is your enemy. You must constantly be aware of how much time is left in the round and how soon the blinds are coming your way. You also need to know whether or not you can survive at least one more round of blinds if you don't catch a playable hand.

If you are a middle stack, you are in no-man's land. One mistake and you're either crippled or out of action. If you lose to a short stack, you take his place on the bottom of the heap. If you go up against a big stack, you have to win or you're on the rail. Meanwhile the clock continues to tick away.

THE CURVE: YOUR ALLY

The curve is the average stack size, which you can calculate by dividing the number of chips in play by the total number of players still left in the tournament. Quite often the tournament clock will do the math for you, and post the average amount of chips per player.

Your place relative to the curve can affect your tournament strategy. If you are well ahead of the curve, you know that you are in good shape and do not need to take any unnecessary chances with marginal hands. Being close to the curve isn't too bad a spot to be in either.

But if you are lagging below the curve, you need to ask yourself, "How far below average am I?" Say that the average is $5,000 and you have $3,800. You're just a little below par, so you aren't in very bad shape. Now let's say that you're down to around $1,500 in chips, $3,500 below the curve. In that case, you will need to find a hand to play sooner rather than later. When looking for that playable hand that might bring your stack size up to average, the size of the blinds is also a consideration. If the blinds are no more than $100/$200 and you have $1,500 in chips, you still have a little room to maneuver. But if the blinds are any higher than that, you're pretty much in a move-in mode. The shorter your stack, the more likely someone will call you. Therefore it helps to have some kind of a hand, or at least play against a tight player who doesn't defend his blinds very often.

The bottom line is this: Always be aware of where you stand in relation to the curve, and adjust your play to maximize your chances of survival.

KEY HANDS OFTEN TURN THE TIDE

You've probably read reports in poker magazines telling how Joe from Iowa defeated Frank from Tennessee to win the North Dakota State Poker Championship. In the final hand, Joe held J-10 and Frank held A-Q. When a jack came on the river, it paired Joe and gave him the title. Sounds like a bad beat for Frank, but was it really?

The description of the final hand might not have included some important points. For example, say there was $10,000 worth of chips on the table, and Joe had $9,600 of them, leaving Frank with only $400. The blinds were $100/$200, and Frank correctly moved in his remaining chips before the flop with his A-Q. Joe had an easy call with his J-10, even if he knew he was beaten at the moment, since it would cost him only a few more chips to see the flop and he would not be seriously damaged if he lost the pot. The point is that, since there was only $800 in the pot, the final hand was not the key hand of the tournament.

The key hand could have gone down like this: With four players left, Joe and Bill each had around $4,000 in chips. Frank and John had about $1,000 each. Joe had the button and raised with the K♠-K♣, making it $800 to go. Bill was in the big blind with the A♦-K♦. Rather than risk all his chips against the co-chip leader, Bill decided to just call and see the flop.

The flop came with the K♥-4♦-2♦. Bill flopped top pair with top kicker, and had the nut flush draw. Joe flopped top set. Bill decided to try and win the pot right there, so he led off with a $1,500 bet. Joe immediately moved in with top set. Bill already had over half his chips in the pot, and with that flop, he felt that he had little choice but to call Joe's raise. The 7♠ hit on the turn. And then, to add some additional pain and suffering for Bill, the 7♦ came on the river, completing Bill's nut flush, but giving a full house to Joe. After winning this big pot, Joe had 80 percent of the chips with only two remaining opponents. This was clearly the key hand of the tournament, not the final hand he played against Frank.

The key hand of a tournament, such as the one described above, always sets the stage for what follows. Although the final hand of the tournament can be the key hand, it seldom works out that way. And oftentimes, there is more than one key hand. Perhaps Joe had been a medium stack with $2,000 but had doubled up to $4,000 before playing that big pot against Bill. Therefore Joe had two key hands that affected his winning result. Get the idea?

TOURNAMENTS USUALLY PROGRESS IN FIVE STAGES

Tournaments usually progress through five stages of play: the early stage, middle stage, late stage, in the money, and final table. For the purpose of this discussion, we are concerned only with freeze-out tournaments with no rebuys.

The early stage includes the first two rounds of the tournament. There are plenty of chips in play relative to the blinds. The middle stage is comprised of rounds three, four, and five. By the end of this stage, around 50 percent of the field has been eliminated. The late stage includes rounds six, seven, and eight. By then you are either in the money or close to it. After round eight about 80 percent or more of the field has been eliminated.

If you survive to the ninth round, you probably are in the money. It may take a few rounds to make it to the final table, but by round 13, you usually are there. In some cases the tournament is over by then. The final table usually has nine or ten players. Sometimes additional time is added to the clock, causing the rounds at the last table to last a little longer.

The longer the rounds, the more skill plays a role in your tournament success. The shorter the rounds, the more luck comes into play. In big buy-in tournaments with $5,000 and higher buy-ins, more chips are in play and each round lasts longer. This means that there are more rounds in each stage of the tournament. These types of tournaments may run for four or five days, and in the case of the World Series of Poker championship event, even longer.

GOOD DECISIONS ARE THE DIFFERENCE

Tournament poker actually is all about making good decisions—in every situation, hour after hour, and sometimes day after day. Not just either/or decisions, but complicated ones based on a multitude of factors.

What is the nature of your opponents? What is your position in the betting sequence? How strong are your cards? How does your chip stack compare with that of your opponents? What are the odds of your winning the hand before the flop, on the flop, and after the flop? What is your table image? What are the likely consequences if you lose the hand? How much will it help if you win it? If you do this, what do you predict your opponent will do? If you do that, how do you think he will react?

In the next chapter, we will give you guidelines designed to help you make the best decisions possible in strategic tournament situations. You will learn how to put these basic concepts of tournament poker into action by using time-tested winning strategies to win the championship.

A Good Tournament Structure

This is a structure from the Fall 2004 Poker Round-Up at the Wildhorse Resort & Casino.

Buy-in: $150   **Starting Chips:** $1,500
Time Limit: 30 min. Round 1-18,
40 min. Round 19-21

Level	Ante	Blinds
1	–	$25/$25
2	–	$25/$50
3	–	$50/$100
4	–	$100/$200
5	$25	$100/$200
6	$50	$150/$300
7	$50	$200/$400
8	$75	$300/$600
9	$100	$400/$800
10	$200	$600/$1,200
11	$300	$800/$1,600
12	$400	$1,200/$2,400
13	$500	$1,500/$3,000
14	$500	$2,000/$4,000
15	$500	$2,500/$5,000
16	$1,000	$3,000/$6,000
17	$1,000	$4,000/$8,000
18	$2,000	$6,000/$12,000
19	$2,000	$8,000/$16,000
20	$3,000	$10,000/$20,000
21	$4,000	$12,000/$24,000

A Bad Tournament Structure

No matter what the size of the buy-in or the length of the levels, this is a bad tournament structure because you receive only 20 times the size of the big blind in tournament chips, and the increments double at each new level. This structure is not player-friendly.

Buy-in: $100   **Starting Chips:** $1,000
Time Limit: 30 min.

Level	Blinds
1	$25/$50
2	$50/$100
3	$100/$200
4	$200/$400
5	$400/$800
6	$800/$1,600
7	$1,600/$3,200
8	$1,500/$3,000
9	$5,000/$10,000
10	$10,000/$20,000

How to Win No-Limit Hold'em Tournaments

"Tournament players follow the rules closely, so it's a bit easier for new players to see how theory works in practice."

–Lou Krieger in *Poker for Dummies*

INTRODUCTION

Now that you have the basic concepts of tournament poker down pat, it's time to put theory into action. In this chapter we detail the winning strategies of tournament poker and show you how to use them in critical situations when the chips are down and your tournament success is on the line.

GET TO KNOW YOUR OPPONENTS

"You need to stay tuned into the game every minute, watching the other players, looking for their unique mannerisms, and noting the hands they turn up at the showdown. Your mission is to get free information from them."

–Brad Daugherty in *No-Limit Texas Hold'em: The New Player Series*

A handful of years ago, everybody who played big buy-in tournaments knew each other. There was Chan, Hellmuth, Green, Lund, Cloutier, Brunson, Johnston, and so on—the members of an exclusive club of poker masters who'd won just about everything there was to win. Not any more. Today so many new faces are playing $5,000 and $10,000 tournaments, as well as smaller buy-in events, that you probably will never get a chance to know them all. And that is why observing how your opponents play is even more important today than it has ever been before.

Tournaments are won one table at a time, so your table and your opponents are what you need to focus on. If you conquer your table, you stay alive. You cannot control what's going on at other tables, but you do have some say about what's going on at your table. Sounds easy, but how do you pull it off? By getting to know and understand your opponents.

In particular, focus on identifying:

1. The hands they play and the way they seem to think about them;
2. Who is aggressive and who is passive;
3. Who will defend their blinds and who will not;
4. Who you can bluff and who will call you every time you try it;
5. Which players are calling stations that you can value-bet hands against; and
6. Which players only come into pots with strong hands.

With these factors and all the other things that you have to be aware of to beat your table, you will spend more time observing and studying your opponents than you will playing hands! In fact, the best time to get a handle on how your opponents play is not when you're playing a hand yourself, but when you're sitting on the sidelines, having folded. Looking from the outside in, you can objectively analyze other people at your table while they are in the heat of battle.

What exactly are you looking for? First, observe the kinds of hands they turn over at the showdown. Notice whether they started with a big pair or big connectors such as A-K. Did they enter the pot with suited connectors or ace-rag? From what position did they come into the pot?

Next, determine whether they are passive or aggressive. You determine this by keeping track of their betting patterns. Do they usually enter the pot with a raise or do they just call? Have they ever just called someone else's raise before or after flop? Do they aggressively bet their hands after the flop, or do they usually just call when an opponent bets into them? Have you ever noticed them slow-playing a strong hand or value-betting a marginal hand? Have they ever been caught attempting a bluff—or calling someone else's bluff—with a weak pair or a drawing hand?

"I also look for what I call 'hand tells,'" Tom advises. "While I'm looking at my cards, I'm also looking at the people on my immediate left. I will know soon enough how the players in front of me act on their hands, so the opponents who must act after me are the most important. A lot of times you can tell just by the way people are holding their cards whether they're going to play or fold. This is very valuable information to have.

"There are times when I've raised from middle position with a hand like A-7 offsuit, a hand I wouldn't normally play, because I could tell that everyone was going to throw their hands away, with the possible exception of the big blind. Watch for players who pick up their cards and hold them in their discard mode. Assuming this is a real tell and not a reverse tell, you can believe they really are going to throw their hands away.

"However, if I have seen someone trying to project a fake tell on past hands by holding their cards like they're going to pitch them and then suddenly putting in a bet or a raise, I know that they're probably giving off a reverse tell. In other words, if they act like they don't care about their cards, it's quite possible that they have a strong, playable hand. And if they act like they do care about their cards, their hand might be weak."

Opponents might also tip off the strength of their hands by "loading up." This is where, after looking at his hole cards, a player picks up the exact number of chips needed to make a call and holds them in one hand. Normally he's going to call. This is especially true of inexperienced players who load up so they won't slow down the game or fumble with their chips when it's their turn to act. They're getting their chips ready to play, which usually is reliable information that you can use to your advantage.

If you have a marginal hand, you want to see the flop cheaply, and you've seen an opponent loading up the exact amount of the big blind, you know that he doesn't intend to raise the pot. Sometimes after the flop, you'll see players loading up, but they often do it to discourage a bet, not because they intend to call one. They act as though they're going to call when they really don't want to call. If you have a strong hand, you may want to put in a little extra raise when you notice this tell.

Also listen for verbal tells. "I sometimes become very talkative at the table," Tom adds, "asking players where they're from and where they usually play. If I see them wearing online apparel, PokerStars T-shirts or caps, I might ask, 'What's your screen name? How often do you play online? Have you played a lot of casino tournaments?' Or if a chap raises and everybody folds, I might ask, 'Pocket queens?' People will give you a lot of free information if you simply ask them for it."

As a spokesperson for PokerStars and the author of a dozen books, Tom is a highly visible player with a recognizable face, which makes getting information a lot easier for him than it is for many of us. Sometimes people want to impress him or ask for his advice and are often truthful about their hands. If a well-known player is at your table, listen to the conversations that players strike up with him. They will often divulge information you can use against them.

Once you know how an opponent plays, you're only interested in finding out whether he is playing that way today, right now. Is he splashing chips and going on tilt even though that isn't something he would normally do? Is a fight with his spouse affecting his play? Get to know your opponents as fast as you can, and then reevaluate how they're playing at the moment.

At first, you might make some mistakes when evaluating your opponents, but as you practice, you'll find that your accuracy will increase. World-class no-limit hold'em tournament players are great observers and incredible readers of their opponents. The only way they got to that point was by spending a lot of time practicing their observation skills and remembering how their opponents play.

"If a wing fell off a gnat at the other end of the table, I'd see it," T.J. claims. "What I'm saying here is that you have to be alert at all times at the poker table."

Learn How Your Opponents Play the Blinds

One of the secrets to winning at no-limit hold'em is taking advantage of how your opponents play when they are in the blinds. Who will defend their blinds and who will surrender their blinds? Watch all of your opponents carefully every time they are in the big blind, in particular. Knowing how they usually play the big blind can help you steal more chips and lose fewer than you ever imagined. Often, the chips you accumulate through thievery are the only things that keep you alive in a tournament. Every time you successfully steal someone's blind, you have earned a free round. If you are able to pick up the blinds one time in each round while basically holding your chip count even, you will eventually make it to the final table just by breaking even in each round.

Sometimes when you are on the button, you can steal the blinds with a raise simply because you know that the big blind will not defend. If you have a weaker hand that you want to take a shot with, you're looking to play it against a passive player who usually will surrender his blind to a raise. And if the blind happens to wake up with good cards and reraises you, it's easy to get away from your hand. Naturally if you get a strong hand, you're more than happy to play it against a blind defender.

You also can steal the blinds from the second seat to the right of the button and from the cutoff seat, one to the right of the button, if you know that the players sitting to your left usually will fold against a raise. Players often give the player in the cutoff seat more credit when he raises than they give the player sitting on the button, who they will call with almost anything from the big blind. When you raise from the cutoff seat, you are taking a bigger risk, of course, since you must contend with the button as well as the blinds. This added risk may be why players often give more respect to these raises.

"If I'm the first player in the pot," Tom says, "I'm often willing to take a shot at the pot by raising with a marginal hand, especially if the player on the button is not a super-aggressive player."

Since the blinds escalate at regular intervals during tournaments, you're always fighting against the clock. The constantly escalating blinds force people to play more hands as the tournament wears on. In the late rounds, players often play much weaker starting hands than they ordinarily would, because they cannot afford to just sit and wait for big cards. They know that if they don't play a hand the rising blinds will eat them up, and they may literally get blinded out of the tournament. This is when it becomes even more important to pick up a few blinds.

As a side note, stealing the blinds is far more important in tournaments than it is in cash games, because the blinds and antes remain constant in cash games and you are rewarded more for patience than for risk-taking. In small no-limit hold'em cash games with blinds that range from $1/$2 to $2/$5, robbing the blinds is not of prime importance. Sure, you might win $7 or so, but the downside is that you could wind up losing a substantial number of chips if you get raised and incorrectly decide to call.

PLAY GOOD STARTING HANDS IN POSITION

"In no-limit hold'em, position is the name of the game. It's everything. If I had position all night, I could beat the game ... and I'd never have to look at my hole cards."

–Doyle Brunson in *Super System*

Starting hands and position are joined at the hip in no-limit hold'em. In fact, your position at the table is more important in no-limit hold'em than in any other form of poker with the exception of pot-limit games. Doyle Brunson, quoted above, understands the importance of position. He is one of the greatest players of all time, and having had the privilege and sorrow of playing against him in tournaments, we heartily agree that he plays late position like a concert pianist. If you only played hands from the last three positions, you would be a winning player.

Superior Position, Outstanding Results

After Phil Hellmuth won the $10,000 no-limit hold'em main event at the World Series of Poker in 1989, he was feeling pretty darned good about himself, and understandably so, since he'd just become the youngest person ever to win the World Championship. But he may've taken things a step too far when he declared that he could beat anyone in the world in a head-to-head freezeout. Amarillo Slim overheard Phil's remark and drawled something like, "Well, son, I dunno 'bout that. I reckon I may be the best head-to-head player in the whole wide world." Naturally, the match was on—a $5,000 winner-take-all freezeout.

But then Slim stalled, telling Phil that perhaps he was right after all, maybe he couldn't beat the young star heads-up. Unwilling to let Slim dodge the bullet, Phil kept after him to play. Finally Slim relented, but with a hedge: The only way he would play Phil was if Phil agreed to allow him to be on the button in every hand. After hashing out the details, Phil agreed and they started the match. It didn't take long to see that Phil had taken the worst of the deal, and Slim won in a breeze. Slim wasn't necessarily the better player; Phil simply could not overcome the power of the button. Hellmuth has since gone on to win nine gold bracelets at the World Series, write poker books, and produce highly successful DVD poker seminars. In Play Poker Like the Pros, which he wrote many years after playing Slim heads-up, Phil wrote: "Being able to act last is a huge advantage in all forms of poker."

It is impossible to overstate the power of being the last person to act in no-limit hold'em, be it a tournament or a cash game. The weaker your position—that is, the earlier you act—the more vulnerable you are. Therefore, you need to have strong starting hands. The stronger your table position, the more powerful you are, so you can play a wider variety of hands than when you are in early position. That's why we say that hand selection and table position are intertwined.

Early Position

Starting Hands

In a typical nine-handed no-limit hold'em game, we suggest that when you are in one of the first three positions after the big blind, you play only the following hands: A-A, K-K, Q-Q, J-J, A-K, and A-Q. If you never played a hand from early position other than these super six, you probably would show a profit over the long haul. The reason you play only these strong starting hands from early position is that most of them can stand a raise from players behind you.

The exceptions are J-J and A-Q, which are more vulnerable to overpairs and certain types of flops. If you have one of these two hands and someone raises or reraises behind you, we suggest that you fold and wait for the next deal. Even if no one raises you before the flop, you could still run into trouble if the board comes with an ace. Your A-Q could be out-kicked, and your pocket jacks might be up against a bigger pair, so you must proceed cautiously with these two otherwise strong starting hands.

Suppose you have raised in early position with A-K, A-K suited, or A-Q suited and someone calls your raise. The flop comes with three small cards, none of which are in your suit. Now what do you do? If you bet and get raised or called, you're in trouble. If you check and the pre-flop caller bets, you're in trouble.

"I throw my hand into the muck," Don answers. "Even though I had premium cards before the flop, why lose valuable chips when I don't hit the flop? I would rather wait for the next hand."

Trouble Hands

Hands such as A-J, A-10, K-Q, K-J, K-10, Q-J and Q-10 are trouble hands that can cost you a ton of chips if you play them from early position. What can you hope for if you get called? With each of these hands, you will be in kicker trouble if you flop a pair if you are called from a late position player. And if you flop a flush draw, you will not be drawing to the nuts. If you are at a table with aggressive

98

players and get raised, you are out of position and will have to throw your hand away. Even when you are playing at a table with all passive players, you can still get into trouble by playing these hands.

Sometimes, of course, nothing works the way you want it to. Don tells this story about a plan that didn't work out during a $1,500 buy-in no-limit hold'em event at the Festa al Lago tournament at the Bellagio in Las Vegas:

"It was the fourth round and the blinds were $100/$200 with a $25 ante. We started with $3,000 in chips, and I thought I had a good read on the table. Six players limped into the pot. Sitting in the small blind with $2,400 in chips, I looked down at a suited A-K. 'This is a good time to move in and pick up the pot,' I thought as I shoved my stack boldly to the center.

"Everyone folded around to the button, who said, 'I have such a big hand, I've gotta call!' and pushed in his case $1,800 in chips. We opened our hands and he showed the 5♠-5♣. Three players announced that they had mucked pocket pairs—sixes, eights, and nines—but our hero could not fold pocket fives. Never fear, the pocket fives were good as gold, and I lost the hand.

"My problem was that I gave the button too much credit. I thought that he would fold any hand except A-A, K-K, Q-Q, J-J, A-K, A-Q. Wrong! I almost asked him why he would put his tournament life in jeopardy when the best he could hope for was to be a slight favorite. I had seen this same player lay down a lot of hands after the flop, and he almost never defended his blinds, but this time he had decided to defend—of all things—his button! I bit my tongue and went back to work with the $600 I had left, gradually getting back into the tournament."

Middle Position

Starting Hands

Good cards to play from middle position—the third, fourth, and fifth spots to the left of the big blind—include all the hands you would play in early position, as well as A-J, K-Q, A-10, 10-10, 9-9, and 8-8.

"If I am the first player to enter the pot, I generally make a standard raise with any one of these hands," Tom says. "However if one or more limpers have come into the pot, I will just call. And if I have one of the top six hands—A-A, K-K, Q-Q, J-J, A-K or A-Q—and limpers are already in the pot, I will make a raise bigger than three or four times the size of the big blind."

Any time you limp with cards weaker than those listed above, you are setting yourself up as a potential target. You still have players in late position and the two blinds to contend with before you're safe. Any of these players could raise, forcing you to fold most of your weaker holdings. If you are in a mid-position and have aggressive players yet to act after you, stick to these recommended starting hands.

"The only time I might lower my middle-position requirements is when I have very passive players to act after me," Tom says. "I also prefer that two or more limpers already be in the pot when I play small pairs and suited connectors, so that I can get a good price on my hand if I hit the flop."

In the previous section, we said that hands such as A-J, A-10, and K-Q are trouble hands if you play them from early position. But now let's assume that you have one of these hands in middle position and you are the first player to enter the pot.

"I would bring those same hands in for a raise of usually three to four times the big blind," Don says. "My goal here is to get the cutoff seat and the button to fold, and then see what the blinds do. If they fold and the blinds also fold, that's fine with me; I have built my stack by winning the blinds and antes. And if the blinds call, I have the advantage of being in superior position from the flop through the river."

Late Position

Starting Hands

You can add the following hands to your starting hand arsenal when you're sitting in a late position: K-J, K-10, Q-10, J-10, any suited ace, small pairs (deuces through sevens), and these suited connectors: 10-9, 9-8 and 8-7. Caution: This does not mean you should call a raise with these hands. It does mean that you can play them for the minimum bet when two or more limpers are already in the pot. You can also consider raising with these hands in certain situations—for example, if you are the first player in the pot and the players in the blinds are weak blind defenders.

You can play weaker hands from late position, especially in unraised pots, than you can play from middle or early position. Being able to open up your starting-hand requirements somewhat is one of the pleasures of playing from late position. If the pot has not been raised, you usually would raise with any of the top six hands. And if one or more limpers are already in the pot, you'll often call with the middle-position hands.

Your raising requirements also may vary when you're sitting in late position.

"If I am the first player in the pot," Tom says, "I will raise with all early and middle position hands, plus a large variety of weaker starting hands. The types of cards I raise with depends on how loose or tight the blinds are, as well as the nature of the player on the button—assuming I don't own the button myself."

In *Super System*, Bobby Baldwin, the 1978 World Champion of Poker, sums up position play beautifully, writing: "My play in the middle and late positions illustrates a saying which applies to every poker game I know: 'Play solid in front and loose in the back.'"

DISCIPLINE PAYS DIVIDENDS

"Caro's Law of Least Tilt: Among similarly skilled opponents, the player with the most discipline is the favorite."

–Mike Caro

Discipline is the cornerstone of tournament play. Using a well-timed, disciplined strategy is the key to longevity in tournaments. Recall that we said earlier that patience is a virtue when you're playing no-limit hold'em. Patience is even more important when you're playing a tournament. In fact, it is the primary ingredient in discipline. But remaining patient and self-disciplined hour after hour, day after day, in big tournament do-or-die situations isn't always easy.

A lot of players become impatient because they've heard that you need to build your stack. They try to force the action; they try to manufacture good hands. These players take risks and make bluffs that are ill-advised. They'll give their chips to you if you can simply last long enough for them to make a mistake playing against you.

How disciplined do you have to be in waiting for premium hands to play? In a tournament that has 20-minute rounds, you should get one good hand to play in each round that will increase your chip stack if you win it. If the tournament has 30-minute rounds, you should get two good hands per round. Sometimes, of course, you don't get any playable hands during a round. Or even two rounds.

That's when your patience is put to the test. As you muck hand after hand, try saying to yourself, "This too shall pass," because most of the time, the cards will turn around in your favor—eventually.

Here's a big difference between cash games and tournament games: In cash games, when you've won a couple of hands and tripled the size of your stack, you can leave the game a winner, but in tournaments, you can't do that—you must continue playing. This is one more reason why being very patient in the hands you elect to play is so important. You can throw off a lot of chips if you don't think about why you're putting them into the pot. You must take time to think about what your next play is going to be, and what you're trying to accomplish with your bet or call.

New players often respond reflexively by making a fast call when they get raised. The "He raised me so I'm gonna reraise him!" mentality will cost you a lot of chips in the long run. One of the things we caution students about is making reflexive plays like this. We warn them about the dangers of making a fast decision when a major portion of their chips are at stake, but too often players get their ego mixed up with strategy. They have a macho thing and can't back down. You'll even see people throw off extra money when it is clear to everyone at the table that they are beaten. That kind of thinking is nonsense—bets saved are just as important as bets earned.

Discipline is particularly important in the early rounds of a no-limit hold'em tournament, because a lot of your opponents are gambling it up with marginal hands. Instead of jumping on the bandwagon and playing too loosely, wait for premium cards to play against them. That way you will have the edge, and they'll usually be taking the worst of it. Be patient. You don't need to gamble early in the tournament, when you have a fair amount of chips in relation to the starting blinds. Your goal is to increase your chips in each round, but you don't need to win a lot of hands to do it. In no-limit hold'em, all you need to do is win one or two hands to double or triple your chips.

BET THE RIGHT AMOUNT

"You do not need to follow the leader—you can raise the amount of chips that you believe is correct, no matter what your opponents have been doing."

–Brad Daugherty, 1991 World Champion of Poker in
No-Limit Texas Hold'em

Learning how much to bet is one of the challenges of no-limit hold'em. When you see top no-limit hold'em players stop, study a hand, think, count out their chips, and then place a bet, they aren't just stalling for time. They are putting their brains to the test with questions such as these: How much should I bet? What do I hope to accomplish here? What does my opponent have? What does he think I have? They're analyzing all the data they have gathered and processing it before they act. The best players can do this fairly quickly, but they always take an extra moment to review how the hand unfolded before they make a final decision about how to play it.

One of the biggest mistakes new players make in tournaments is either raising too much or raising too little. When you are the first player to enter the pot, we suggest that you raise about three to four times the size of the big blind during the early rounds of a tournament. Make this your standard raise no matter what the strength of your hand. Of course, opinions vary when it comes to exactly how much the standard raise should be. T.J. Cloutier thinks it isn't so bad, particularly in the early rounds, to raise slightly more than three to four times the big blind if the situation is right. But most top players agree that sticking to a standard amount when making your opening raise is the right decision.

The purpose of doing this is to make it difficult for your opponents to determine the strength of the hand. If you raise more when you have a strong hand and less when you have a weak hand, your opponents will pick up on that. In essence, the size of your raise will be giving away the strength of your hand. That's something you don't want to do. If you decide to take a shot at the pot with a 9-8, raise the same amount you would if you had pocket aces. That way your opponents cannot get a read on you.

Once in a while, you might want to mix things up a bit. For instance, if you don't want to get called, you might try deviating from your standard raising pattern.

"This usually is when I have a hand such as pocket nines or tens in late position," Tom says. "These are hands that I don't particularly want much action with, so I may raise four to five times the size of the big blind to discourage a call.

"Another time I might raise more is when some limpers are already in the pot. For every limper, I might escalate my raise one notch. For example, if one limper is already in the pot, I might bring it in for four to five times the size of the big blind instead of three times the big blind. With two limpers, my raise would be five to six times the big blind. The purpose of making a larger raise is to make it more expensive for the limpers to see the flop."

In addition, you might raise more than the standard amount when you are in late position and the big blind is a liberal blind defender. If you are up against this type of loose player and have a big pocket pair—queens or better—you want to "sell" your hand for as much as you can. This means that you are trying to get your opponents to call as big a bet as possible when you have a premium hand that you think is the best hand.

Factoring in Your Opponents' Betting Patterns

Always be aware of the tendencies in your opponents' betting, raising, and calling standards. The size of your bet depends on the types of opponents you are up against and what you are trying to accomplish. When you're up against professional-level players, playing in a straightforward manner is often the most effective tactic. In other words, if you have what you think is the best hand, fire in a pot-sized bet. You want some action on the hand, and you know that they will be suspicious of any other type of bet. Whether you have a hand or are bluffing, putting in a pot-sized bet will seem normal to this caliber of player, but it won't cause any alarm bells to go off in their minds. A pot-sized bet will make it expensive for them to come after you, forcing them into a tough decision. A bet like this says: "I have something. And if you want to play, let's go at it."

If you're up against less experienced players and you want to get some action on the hand, you may want to under-bet the pot. Occasionally an underbet will fool even a good player, but usually it is more effective against a new player who doesn't yet grasp the game completely and doesn't understand the nuances of the betting in no-limit hold'em. The underbet may seem like a bargain price for their hand, so they often will go after you with cards they probably should not play.

Making a Double Bet

Players who are accustomed to playing limit hold'em often come into a no-limit pot by raising an amount that is twice the size of the big blind. Usually, this is a mistake. If you have a big pair, you need to make a larger raise than this in order to thin out the field before the flop. If you have a marginal hand, such as a small pair or suited connectors, and you might be able to see the flop for the minimum bet, why raise at all? The double bet before the flop won't move opponents off their hands, and it will reopen the betting at a time when all you have is a drawing hand. How much sense does that make?

Even after the flop, some players bet or raise an amount that is twice the size of the big blind with drawing hands like flush or straight draws—the idea being to build a pot so they can win more if they make their hand. But building the pot is not a viable strategy unless you have a strong hand. With a drawing hand, the double bet reopens the betting for aggressive opponents, and this in turn might make the cost of drawing much higher than you intended. Instead take a free card if you can, or keep anyone from calling you by making a big bet, which will allow you to win the pot right there. If you have a strong hand, certainly you want to build the pot, but still, making a mini-bet is not the way to do it. Instead make a bet that is the size you think your opponents will call without making it too cheap for them to draw. And as for drawing hands, we believe that you would not be making a huge mistake if you never bet a drawing hand in no-limit hold'em.

Underbetting the Pot

An underbet is a bet that is disproportionately small in relation to the size of the pot. When you under-bet the pot, you usually are showing weakness—one thing you don't want to do, especially in no-limit hold'em. Good players pick up on that. Therefore if you think you have the best hand, you should usually bet bigger, not smaller. Why? Because making a bet that is too small can be dangerous to your tournament health. A small bet simply reopens the betting and gives aggressive players sitting behind you an opportunity to steal the pot away from you.

For example, suppose there is $100 in the pot, you flop top pair with a weak kicker and bet $20 or $30. Based upon your small bet, an experienced opponent will sense that you are weak, and he may take the pot away from you with a raise—even if he doesn't have a hand.

Now let's look at a scenario in which you might make an underbet. Suppose you are in an early position and you flop bottom set. In this situation, you make a small bet at the pot to lure your opponents in. You actually want somebody to come over the top and try to take the pot away from you, which would allow you to reraise. Here's an example: Suppose you are in the big blind with pocket threes in an unraised, multiway pot, so you get to see the flop cheaply.

The flop comes with the J♦-10♦-3♠. With the J-10 suited on the board, there are a lot of drawing possibilities. Your opponents may be in the pot with hands like K-J, K-Q, J-10, or suited cards that give them a flush draw. This is a very good spot to lead into the field with a small bet. Many times, your opponents will come after you on the flop, and they often will be very aggressive with their hands. That's perfect because now you can come over the top of them and tax them heavily if they want to continue playing the hand. So in this case, a small bet is correct.

A lot of times you can win much bigger pots if you lead into them with a strong hand, giving someone the opportunity to come over the top of you. If you check-raise, many times you will get one bet out of your opponent, but they usually will fold to your raise unless they have a very strong hand. You often can make more money by leading at the pot, but you need to have the right kind of board.

The size of your bet also depends on the type of opposition you're up against. The more inexperienced your opponents, the more inclined you might be to make a small bet. Still, if there is $100 in the pot, you should bet $40 or $50, rather than only $20 or $30. In other words, make a bet that is about one-half the size of the pot in the hope that someone has enough of a hand to come after you.

But if you don't have a big hand, such as a set, you're much better off making a decent bet at the pot, either a pot-sized bet or possibly two-thirds to three-quarters the size of the pot. In no-limit hold'em you can bet enough chips

111

to make it too expensive for people to play their drawing hands. This doesn't mean they won't draw to them, it simply means they're making a mistake if they do.

In summary, if you figure to have the best hand, always keep in mind the nature of your opponents when deciding how much to bet after the flop. Avoid the mistake that inexperienced players make when they bet only a twice the minimum on the flop without thinking things through. If your opponents are calling stations, make a larger bet that will tax them for the privilege of trying to hit a card. If they are not calling stations, or if they are overly aggressive, just make a standard bet. That way, you can penalize them by reraising if they decide to come after you.

Betting into a Dry Pot

Tournament players often make the mistake of betting into a pot that has one player all-in against two or more opponents with no side pot. This is known as a **dry pot**. Many times, one of the active players bets on the flop with no hand at all or with only a drawing hand. This bet actually protects the all-in player by forcing the other active opponents to either fold or call. What is he trying to accomplish by betting?

"I have a slightly different slant on that," Don says. "Suppose I have a K-Q, for example, and the flop comes 9-high. Even though we have an all-in player, I may bet into this pot just because I think that my K-Q will be good as long as I hit one of my overcards. I would never make this play at the final table, of course, but it's something that I might do in regular tournament play. In other words, you might bet into a dry pot when you think that nobody else, including the all-in player, can beat your hand. You certainly would not bet with a 4-2, for example. Why try to create a side pot unless you have a decent hand?"

Be aware that sometimes in dry pot situations, one of the other active players might check to you with the solid nuts just because he's hoping to eliminate the all-in player. A player often will check fairly strong hands not because he is setting up a check-raise, but because he doesn't want to force anybody else out of the pot. He does this even when he knows that he has the all-in player beaten and just in case the other active players in the pot make better hands than his.

BUILD YOUR STACK

"In life the strong survive and the weak perish. Big fish eat little fish. In tournament poker the same law of the jungle applies. Big stacks prey upon little stacks. Chips are power!"

–Mike Sexton in *Shuffle Up & Deal!*

The number of chips you have in relation to the size of the blinds affects your tournament strategy—especially at the start of the tournament and in the very late rounds.

In the beginning rounds when the blinds are very small in relation to the number of starting chips, you have less reason to try to build your stack by stealing blinds, playing marginal hands, or highjacking your opponents.

In the late stage of the tournament, the reverse is true. The blinds are usually so big in relation to the size of your stack and the number of chips in play that many times you must try to steal the blinds and play marginal hands just to maintain your chip status. This is why people can become misguided about how to play no-limit hold'em by watching the World Poker Tour and other televised tournaments. They only see the final table of the tournament, where players at a shorthanded table are making aggressive plays with marginal hands. If those same players had played that way during the beginning stage of the tournament, their aggressive tactics invariably would have backfired on them.

How many times the size of the big blind do you need to have in chips in order to feel comfortable? Any time you have 50 times the size of the big blind, you have a big stack with plenty of chips to maneuver with. With fewer chips than that, say 30 times the size of the big blind, you have enough chips to play with, but you have a much smaller margin of error.

How many hands do you need to win in a 30-minute tournament round? You should be happy if you can win one or two hands. That's the rule of thumb, though a lot of players have the misconception that your goal is to double-up in each round. No, doubling up is strictly a bonus. And that will happen sometimes, but the main thing is to add to your stack each round by making intelligent bets and raises, picking your spots carefully, and getting lucky enough to catch a few strong hands that hold up.

Every time you finish one level, you want to have more chips than you started with. If you can do that, you will make more final tables, win more tournaments, and become very successful. You cannot win a tournament in the first stage, and you can't win it in the second stage. You win tournaments in the middle and latter stages—not the first four or five rounds.

What you can do in the early rounds is lose the tournament—and a lot of players do exactly that by taking unnecessary risks. Sometimes they simply take a bad beat, say, when they have a big pair against a lesser pair and their opponent hits a set. In other words, you sometimes get knocked out not by playing incorrectly, but by getting unlucky. Other times, players simply gamble too much and risk getting broke far earlier in the tournament than they should. They forget that they can't win the tournament in the first few rounds. They think that they have to accumulate a lot of chips early on, but what they really have to do is slowly build their stack and survive.

During the first one or two rounds, while you're still observing your table and figuring out a lot of things about your opponents, your efforts at building your stack may move at a slower pace than you would like. The ideal situation is to triple- or quadruple-up in the first round or two, but be happy if you can increase your stack by 20 to 50 percent. If you can do that, you're doing just fine. If you go into the third level and you've doubled-up or close to it, you're in very good shape.

"But still, I always keep my eye on the amount of chips I have in relation to the blinds," Don says. "I take a number—it may be 20, 30, 40, or 50 times the blind—and if I have that number, I'm fine no matter what the size of the big blind. In fact, any time you have 30 or more times the size of the big blind after the first couple of rounds, you have enough chips to work with."

Weathering a Drought of Cards

You cannot manufacture good hands in a tournament. Sometimes you will go through a dry spell of cards, and even if you want to take a shot at stealing the blinds, there's not much you can do if someone beats you to it, except be patient and wait for a better situation. Just because you feel the need to build your stack—the need for greed, so to speak—by 30 to 50 percent in each level doesn't mean that things will always happen that way. That's the ideal situation, but sometimes you just have to wait it out. If you wait too long, of course, the blinds and antes will get to you and force you to make a decision with a more marginal hand.

If you're fortunate, you will find a good hand to play. And hopefully, you will get action with your big hands, so that you can double-up and build your stack. In other cases, you may get pocket aces, make a raise, and watch as everybody folds, including the blinds. "Gee, that was sort of unlucky," you say to yourself. At these times, remember than you also can go broke with aces. No hand is an ironclad cinch.

KEEP AN EYE ON THE TOURNAMENT CLOCK

"Think of the tournament as a pie that is divided into as many pieces as there are time periods."

–Shane Smith in *Poker Tournament Tips from the Pros*

A poker tournament is similar to a football game, which is divided into timed quarters. Eventually the time runs out and the game is over. In a poker tournament, the game isn't over until one player has won all the chips, but like in football, you know how much time you have left in the round. And there's one other important question you should always know the answer to: How does my chip stack compare with the average stack?

Tournament clocks, which are projected on a big screen, tell you what the limit is, how much time is left in the round, how many players remain in the event, and the size of the average chip stack, so that you can calculate where you stand in relation to the rest of the field. Online clocks do the job very quickly and efficiently, but sometimes the tournament clocks in casinos fall behind a little bit.

"I know how many players started the tournament and I know approximately how many players are left," Don says, "so I automatically know how many chips are in play. I divide the number of chips in play by the number of players left to calculate the average chip count. If I find that I have the average number of chips or higher—in other words, if I am right on the curve or higher than the curve—I know that I am progressing very nicely."

Knowing when the limits will change also has an impact on your strategy. Suppose you're in bad chip position, and by glancing at the tournament clock, you realize that you probably will be taking the blinds once more before the limits rise. In this case, you might consider making a move now, before the blinds get so high that you won't be a factor no matter what you do. Here's another example: Say that in three more hands, you'll have to take the big blind. Should you take a chance right now with a marginal hand when the blinds are smaller, or should you wait? The clock can help you make this decision.

In tournament play, you're always playing against the clock as well as your opponents. Sure, you can sit there and patiently wait for good cards in the early rounds, when you have 30 to 50 times the big blind in chips. But in the later rounds when you have only 10 times the size of the big blind, you can't do that. You will have to make a decision fairly soon. The clock can help you formulate your strategy—use this important tool to your advantage.

PLAY A BIG STACK WISELY

"Noting the relative chip counts and the positions of the finalists, I pondered what might take place when they vied for the $1,795,000 first-place prize. Would we see a cakewalk or a comeback? Would Negreanu attempt to use his big stack to bully his opponents?"

–Lee Munzer in *Card Player* magazine on the final table at the 2004 Five Diamond World Poker Classic at Bellagio

A big stack is a thing of beauty in no-limit hold'em tournaments. Used correctly, a big stack can intimidate and annihilate the enemy. But used frivolously, a big stack can be decimated. In this section we'll give you some tips on how to use a big stack as a weapon of mass destruction, but first let's talk about how to protect and preserve it.

One of the biggest mistakes tournament players make is frittering away a big stack. They go on a massive rush early in the tournament and accumulate a lot of chips, often by gambling and playing overly aggressive. Then they make a fatal mistake: They don't change gears and slow down to protect their precious assets. They keep on playing the same way—being overly aggressive with marginal hands—and they destroy themselves before they make it to the money. We've seen one-time chip leaders finish out of the money because they refused to lay down a 10-9 before the flop to an opponent's raise, or because they moved in with a 9-8.

Even with a big stack, you still have to give your opponents credit. When you've built a massive chip stack by doing a lot of gambling, your opponents know that you gamble and that you don't necessarily have a good hand when you raise. "I'm gonna look him up!" they say to themselves. "He may knock me out of the tournament, but I'll take that chance. The next time he raises, I'm coming after him if I have a hand." They don't think they need an excellent hand to go up against the bully with the big stack—just a good hand.

To counter this mentality, change gears—go from an aggressive mode to a patient mode. Raise only when you have a big hand or a good hand, not the mediocre hands you may have played aggressively while building your big stack. Your opponents will remember some of those marginal hands you raised with earlier, and if they haven't given you credit for changing gears, they will call you with their own marginal hands. So shifting gears will help you preserve a big stack and even add to it.

Here's another factor that comes into play: Suppose you've accumulated a large stack by having legitimate hands and getting good action on them, meaning you've shown nothing but strength on the hands you've turned over at the river. Now you can take advantage of that solid image by raising with a marginal hand, because your opponents will be much more likely to give you credit for a strong hand. When you have a strong table profile, this is how you can preserve your stack and add to it by taking a few more risks.

Usually, however, when you see someone with a huge amount of chips early in the tournament, it's because he got lucky with the worst hand a few times. If that's the case and you're up against observant opponents, they are going to look you up—even if they have to risk getting broke—because they don't necessarily think that you have a big hand. And they're probably going to be right.

Beware Forcing An Opponent to Play a Hand

When you have a big stack and are thinking about coming into the pot with a raise, be aware of the types of players sitting behind you. Sometimes your raise is going to force someone with a small stack to play because of his chip position, when you really don't want him to play with you. Your opponent might be sitting there thinking, "Well, the blind is coming to me in a couple of hands and I only have twice the big blind, so I'm gonna play."

Suppose you raise from middle to late position with a hand like J-10, and a guy in the blind has only one or two more blind bets left in his stack. He is going to have to call you. And even if he has only a queen-rag, he's a favorite over you heads-up. You've forced the guy to put his chips in whether he wants to or not. This is not the time to raise with a marginal hand. What you don't want to do is double up a short stack when you don't have much of a hand yourself.

If you are the short stack in a situation like this, be aware that you're only two hands away from being the chip leader or a chip contender at your table. Even with a very short stack, if you double-up twice, you will have plenty of chips to play with. And sometimes, you can triple-up on one pot, if the amount of the blinds, antes, and your opponent's chips are high enough. Winning two hands in a row can dramatically change your situation for the better. On the flip side of the coin, if you lose two hands in a row, you can go from the penthouse to the outhouse in a hurry.

This gets us back to the importance of preserving a big stack. Once you've accumulated a decent stack, don't take a lot of reckless chances. In this situation, you really want to play your best game. Play solid, selectively aggressive poker.

A Weapon of Mass Destruction

Now comes the fun part: Wield a big stack like a weapon of mass destruction to destroy your table. When you have a big stack, a lot of players with medium or short stacks will be afraid to confront you. They don't want to risk getting broke, especially if they're anywhere close to the money and it's in the latter stages of the tournament. They realize that if they can hang on a little bit longer, they at least will have a money finish. When you have a big stack and can break them without seriously risking your own chances in the tournament, they will try to avoid you. Any time you have a big stack and can put somebody all-in without putting at risk a major portion of your stack, you have a huge psychological advantage. Your opponent will have to have a much better hand than yours in order justify the risk of getting broke to the hand.

Big stacks are especially intimidating to players who are playing excessively tight. These rocks are the players you can rob. When you're in position, it doesn't matter what your two holecards are, you can make a positional play at the pot—meaning a raise—against opponents who most likely are going to lay down their hands. On the other side of the coin, if based on your observations you know that the short stacks are willing to gamble with you, don't try the same play. These are not the kinds of players you want to put all-in with marginal hand.

Here's a humorous true story from Don about a player who was willing to lay down a lot of hands because he really, really wanted to make it to the final table:

"I played a tournament recently where the buy-in was $300. "We got down to sixteen players and one player at my table kept calling over to his friend at the other table, 'I will make the final table. I'll bet you $100 I make the final table!' Well, I raised his big blind every time without even looking at my cards. And you know what? He showed me an A-Q that he had laid down, and he also folded pocket jacks against me. Sure enough, he made the final table; he finished in ninth place."

But he forgot the big picture. He was so anxious to make the final table, he gave up his chance to win the tournament. Don picked up on the fact that he really wanted to make it to the final table and took total advantage of the guy. Shame on him!

PLAY A MEDIUM STACK WITH DISCRETION

"If the cards break even, a good player will win the money because he makes fewer mistakes than a bad player makes."
–T.J. Cloutier in *Championship Hold'em*

Playing a medium stack correctly is essential to your tournament success. Obviously the more chips you have, the better off you are, but most of the time you will have to do battle when you have less than a big stack.

"I believe that a medium stack is much more difficult to play than either a large stack or a short stack," Tom says. "With a medium stack, you must make far more difficult decisions on each hand you play. If you go up against a big stack, you can get broke or crippled. If you go up against a short stack and lose, they double-up and you become the short stack.

"If you make the correct decision against a big stack, you may double through and become a big stack at their expense. If you win against an all-in short stack, you have eliminated a player, increasing your chances of making the money or moving up on the pay scale if you're already in the money. With a medium stack, you need to balance surviving with accumulating enough chips to be a contender for the title, not just a finish in the money."

There are certain advantages to having a medium stack. First, you can bust a short stack just as easily as a big stack can. The short stacks know this and probably will be wary of playing with you. Second, even the big stacks know they must be careful playing pots against you. If they make a mistake, you could double through them and take their place on top of the heap. You can become the big stack while they become a medium stack.

PLAY A SHORT STACK CAREFULLY

"I've always thrived under pressure throughout my poker career. When my back's against the wall, it often brings out the best in me."

–Daniel Negreanu, 2004 Tournament Player of the Year

"I tell people that I play a short stack well because I have had so much practice with one!" Tom says. "I have played tournaments where I lasted very deep into the tournament with very few chips. In every tournament I've won, I was in what appeared to be a hopeless chip position at some point.

"How did I survive to come back and win? First, my personal philosophy is the same as that of Winston Churchill: Never, ever, ever give up. Second, I try to find the best spot for my precious few remaining chips. If I have a premium hand like a big pair or A-K, it is easy to put my chips into the pot. But when I have a less than premium hand, I try to decide whether this is the best spot for my chips, or whether I should wait for something better. My position at the table in relation to the blinds and the type of players in the blinds often influence my decision. In other words, I am looking for the best hand or the best situation to put my case chips in the pot.

"Always try to avoid allowing your chip position to deteriorate to the point that if you do enter the pot with a raise, you're not a factor. If you only have two or three

126

times the big blind, you will get called when you raise. A top tournament player told me, 'I'd rather move in with absolutely nothing, even 7-2 offsuit, as long as I can be the first player in the pot.' He would rather take a chance while he can still make a big enough raise that his opponents will have to think twice before calling him."

But what if you don't get the opportunity to make a move at the pot because someone else always beats you to it, and you don't have a strong enough hand to call? Since you can't manufacture a good hand out of thin air, sometimes you have to grit your teeth and wait for the big blind to take your stand. If it is highly likely that you are going to get called because you are short-stacked—and you have had nothing but weak starting hands—waiting for the big blind is not the worst strategy in the world.

Another nice thing—relatively speaking—about playing a short stack is that your decision is often made before the flop. In some ways, you actually have fewer decisions to make when you have a small stack than when you have a large or medium stack. You simply move all-in and hope for the best. Your opponents can only call you or fold. If someone raises in front of you, you decide to play by going all-in. Either way, you get to see all five community cards, and nobody can bluff you out of the pot.

PLAY AGGESSIVE POKER

"If a hand is not strong enough to raise with, it is not strong enough to call. If you don't believe me, just watch the final table at any major poker tournament. It is common for the entire final table to be played without ever seeing a player call as the first one to enter the pot."

–Chris Ferguson, 2000 World Champion of Poker, in *All-In* magazine

No-limit hold'em is a game that requires aggression. You must be willing to jockey for position and grab the advantage over your opponents. It definitely is not a game for the passive. Nobody gives you anything for free in no-limit hold'em—you have to wrench it from them with cunning and aggressive play. The advantage of playing this way is that you force your opponents to react to you, rather than you having to react to them. As the old saying goes, "A bettor be, a caller never."

Be aware, however, that in no-limit hold'em tournament play, this axiom is not true 100 percent of the time. There are times when you might consider being passive. For example, say you have a marginal hand, such as a small pair or a 9-8 suited, and two or three players already have entered the pot for the minimum bet before the flop. In this scenario, you might just call. You're hoping to see a cheap flop and then milk it for all it's worth if you hit it. Other than that, there is practically no hand that you should not raise with before the flop if you intend to play, especially if you're the first one in the pot.

If you're going to call a bet, you should have a strong enough hand to be able to reraise if someone raises behind you. Suppose you entered the pot by raising the standard amount with pocket aces or kings, for example, and a player raises the pot behind you. You can reraise him, knowing that in all likelihood he's going to call, and you still have the best hand.

Now let's say that you have a J-10 and decide to call an opponent's standard raise. If a player raises behind you, you have to fold because your hand is not strong enough to call a second raise.

Buying Pots That Are Up for Sale

Some pots in no-limit hold'em are for sale, and you can buy these bargain pots with an aggressive bet. Suppose you come into a hand from late position with a small pair or suited connectors. The flop doesn't hit you, but it's possible that it doesn't hit anybody else either. If everybody checks to you, you can often fire a bet at the pot and pick it up on the spot. Buying a pot that is up for grabs is one of the rewards of playing aggressively. But be careful: Some tournament players are using the check-raise a lot more often than optimal no-limit hold'em strategy indicates. If you get check-raised when you try to buy a pot, don't be proud. Get rid of your hand. Trust us, they have the goods.

Watch Out for Early Limpers

When you are in attack mode, always be wary of early-position limpers. Some crafty players will limp in with a good hand, trying to trap an overly aggressive player—and anybody else they can lure into the pot—either before or after the flop. This doesn't mean that everyone who limps in from up front has a big hand, simply be alert to the possibility.

If a good player or a tricky player limps into the pot from early position, a red flag should start waving in your mind; bells should start ringing in your head. Be wary because this opponent is going against conventional no-limit hold'em wisdom, which is to play aggressively. Many players who are new to the game or trying to convert from limit to no-limit play come into the pot with a variety of marginal hands because that's how they're accustomed to playing in limit games. Because they often don't have a good sense of hand values, their tendency is to call rather than raise, and this mentality actually makes them more difficult to read.

Still, a red flag should go up whenever someone limps into the pot from up front. This is one more reason why you want to determine as soon as possible which players at your table are new to no-limit hold'em. This is especially important after the flop. Why? Here's an example: Suppose an opponent checks to you on the flop. You've played a marginal hand from middle position and missed it, but you think a bet might win the pot. So you fire some chips into the middle, but—oops—your opponent calls. The call usually means you opponent has something, even if he isn't a sophisticated player. Be wary when trying to bluff this type of player. If he calls you on the flop, there's a good chance he may continue playing the hand, especially if he has flopped middle pair or even bottom pair. Converts from limit hold'em are accustomed to calling a bet on the flop with a lower pair because they want to see the turn card, and a lot of times the pot is big enough to justify their call. In no limit hold'em, it is seldom correct to do that. But inexperienced no-limit players often do not understand this concept. Therefore if your hand doesn't warrant further betting action, you had better slow down.

BLUFF WHEN THE TIME IS RIGHT

"No-limit hold'em is all about bluffing."

–Juan Carlos Mortensen, 2001 World Champion of Poker

Bluffing is one of the most powerful—and perilous—weapons in no-limit hold'em. When you pull off a successful bluff, you're the happiest camper in the woods.

It's more satisfying than turning up pocket aces at the showdown and winning a huge pot. Anybody can play two aces, but not everybody can successfully bluff in the right situations. However when you get caught trying to pull off a bluff and are forced to show your 7-2 offsuit or some other miserable hand, you want to slink away and hide in a dark corner. Don't let getting caught in a bluff stop you, however. If at first you don't succeed, try again when you think the time is right.

When Not to Bluff

Be sure that you know your opponents very well before you try a bluff. Who is most likely to fold if you bet? Who is most likely to call? You should not attempt to bluff a **calling station**, a player who hates to fold a hand and calls far more often than optimal strategy dictates. Because so many new people are experimenting with no-limit hold'em these days, you often will run into a gang of calling stations in low-limit tournaments. We repeat, don't bluff if you think you're going to get called.

Most bluffs are made from late position when everybody has passed to you. If you are in late position and believe that a bet will win the pot for you, fire one in. However, you should not bluff bet if you know that your opponents—in this case, the small and big blinds—are probably going to call you. That is, if he's not the type of player who will fold when he has any kind of hand at all, don't try a positional bluff against him.

The smaller the pot, the easier it is to pull off a successful bluff. The larger the pot—that is, the more players already in the hand—the more likely someone will call your bluff. More players in the pot usually means that there is more strength out against you, making it more likely that someone will wake up with a real hand or one that they believe is strong enough to call a bet.

When you try to bluff in a multiway pot, somebody is bound to think, "I'm gonna play sheriff here and look you up." And they will call. This is especially true during the early rounds of small buy-in tournaments with rebuys. This is not the time to bluff, because players will call your bluff bet with a remarkable variety of marginal hands. In fact, we suggest not bluffing in rebuy tournaments until after the rebuy period has ended. This is a rule of thumb that will serve you well.

When to Bluff

In addition to inexperienced players bluffing when they shouldn't, they often do not bluff when they should, passing up good opportunities to pick up a pot with a bluff bet. The time to bluff is when you can make a significant enough bet that calling without a decent hand can really hurt your opponents. If you have a fairly marginal hand that you don't think will win a showdown, but it appears that nobody else has a decent hand either, you might try a bluff. In this situation, a modest bet of one-half to two-thirds the size of the pot will most likely win the pot for you.

Here's another bluffing opportunity: Say everyone has passed to the blinds, and the action will be blind against blind. You are the big blind, and the small blind limps into the pot. You might raise to try to pick up the pot, even if you don't have much of a hand. Now suppose you are the small blind and believe that the big blind is the type of player who will fold against a raise. In this scenario, you might raise with any two cards, trying to take the pot away from the big blind.

"I played a medium buy-in no-limit tournament in which the player to my right kept raising and taking down pot after pot," Don recalls. "After a while, I decided that the next time she raised, I would go all-in, no matter what two cards I held. The next time she was in the cutoff seat and I was on the button, she raised. I pushed all my chips to the middle, everybody folded around to her, and she laid down her hand. 'Well, you've got me this time,' she said. I hadn't even looked at my hole cards!"

This is an example of understanding the situation and reading your opponent, two things that you must be able to do if you want to become successful at no-limit hold'em.

Four Types of Bluffs

There are four types of bluffs you can use in order to win the pot without having the best hand. Each bluff we describe is based on position, card value, and the situation.

The Semi-Bluff

A semi-bluff is executed with a hand that probably is not the best hand at the moment but could improve on the turn or river to become the best hand. Most semi-bluffs are made when a player has a straight or flush draw, especially if the hand also contains overcards. You always have a better chance to succeed when you have fewer opponents and are in late position. The first player to act after the flop will often win the pot with a bet.

The object of semi-bluffing is to win the pot right there with your bet. If you get called on the flop, you might check and try for a free card. If you get no help on fourth street, you might continue the semi-bluff by betting again, in the hope that the second bullet you fire will get the job done. But even if you get called on fourth street, you could still improve to the best hand at the river.

Let's look at a scenario in which you might try a typical semi-bluff. Suppose you are in the cut-off seat, and two players have limped into the pot in front of you. The button and the blinds are still to act. Your hand is the A♦-9♦, and you flat-call the opening bet. The flop comes Q♣-9♥-4♦, giving you middle pair and a three-flush.

There are several possible ways to play this hand:

1. If it is checked to you on the flop, how much should you bet? We suggest that you bet the size of the pot or a little more, up to one-and-a-half times the size of the pot. Your goal is to win the pot immediately, knowing that if you get called, you still have outs.
2. If someone bets in front of you, you have two choices: Raise or fold. Calling is not an option. You have second-best pair with an ace kicker, plus a backdoor flush draw. And if you decide to raise and an opponent reraises, you fold. Do not chase.
3. If you raise and someone calls, you have outs to this hand, plus you are in superior position. Your hand could improve on fourth street. If it does, you bet it, of course. But if your hand fails to improve, you have two choices: Continue to semi-bluff by firing in another bet; or check and take a free card.

At the river, your strategy depends on your analysis of the situation. Let's assume that you have not improved, and a blank comes on the final card. Do you think your opponent was on a flush draw and missed? If so, he can't call a bet, so you might as well check. If you think that he has top pair but believe that he may be uncertain about whether or not his kicker is any good, you have to decide whether or not he will fold to a bet. If you decide to bet, you need to make about a pot-sized bet, making it expensive for him to call you. If you had also bet on fourth street, this play will represent a strong hand and make your opponent think you are trying to get paid off.

If you checked on fourth street and took a free card, your bet might look suspicious. In that case, you might be better off checking and hoping your hand is good. As always, you have to evaluate your opponent. In our example we assumed three players were in the pot and one of them folded on the flop. But if both opponents had continued to play after the flop, it would be better to back off. At least one of them has the top pair and is unlikely to fold against your semi-bluff.

The Stone Bluff

A successful stone cold bluff—one you make with zilch, no hand whatsoever—is an art form. You can try a stone bluff before the flop, on the flop, on the turn, or at the river, but most stone bluffs are made on the flop. Total bluffs work best against one or two opponents at the most, because the more people who have put money in the pot, the more likely it is that you will be called.

Let's look at a scenario where you might try a stone bluff. Suppose you have the Q♥-9♥ in late position. One player has limped into the pot for the minimum bet in front of you. You call, and the big blind just calls. The flop comes K♠-7♣-2♦.

137

The big blind and the limper both check. You fire in a bet—with absolutely nothing. Your goal is to make your opponents fold if they are holding second- or third-best pair, or just an overcard.

Now suppose one player calls. The turn card is a blank such as the 5♥. If your opponent checks to you, you can bluff at the pot again. If he is holding any king with a bad kicker, such as the K♦-6♦, or second- or third-best pair, he will have a very tough time calling another bet. If you get called a second time and the river card is a total blank such as the 3♠, you can fire the third bullet at your opponent.

This play obviously has a certain amount of risk attached to it, but it can be very rewarding if you are successful. Not too many people are capable of firing that third bet. You really need to know the mindset of your opponent. The late Stu Unger was a master of this kind of bluff. He had an uncanny knack for knowing when his opponent was willing to fold in this type of situation.

If you choose to make a stone bluff on the turn or river card rather than on the flop, it should be because you believe your opponent is weak. If your read is correct, he will fold.

The Positional Bluff

When you are on the cutoff seat or the button and are the first player to enter the pot, you can attempt a positional bluff. Come into the hand with a raise to try to drive out the players behind you and win the blinds. To be successful with a positional bluff, you must know how your opponents play when they are in the blinds. You should be fairly certain that they will not defend their blinds unless they have a very strong hand. If you really know your opponents, you can even make this play from two seats to the right of the button.

You can also make a positional bluff when you are the small blind and everyone has folded to you. Raise if you think the big blind will fold. Caution: Don't overwork this play from the small blind. Use it sparingly because if you continuously raise the big blind, he will notice it and play back at you.

When you are in the big blind, everyone has folded, and the small blind simply completes the bet, you can make a positional bluff. Normally, the small blind is hoping to see a cheap flop and will lay his hand down to a raise. Use this play sparingly as well. If you try it too frequently, the small blind will eventually limp in with a big hand and then trap you with a reraise, which would almost always force you to muck your hand and lose money to it.

The Situational Bluff

Successfully pulling off situational bluffs requires expert timing. Often, you try a situational bluff just before your back is to the wall. For example, suppose your chips are eroding, and you have only four times the big blind in front of you. You need to gather some chips to survive. Alas, the blinds are fast approaching. You push all your chips into the pot with almost any two reasonable cards, even an ace-rag, in the hope of winning the pot right there.

If you are successful in getting everyone to lay down their hands, you'll pick up enough chips for another round. The extra chips you earn for pulling off a successful situational bluff will hopefully give you enough time to pick up a legitimate hand and accumulate more chips. Using the situational bluff, you sometimes can pick up enough chips to get back into the tournament and make the final table.

MIX UP YOUR PLAYING STYLE

"You never want to get yourself stuck in an identifiable pattern. You must mix up your play. If you do, you'll always keep your opponents guessing."
–Doyle Brunson in *Super System*

Skilled tournament players know how to change their style of play based on what they know about their opponents, the situation, and their chip count. They don't always raise from early position with premium hands; they sometimes play suited connectors out of position; and they occasionally smooth-call a raise with the best hand. Their ability to mix up their playing styles makes them hard to read.

Players who always play the same way are easy to read. They are at a distinct disadvantage in tournament play, especially against observant opponents. People who always play a very straightforward game with little or no creativity, those who always play by the book, are called A-B-C players. They are predictable, and they sometimes do reasonably well against weak opponents who don't notice that their style never changes, but they run into trouble against observant, aggressive players. Top players paint a bulls-eye on the foreheads of predictable opponents, and only give them action when they believe they have them beaten or can bluff them.

The Value of Deception

When you mix up your play, you keep your opponents guessing about what you have and what you're going to do next.

"You want to create confusion in the minds of your opponents," is how Tom put it in *Championship Tournament Poker*.

Deception is the name of the game. It is what gives you an advantage over your opponents. Play a solid game for the most part, but mix up your style often enough to be unpredictable. And when your opponents are forced to guess, the chances are good that they will guess wrong.

For example, let your opponents know that you will occasionally raise with a 9-8 suited or bet a drawing hand

141

on the flop when it is checked to you. Occasionally come over the top of an aggressive opponent when you think he is bluffing, even if your hand is marginal. Slow-play a big hand every now and then to let your opponents know that when you check, they cannot automatically take the pot away from you by betting.

Changing Gears

Going from tight play to loose play and vice versa is known as changing gears, and it is one way you can mix up your style of play. If you have a sudden, major change in your chip status, you have to change gears. You might need to change gears just before or just after the blinds and antes increase. And if you are on a short stack, the approaching increase in the blinds may force you to take a few more chances with hands you wouldn't ordinarily play in order to avoid getting blinded out of the tournament.

Another time you might change gears is after you win a big pot to become the chip leader at your table. If you were playing a very conservative game up to that point, you can now open up your game a notch and play more aggressively. Conversely, suppose you have lost some pots and are short-stacked. Now you gear down into survival mode by tightening up your play considerably.

In addition to changing gears when you need to, be on constant alert for opponents who have changed gears. Look out for someone who has been playing conservatively then inexplicably raises three pots in a row. Take notice when an aggressive player flat-calls a bet instead of putting in a big raise. When your opponents change gears, you need to adjust your play accordingly.

As a side note, we have found that there comes a time in many tournaments when almost everybody at the table seems to shift into overdrive. When the blinds and antes get very high, a buzzer seems to go off in the minds of some players who have been playing conservatively throughout the tournament. Suddenly they start shoving chips into the pot with reckless abandon. They know they need chips to survive the higher limits, so they start taking big risks with marginal hands. To say that they have changed gears is an understatement. At the same time, some of the bigger, wiser stacks that gambled earlier in the tournament start backing off to protect their chip position. But sometimes a big stack will jump right in, happy to join in the fun of the feeding frenzy. Many times he'll wake up to find himself on the rail, wondering how all his chips disappeared. The moral of the story is this: Change gears when you must, to either preserve or build your stack, and stay clear of temporary table mania created by players who impetuously change gears when they get desperate for chips.

USE SURVIVAL TACTICS TO STAY IN THE CHASE

"Every tournament ace has to be able to scale it back sometimes and play extremely tight poker for at least a little while."

–Phil Hellmuth, 1989 World Champion of Poker

You can't win it if you're not in it, and you can't win it until you make the final table. Learning how to survive is the key to tournament success.

"Earlier I talked about how I won a lot of tournaments coming back from a short stack," Tom says. "I used survival tactics to get there."

As the limits increase, survival becomes more important. Each rise in the antes and blinds requires a different survival approach, and each stack size requires a special strategy. A big stack needs to be protected and increased. A medium stack needs to be built into a big stack when opportunity knocks. A small stack needs to double through somebody, anybody, to become a contender.

You must survive long enough in the tournament to accomplish these goals and give yourself a chance to get lucky. Easier said than done, of course. You need lots of practice, ample patience, some luck, and a winning attitude. And you must have enough heart to push all your chips into the pot when necessary—even if you don't have a premium hand. You can't make an omelet without breaking eggs, and you can't win a no-limit hold'em tournament without taking some chances.

LET THE ODDS HELP YOU MAKE TRICKY DECISIONS

"I don't trust on luck. I have to think fast and figure my percentages. I can't relax for a second. I tell you, gambling is hard work!"

–Johnny Moss

You're watching a televised tournament with the chips flying across the green felt when suddenly, the action comes to a halt as Howard enters a trance-like state of semi-consciousness that the commentator refers to as the think tank.

"He's calculating the pot odds," the speaker whispers, "deciding whether he should call Daniel's raise."

In other words, he's adding up how much money is in the pot and comparing it to the number of outs—cards that will complete his hand—he has. If Howard concludes that he will be getting the proper odds, he probably will decide to call Daniel's bet.

He might also be trying to figure the implied odds for his hand. All the top pros know that with the right odds and a bit of luck, they can win a lot more chips than just those that are in the pot at the moment. They try to calculate how much they could win after the final round of betting. This is how they arrive at the implied odds for their hand. They might decide that if they make what appears to be a loose call on the flop, they'll stand a favorable chance of winning a huge pot if they get lucky and hit their draw.

Pro players are experts at calculating pot odds and implied odds, and they often consider other factors as well. A top-notch player might call a bet from late position before the flop because he knows in his heart that even if he doesn't make his hand, he can still bet or bluff on the flop and take the pot away from his opponent. If he decides to fire a big bet into the pot, his opponent may not be either willing or able to call.

"This is one of the beauties of no-limit poker," WPT commentator Mike Sexton has said. "You can win a pot without a hand!"

In *Championship No-Limit & Pot-Limit Hold'em*, T.J. Cloutier makes some additional points about math and its relationship to tournament poker:

"The math of poker should be in the back of your mind all the time. For most top pros, it is automatic. They can make their decisions quickly because they understand the numbers. But in tournament poker, pot odds aren't always the most important factor in deciding whether to play a hand. The odds go out the window a lot of times because you can't go back to your pocket for more chips, and that should be a determining factor in each and every hand.

"Your thinking in critical tournament situations must be different from how you think in a side game. You should take the math into consideration, but if that's all you're thinking about—if you forget about the fact that if you don't win the pot, you will either be out of the tournament or you will take a big hit to your stack--you're putting too much importance on it."

TRUST YOUR INSTINCTS

"Your first instincts are better than 95 percent correct if you're a poker player. That's because your first instinct comes from all the training and practice and skills you've learned over the years."

–T.J. Cloutier in *Championship No-Limit & Pot-Limit Hold'em*

Poker instincts are based on your past experiences, your analysis of what has transpired, and your knowledge of how your opponents play. In other words, instinct is connected to experience. Doyle Brunson emphasizes recall as an important part of instinct, saying "All good poker players have tremendous recall. They reach back into the depths of their minds and remember what a certain guy did in a similar situation." As you play more, you'll get better at analyzing players and situations and recalling your analysis from your memory bank.

Trusting your instincts in the play of a hand is often referred to as having a "feel" for the game. Players who have a feel for no-limit hold'em follow their gut in the play of the hand. Quite often your first instinct is the correct one, but you should still pause to consider it. If you're going to make a major decision based on your chip count, take your time. Think it through. If you're wavering on the edge, go with your instincts. You'll be surprised at how often you are correct.

Online Instincts

When playing online, you don't see your opponents and are often up against people you've never played with, so your instincts do not come into play as much as they do in live games, where you are face-to-face with your opponents. In online tournaments, you can't rely on your read of an opponent by looking at his facial expressions, and players change tables frequently, so you don't have a whole lot of time to observe them.

You have to rely on other factors when playing poker online, including the length of time it takes your opponents to make decisions. Does a player stall and then suddenly raise? This often means that he has a big hand. If a player calls a lot of small bets in order to see the pot, he probably is a loose player and may be tough to bluff. But he might also be the type of opponent that you can make a value bet against when you have a good hand.

Whether you're playing online or in a traditional casino, the players who can adapt the quickest and think the best on their feet are the ones who earn the richest rewards. The player who can weigh the many variables in no-limit hold'em the quickest and make adjustments the fastest has the best chance of success.

KEEP FIT PHYSICALLY AND MENTALLY

"TV has basically revealed that poker—especially no-limit hold'em—is a battle of wits. So, people who were never even drawn to card games have gravitated toward what is clearly a form of engaging in psychological warfare."

–Josh Melina, actor and co-creator of
Celebrity Poker Showdown

Poker is all about making good decisions. In all poker games, and especially in tournament poker, the quality of your decisions directly affects your results. The players who make the fewest mistakes in judgment are the winners over the long haul. When you are physically fit and mentally alert, you make better decisions than when your body is out of shape and your mind is asleep at the wheel.

No-limit hold'em tournaments are endurance contests that require physical stamina and mental sharpness. Big buy-in tournaments often require twelve or more hours of play on the first day, with survivors coming back to do battle for another ten hours or so on day two. To complete a championship event, you'll be required to play for nine or more hours a day over four to seven days, making stamina an increasingly important prerequisite to winning.

Proper exercise increases stamina and energy level, which will help you make better decisions and maintain your focus in the heat of battle. If you want to play your best game, get fit! It's that simple.

6

The Five Stages of Tournaments

"It's round five and my character is being tested. I've lost over half my chips and I'm right back to where I started the day with 20,000! Which is better: to have had it and lost it, or to have never had it at all? With Howard [Lederer] taking up the nickname 'Professor,' maybe I'll be known as the 'Philosopher!'"

–Tournament ace Kenna James in *Bluff* magazine

INTRODUCTION

No-limit hold'em tournaments usually progress through five stages of play. In this chapter we discuss each tournament stage and the special strategies you'll need to survive and thrive in each of them.

STAGE ONE: EARLY STAGE

In rebuy events, **Early Stage** lasts until the rebuy period is over, usually three levels of play. In this kind of event, we suggest that you play solid-aggressive poker during the Early Stage. Your goal is to build your stack. Be aware that many of your opponents in low-stakes rebuy events will be loose-aggressive players who call and raise with marginal holdings. They don't care if they lose their chips because they are prepared to rebuy. Remain patient and eventually you will find a hand that might double or triple your stack. After the rebuy period has ended, loose-aggressive players often will change their style and play fewer hands because they realize that they can be knocked out of the tournament if they continue playing recklessly.

In a freezeout tournament, the Early Stage ends when the antes come into play, which is usually at the start of the fourth level. Again, we suggest that you play solid-aggressive. Limit your blind stealing, seldom—if ever—bluff, and play the right hands in the right position. From the start, observe your opponents carefully. Good observation will give you insight into which moves you can use or should not use against certain opponents. Your goal is to increase your stack 50 percent or more at each level. If the blinds are $25/$50, and you start with $2,000 in chips, you have 40 times the big blind. Your goal is to increase the size of your stack 50 percent or more at each level so at the end of Levels 1, 2, and 3, you'll want to have $3,000, $4,500, and $6,750 in chips respectively. By the end of the second round with the blinds at $50/$100, you'll have 45 times the size of the big blind, and by the end of level 3, with the blinds at $100/$200, you'll have almost 35 times the big blind.

Early Stage Starting Hands

In the early rounds of a tournament, evaluate the players at your table to find out who are limit players, who are novices or internet players, and who are experienced, professional-level players. During the first round or two of a tournament, you should play solid poker and seldom bluff. You first have to decide what hands you should enter the pot with and from which position. Then you must consider what types of opponents you are up against. In particular, what is the playing style of the player to your immediate left and the other people who get to act after you?

During the first round or two, stick to the top hands—A-A, K-K, Q-Q, J-J, A-K, and A-Q—when you're sitting in early to middle position. Later in the tournament you can modify these starting requirements. As the blinds and antes escalate to a very high level, you'll often have to lower your raising requirements or else risk getting blinded out. But unless your chip status or your opponent's chip status causes you to deviate from your standard starting-hand requirements, stick with the premium hands.

If somebody has already come into the pot for a raise, stay away from suited connectors up to and including

J-10, no matter what your position. If you raise or call a raise with a drawing hand and get played with, you could lose all your chips on nothing more than a draw far too early in the tournament. This is not the time to play those types of hands. In fact the only time you might play suited connectors up to and including J-10 is from very late position in unraised pots. That way you're getting a fairly good price for the hand, plus you have superior position.

There are a few other liberties you can take if you are sitting in late position, especially if conservative players are sitting in the blinds.

"In my opinion, which varies somewhat from Tom's advice," Don adds, "I do not believe in playing suited connectors in late position if any other players have already entered the pot. If I do play them from a late position, I raise with them to try to steal the blinds. Too many times in my tournament experience, playing the small suited connectors burns way too many chips, chips that you'll wish you had later in the tournament."

Tom counters with the following argument: "I still like to take a few more risks while the blinds are very small early in the tournament, but only when I'm in a late position. I agree that small suited connectors can be big chip burners because you have to catch the flop just right. And the circumstances have to be just right. You have to be in late position in an unraised pot with some players already in it. I agree with Don that when you're the first player in the pot, you should either fold or bring it in for a raise to try to steal the blinds. I'm also suggesting that you can play the middle suited connectors during the first round or two when the blinds are relatively small in relation to the chips in play.

"You certainly don't want to play the small suited connectors as drawing hands after the flop for any serious amount of chips. That would be a big mistake. If you catch part of the flop and can still get away from your hand without risking too many chips, that's a reasonable strategy. But if you're the type of player who wants to stick around to see another card or two when you catch a piece of the flop, these types of hands can cost you a lot of chips, so you're better off not playing them to start with."

STAGE TWO: THE MIDDLE STAGE

In rebuy no-limit hold'em tournaments, the **Middle Stage** begins at the end of the rebuy period, usually the fourth level, and continues through about the next six or seven levels. The Middle Stage of a freezeout event begins when the antes kick in, usually the fourth level, and runs through the fifth and sixth levels. By the end of Stage Two, approximately 50 percent of the field will have been eliminated.

By the fourth level, chip stacks are beginning to be defined. You will see players with large stacks, medium stacks, and small stacks. Now you can open up your game a bit and start to attack the blinds more often when you are in position. Be aware, however, that if either of the blinds is short-stacked, you may be forcing them to play hands that they might otherwise have thrown away. Any time you attack short-stacked blinds you like to have two big cards rather than medium or small suited connectors.

Raise if you are the first one in from a middle position or later. Be willing to use the bluff more liberally when you are sitting on the backside. If you have created a solid-aggressive image in the early stage, now is the time to capitalize on it. Even though you have established yourself as a solid-aggressive player at your starting table, you will have to reestablish your image every time you change tables.

Your goal in the Middle Stage is to substantially increase your chip stack. You want to accumulate a much larger than average chip stack in order to position yourself to go deep in the tournament, make the money, and win the final table.

"The second phase of play is the long one, where action is only spasmodic," 1978 World Champion of Poker Bobby Baldwin wrote in *Tales Out of Tulsa*. "This is the time of tedious jockeying, patience, and more than that—the time for iron control. A time for the strong to survive."

STAGE THREE: THE LATE STAGE

The late stage of a tournament is usually comprised of rounds seven, eight, and nine. By the end of round nine, you are either in the money or so close to it that you can smell it. In many instances you will be playing shorthanded until a table breaks and the empty seats at your table are filled. In these rounds, we suggest that you play aggressively according to your table position. Actively attack the blinds; if you are successful a mere one time per round, you will have earned enough chips to pay for your blinds and antes for the next round.

Do not play the role of sheriff or terminator. You do not have to call raises or bets with marginal hands. Leave that to the other players. Unless you have a strong hand, don't try to knock players out. Be careful when you raise with marginal hands as you may force a short stack into playing against you. This is another good reason to always keep track of your opponents' chip stacks.

With a medium stack, you certainly do not want to double up a short stack and become one yourself. You would rather attack medium and big stacks because they do not want to play against you. Why? Because you can cripple or even knock out a medium stack, and a big stack has to be careful not to double you up. If that happens, he'll become a medium or small stack while you take over his position as top dog.

157

If you are a short stack, you must find a hand and go with it. Do not allow yourself to become so low in chips that you will get played with no matter what you have. Since you do not have enough ammunition to scare anyone out of a pot, your opponents will come after you.

If you have a big stack, determine who is trying to hang on to make the money and move up the ladder. These players will lay down hands and allow you to accumulate even more chips. You want to preserve your chip stack, but you don't want to play timidly in the process. Continue your controlled aggressive style of play. Your goal is to make it to the top of the food chain—the final three spots.

STAGE FOUR: IN THE MONEY!

Congratulations, you're in the money! The medium and higher stakes tournaments with large fields normally pay a minimum of two tables, but sometimes pay three or four tables, depending on the size of the field. At the World Series of Poker, it is not unusual for 10 percent of the field to finish in the money. The WSOP organizers believe that by paying more participants, they'll induce players to use their winnings to enter more events and build larger fields.

In Stage Four of the tournament, play changes dramatically. Players who had been holding on by a thread in order to cash often loosen up their play considerably. Now they want to gamble; they are in a double-up or get-up mode. Play carefully against the short stacks. Unless you have a premium hand, let another player attempt to bust them.

In a three-table payout tournament, you will receive the same amount of money whether you finish 27th or 19th. Play a solid-aggressive game. Try to pick up the blinds and antes at least once a round. Remember to consider your table position in relation to the short stacks so that your raise does not force them to play marginal hands. You'd prefer to raise the medium and large stacks that will lay hands down to your raise. As the table shrinks to seven players or less, some players just want to survive to the second table so that they will receive more money. Try to determine who these players are and use them as your targets.

The Second Table

At the second table of large tournaments, the payouts for places sixteen through eighteen are usually the same. Spots thirteen through fifteen receive a little more money, and places ten through twelve receive still more money.

At the second table, stay with your solid-aggressive game plan, steal the blinds and antes, and try to build your chip stack for the final table. Don't be in a rush to attack the short stacks with marginal hands. You do not want to double them up.

If you are a big stack, players do not want to play against you and take the risk of getting knocked out of the tournament. If you are a medium stack, play solid-aggressive and try to steal the blinds occasionally. Be wary of the small stacks because they will play with you if they have a hand, hoping to get back into the tournament. The same is true for other medium stacks.

If you are a small stack and you get a hand, go for it. You need to double up a time or two in order to get back into contention. If you are the first player in the pot, you can either raise or go all-in with hand like A-10, K-Q, K-J, K-10, Q-J, and Q-10. If an opponent decides to play with you, hopefully you will have either the best hand, or enough outs on the flop to double-up.

The last ten players in action assemble at the final table, and as soon as one player is eliminated, actual final table play begins. That's when the camera crew descends en masse in televised events. When Greg Raymer sat down with nine other players at the 2004 World Series of Poker championship table, he knew that the next player eliminated would not make the TV cut. Here is how the 2004 champion described his strategy in *Cigar Aficionado* magazine: "I sized up who was playing it safe and took advantage of that. In about two hours I went from $5 million to $8 million by pushing people around and stealing blinds and antes. I cared about being on TV, but no so much that I would let it affect my winning the tournament."

160

STAGE FIVE: THE FINAL TABLE

You've finally made it to the championship table! In nearly all of the big buy-in tournaments, as well as some medium buy-in events, the tournament stops for the day when it's down to the last nine players, who will come back the next day to play for the championship. Go home, relax, and plan your final-table strategy. Get a good night's rest so that you will be fresh and eager when the last leg of the race begins.

The championship table will probably be made up of players that you have faced at one time or another during the tournament. You should have a read on their play, but if you don't, ask a friend who might know them. If no information is available, your first task is to study the players you don't know—their chip stack, their table position, and how they play. What is their modus operandi? Are they protecting their chips, or are they willing to gamble? Knowing their styles allows you to adjust your play and take advantage of them.

As soon as the director says, "Shuffle up and deal!" remember that your goal is to get to the final three. That's where the big money is. If you are a big stack, one of the chip leaders, you can afford to play solid-aggressive strategy. Do not call a raise or reraise without a premium hand. You want to pick up the blinds at least once a round and maintain your big-stack status as players get eliminated.

161

If you are a medium stack, play carefully. Raise the blinds to maintain your chip status, do not go after the short stacks with marginal hands, and do not be afraid to raise the big stacks when you have a hand. As players get eliminated, hand values change, and your skill at shorthanded play becomes more important. If you are down to five to six players and you are below the average in chips, you may take a gamble to move up the ladder.

If you are a short stack, be prepared to find a hand and go all-in. It pays to gamble when you're on the short end of the stick. If you are fortunate enough to win one or two hands, you will be one of the chip leaders.

There will be quite a jump between the fourth-place prize and the third-place money. Your opponents will notice it, too. So when you get to four-handed play, try to determine which player is just trying to survive and climb one more step up the ladder. If you are a big stack, keep going after the blinds, while protecting your big stack and hopefully building it.

If you are in third chip position with a medium stack, you must steal blinds to maintain your stack size. Be selectively aggressive and be prepared to bluff a little more often. Be aware that the big stacks do not want to double you up, and they will only play with you if they have a premium hand.

If you are the short stack, get ready to gamble! Don't allow yourself to be anted and blinded out of the tournament. Your goal is to catch up to the bigger stacks, so you must take chances with some marginal hands. If you are successful, you will become a big stack. If you fail, at least you will have given it your best shot and will receive a nice payday for your valiant effort.

Now there are three players left to do battle for all the marbles. If you all have roughly equal amounts of chips, you might make a deal and play for the trophy. For example, if $300,000 is in the prize pool, you might each take $90,000 and play for the remaining $30,000 and the trophy. But if you decide to just go for it, you will see the play really open up. Bluff raises will be frequent, reraises will be common, and all-in moves will occur. Unless one player is short-stacked, be prepared to move your chips in; do not sit on them.

If you are the short stack, your goal is to double-up and get back in the tournament, so be prepared to play a lot of hands. If you are the big stack, go after the blinds but only when you have a real hand. Your goal is to get rid of one player so that you can play heads-up for the championship. If you are second in chips, you must play a few more hands. If you're up against the short stack, be sure that you have a hand, because the short stack will be more inclined to gamble with you.

Heads-Up for the Championship

Now only two soldiers are left standing on the field of battle. The big money and the trophy are on the line, and your skill at playing heads-up is so important. Are you going to chip away at your opponent's stack by limping on some hands and raising on others? Or are you going to just move all your chips in? We strongly suggest chipping away. You can afford to play a lot of hands heads-up, and if your reads are accurate, you will increase your chips with this strategy.

In *Championship Hold'em Tournament Hands*, T.J. Cloutier describes how he used the chipping away strategy in a classic duel against Chris Ferguson at the championship table of the 2000 World Series of Poker:

"When we started playing heads up, Chris had $4,700,000 in chips and I had $400,000, and at one point, I took the lead away from him. I kept chipping away, which means that I was trying to get Chris to take me off in spots, and he did. When I had the best hand, I tried to let him pay, but not so much that it would make him drop his hand. I wanted to get paid on all those hands—that's what chipping away means. In other words, I tried to make bets that I figured he would call."

By using this strategy rather than just moving all-in every chance you get, you can outplay your opponent. Give him plenty of room to make mistakes, and then punish him for his errors by scooping up his chips. Before long, you might find yourself in the winner's circle counting the cash and polishing your shiny new trophy.

7

Winning Strategies for Low-Stakes Events

"Whether it cost you $10 to play a small tournament or $10,000 to play a WPT tournament, the joy of winning is the same. It's that 'I've done it!' feeling. You're the champ!"

–Mike Sexton, World Poker Tour TV Commentator, in *Shuffle Up & Deal!*

INTRODUCTION

In the wide world of tournament poker, the amount of the buy-in attracts various groups of players. Tournament buy-in levels are similar to casino cash games, where one group of people play $4/$8 hold'em and another plays $20/$40. Some people play only the $100 to $300 buy-in events on the tournament circuit, and others play $500 to $1,000 tournaments. The players in the top tier only enter events with buy-ins of $5,000 and higher. Tom is well known throughout the broad spectrum of the tournament circuit, while Don is best known for his play in medium buy-in events.

Even the best tournament players in the world started out playing low-stakes tournaments and moved up the buy-in scale as they became successful and built their bankrolls. Your goal might be to improve your game and move up a notch in the tournaments you play so that, eventually, you will be comfortable playing high buy-in events. However, if you feel most comfortable in $20 tournaments, stay put.

Don has one tournament wish: "I want to sit down in a $20 tournament and have Tom McEvoy seated to my left and T.J. Cloutier seated on my right. I will then just sit back and spend the next three hours laughing!"

What Don means is that many players accustomed to entering only the big buy-in tournaments are unsuccessful in smaller buy-in events because they are unable to adjust to the different style of play. Daniel Negreanu, 2004 Tournament Player of the Year, expressed a similar view in his *Card Player* magazine column, saying, "I don't do as well in smaller tournaments with faster structures. Fast-paced tournaments are played predominantly pre-flop, while the big WPT events I'm accustomed to playing reward post-flop play."

Some players who have developed big bankrolls and strong playing skills don't play any tournaments other than World Series of Poker or World Poker Tour championship events. They don't want to play any events with buy-ins less than $5,000. A buy-in of $2,500 seems to attract a large number of players. Top names who play the biggest buy-in events will often play $2,500 tournaments. Interestingly, a recent $2,500 tournament attracted 380 entrants, and the $3,000 buy-in tournament that immediately followed drew only 210 entries. As it turned out, the prize money was higher in the lesser of the two events.

Playing small stakes no-limit Texas hold'em tournaments allows you to get your feet wet and find out whether you enjoy tournaments as much as, if not more than, live play. You will also become familiar with the different strategies that are used in tournaments versus live play. Small buy-in events are safe places to practice what you have learned from reading the best books on no-limit Texas hold'em tournaments.

A low buy-in tournament is a training ground where you can learn to compete in higher buy-in events. Once you feel comfortable at one level, you can move up a level and play in a bigger buy-in tournament. After playing a few small tournaments, you will develop your own unique style, as all the great no-limit tournament players have done. And no matter how good you become, you can always use small buy-in no-limit hold'em tournaments as a testing ground for new plays that you plan to implement in higher limit tournaments.

What separates the stars of no-limit Texas hold'em tournaments from the rank and file is their ability to read their opponents. Small stakes events can help you develop this skill. With enough practice, you'll be able to put a player on a hand and base your strategy on that read—key skills in no-limit hold'em. For example, suppose you decide that Player A is a rock who will not raise unless he has pocket aces, kings, queens, or A-K suited. If Player A raises and you have 10-10 in the hole, you know that the correct play is to fold. On the other hand, Player B seems to raise with less than premium hands. You've seen him raise with cards such as A-x, K-Q, or J-10, so you might call Player B's raise with that 10-10. The bottom line is that when you are able to put your opponents on the correct type of hand, you can make a much more educated decision on how to play against them.

HOW TO WIN SMALL BUY-IN TOURNAMENTS

Now we're ready to step into the arena of low buy-in tournaments. A **small buy-in** no-limit hold'em tournament is one in which the buy-in is $100 or less. Most low-stakes tournaments are rebuy events in which you can rebuy during the first three levels of play and make an add-on at the end of the rebuy period. Most small stakes tournaments also have short rounds. As you read this section on how to win these beginner tournaments, keep that in mind.

How Much Should You Invest in a Rebuy Event?

When you play a multiple rebuy tournament, you should have a plan for how many rebuys you are prepared to make. In a $20 buy-in tournament, each rebuy and add-on usually costs $10, and as a rule of thumb, we suggest investing a maximum of two rebuys and an add-on.

"In my opinion that is all a $20 buy-in tournament is worth," Don says. "I want to be able to win at least 50 times my investment. If I've invested $50 in a tournament that awards $2,400 for first place, I'm close to my goal. But if I make four or five rebuys plus an add-on, the best I can hope for is 30 to 40 times my investment. If I have to rebuy that many times just to stay in action, I figure it's just not my night."

If you have not accumulated chips by the end of the rebuy period, extra rebuys will not serve any useful purpose. For example, if 10 minutes are left in the rebuy period of a $20 buy-in event and you go broke, rebuying makes little sense. The amount of the blinds at the third level—usually the last level at which rebuys are allowed—are at least triple the amount they were in the first level of play. The $300 in chips you'd receive for this additional rebuy is virtually insignificant at the fourth level where the blinds usually are $20/$40. Your small chip stack at that stage will not intimidate your opponents; in fact, you will be the target of the taller stacks. Save the money and use it for your next tournament.

Now let's look at a typical $40 buy-in no-limit hold'em tournament with unlimited $20 rebuys. As soon as you sit down, you are allowed to rebuy.

"I take the rebuy immediately," Don suggests, "because it allows me to cover everyone at the table, initially. That is, I will have more chips than players who do not rebuy right away, and of the same amount as the players who do."

Players who do rebuy immediately tend to play more often against the shorter stacks, because they know that they cannot go broke against them.

While in the rebuy period, a lot of players like to gamble because they know that they cannot be eliminated.

"During this kamikaze period," Don says, "my strategy is to play rather tight. My goal is to accumulate three or four times the amount of chips I started with so that with the add-on, I am in a favorable chip position when the real tournament begins."

Playing after the Rebuy Period Is Over

When the rebuy period ends, the real tournament begins, and the entire texture of the tournament changes. Players try to play better because no one wants to get knocked out. This is when you can start making some moves from the backside, but be aware of which players have not changed their loose play and still want to gamble as much as they did during the rebuy period.

About three or four levels after the rebuy period is over, players will be required to start posting an ante on every hand. The antes in small buy-in tournaments usually come into play at the $150/$300 level, in which the ante will be $25.

Once the antes kick in, you can throw your game into a higher gear. Assuming you have a reasonable amount of chips relative to the size of the blinds (roughly 15 times the size of the big blind) you'll be in a good enough chip position to start stealing the blinds when you're sitting on the backside—two seats to the right of the button, say. If you have control of your table and have presented yourself as a tight-aggressive player, most of your opponents will respect your raises. If you win the blinds and antes once a round, you will have earned a free round.

By the time the antes begin, between 50 to 60 percent of the field will have been eliminated. From this point onward in the tournament, most hands will be played heads-up or three-way. Because most pots are played shorthanded, medium pocket pairs, as well as A-K, A-Q, and A-J, go up in value. Now you want to start accumulating chips by judiciously raising in position when you can be the first player in the pot. However, if you raise and get called by a player sitting behind you or by one of the blinds, you must give them respect for having a hand. Hopefully you will have been at the table long enough to get a read on the players and know who is playing loose, who is timid, and which players will defend their blinds with practically

171

any two cards. Be wary of raising short stacks in the blinds, because they often will realize that their chip position is precarious and may defend with any two cards. Do not pick on these blinds without a good hand, at least A-Q, A-J, or a medium pair. Be wary of playing K-Q (suited or not) because this hand is a dog against any ace—and you'd be surprised how often one of the blinds wakes up with one of these in his hand.

Playing the Later Rounds

As players are eliminated in the later rounds, the tables get shorthanded, and the blinds come around more rapidly. This means that you must be selectively aggressive as you accumulate chips. When you get down to two tables in a tournament that pays only one table, you want to know who is just trying to hold on so that they will make it into the money. These opponents are prime candidates for having their chips stolen. Earlier, Don discussed a tournament he played in which a player at his table announced that he'd made a bet with his friend that he'd make the final table. Don raised his blind every time and the guy laid down A-Q and pocket jacks. That's a perfect example of taking advantage of a player whose only goal is to make the final table.

As players continue to get eliminated and the action gets down to 12 to 14 players with two shorthanded tables of six to seven at each table, you'll be in the best spot to accumulate chips—not necessarily by earning them, but by stealing them. Hopefully everyone will be holding on to make the money, in which case they will only play the biggest hands. If you raise with a mediocre hand trying to steal the pot and you get reraised, be prepared to give it up and wait for the next opportunity. Your game is fast, aggressive, and somewhat loose, though not reckless.

Playing the Final Table

At last you're in the money! It's time to change gears again. At the final table with 9-10 players, you must go back to your solid-aggressive play. Do not try to knock players out with marginal hands. Remember that you only have to win the antes and blinds once a round in order to earn a free round. Your goal is to be one of the last three players—that's where the money is. Once you are playing three-handed, you want to be selectively aggressive. Ideally two of your opponents will go to war with each other, and one of them will get knocked out. If this happens and you are heads-up, you'll be in a great position to win the tournament, especially if you have studied your opponent, his betting patterns, hand selection, and so on. Even if he has you out chipped 3 to 1 or 4 to 1, you are only two hands away from winning the tournament.

"Once I have second place locked up and I am behind," Don advises, "my style of play is very aggressive. The chip leader is looking to knock me out with a big hand, while I am looking to chip away at his stack. Sooner or later most chip leaders will get frustrated and make errors that I can take advantage of to win the tournament."

Tournament Talk

Don's Top 12 Tips for Winning Small
Buy-In Tournaments **By Don Vines**

1. Have a rebuy strategy. Decide in advance how many
rebuys you are prepared to make. We believe the
maximum amount that you should invest is two rebuys
and an add on.

2. Set a goal as to how many chips you want to have in
front of you after each round. For example, your goal
might be to increase your chip stack by 50 percent at
each level. This does not mean that you stop playing
once you have reached that goal. Nor does it mean that
if you fail to make the goal, you should start playing more
hands. Maintain your composure, remembering that it
only takes one winning hand for you to double-up and
get right in the thick of things again.

3. Play assertively aggressive from the start. Be selective
in the hands you play, but play them strong once you
decide to play.

4. Play straightforward poker. In the early rounds
particularly, tricky plays do not work. Players often are
looking for an excuse to play big pots because they
know that if they go broke, they can rebuy.

5. Keep track of how your chip stack compares to the average. During the rebuy period, this is impossible because you cannot know the number of chips in play. But after the rebuy period, the tournament director usually will announce how many chips are in play and the number of players remaining. Most tournament clocks will give you that information as well. If you have 30 times the size of the big blind, you're in good shape.

6. Read your table as quickly as possible. Determine who is playing loose, who is playing tight, who is aggressive, and who is passive. This is not easy in the beginning, but if you observe and concentrate, you will be able to identify who is doing what, and that information will give you an advantage when the right moment arrives.

7. Take advantage of tight players. These rocks will lay hands down unless they have the stone mortal nuts.

8. Take advantage of weak players. These players will play hands out of position. And they will call your ace-big-kicker with ace-anything, which gives you a substantial advantage.

9. Watch the clock. Know when the round will end and the blinds will increase. Remember that your chips have more value in relation to the blinds and antes when the blinds are small. When the blinds increase, your chips lose value. Be prepared to play a little stronger from the backside in the five minutes or so before the blinds increase.

10. Change gears. Be willing to change gears from fast to slow, from being too aggressive to being more passive. In a rebuy tournament, you may have to change gears several times. During the rebuy period, you'll play aggressively when you think you have the best hand. You do not bluff. After the rebuy period when players realize that they can get knocked out, then you can put pressure on players by betting aggressively. Only do this from the backside, as betting into a player exposes you to being raised, in which case you may have to give up the hand. In no-limit hold'em, it is more difficult to call a raise than it is to make a raise.

11. When you have built a large stack of chips, conserve them. A big chip stack is a weapon and should not be frittered away with excuses such as, "Oh well, my opponent did not have many chips, so I thought I'd go after him."

12. Practice, practice, practice. The more tournaments you play, the more comfortable you will become. You'll even grow to love them. Tom plays a mix of 60 percent tournaments and 40 percent live, while Don plays a mix of 90 percent tournaments and 10 percent live.

Winning Strategies for Medium- and High-Stakes Tournaments

> "Professionals overemphasize skill. Amateurs over-emphasize luck."
>
> –Tex Sheahan in *Secrets of Winning Poker*

INTRODUCTION

You've felt the thrill of victory at the championship table of several small buy-in no-limit hold'em tournaments. You've played deep into a lot of other events, only to suffer the agony of defeat a few steps short of first place. You know how to read your opponents, use position to your advantage, and adjust your strategy in critical situations. You're patting yourself on the back for consistently using good tournament strategy. Now you want more. You're mentally ready to play with the big boys and girls.

It's time to move up the tournament ladder and test yourself against tougher competition in higher stakes events where the financial risks are much higher, as are the monetary rewards and personal satisfaction. We want to help you in your ascent to the top by giving you our best advice on how to move up, what to expect in higher buy-in events, and how to adjust your strategy to win them. We consider $200 to $500 to be a **medium buy-in**, while the next level, **big buy-in** tournaments, begins at $1,000 and more.

When most players start to move up the tournament buy-in ladder, they usually continue to play mostly lower buy-in events in which they have had success, then gradually begin to dip their toes into the deeper waters of $500, $1,000, or $1,500 tournaments.

When you decide to move up, evaluate the initial higher stakes tournament you're thinking of playing. You want your maiden voyage to sail as smoothly as possible, so be sure to consider the following factors:

1. Number of entries,
2. Quality of players,
3. Amount of money you can win,
4. Number of chips you start with,
5. The length of the rounds, and
6. Whether you sincerely believe you can win it.

Higher buy-in tournaments have a steep learning curve. Accept this as fact. Our goal is help lead you to the final table as soon as possible.

Building Your Bankroll

We advise against putting too much money into higher buy-in tournaments before you're ready, and you won't know that for sure until you've established a winning record in the lower buy-in events. After cutting your tournament teeth in smaller events, you're going to want to move up, but you don't want to jeopardize your financial stability when you do it. The lessons you learn from playing against the toughest competition shouldn't be overly expensive. Keep enough money in reserve so that you can return to playing the lower buy-in events if you need to.

To build a big enough bankroll to play higher buy-in tournaments, try this method: Every time you win a small buy-in tournament, put around 10 to 20 percent of your winnings into an envelope. The money in the envelope is for future tournaments with bigger buy-ins than the ones you usually play. For example, don't play a bigger tournament until you have put aside enough money for a $1,000 buy-in tournament. That way, playing it won't strain you financially. In a sense, you are rewarding yourself for success.

You also can use part of the money in your reserve envelope to play satellites for the more expensive

181

tournaments you want to play. Not only are satellites good training grounds, they give you the chance to win a seat in a higher buy-in tournament for a fraction of the cost. You can turn a toothpick into a lumberyard, just like Tom did in 1983 when he won a one-table satellite for a seat for the World Series of Poker, then became the first satellite player ever to win the World Championship. Amateur player Chris Moneymaker did it in 2003 when he won a $40 satellite online at PokerStars and went on to win the championship. We won't go into detail about how to win satellites in this book, but you can get all the winning tips you need in *Win Your Way Into Big Money Hold'em Tournaments* by Tom McEvoy and Brad Daugherty.

Understand that you won't win a lot of the tournaments you enter. You can win 70 to 80 percent of the time when you play cash games, but that is not the percentage you will realize in tournament play. Only the very best tournament players finish in the money 20 to 25 percent of the time. The upside is that you can get a big return on your money in tournaments. It's a numbers game. If you just want to take an occasional shot at a medium buy-in tournament because you don't have a big enough bankroll to play them regularly, that's okay. But to be consistently successful playing medium and higher buy-in tournaments, you will need a big enough bankroll to cover at least 20 tournament entries, assuming that your skills are developed enough to be competitive.

What If You Lose?

If you try playing a higher-level tournament and you lose ten or eleven events in a row without at least finishing in the money in a few of them, it's not only damaging to your bankroll, it may prove that you are not ready for the move. Bad luck isn't the only thing that has kept you out of the winner's circle; you're just not a seasoned enough player yet.

If you consistently lose after trying an upward move, reevaluate your game and if necessary, drop back down to the lower buy-in tournaments until you further hone your skills.

In addition, you should try to assess whether you've stepped too far outside the boundaries of your comfort zone. If you're playing tournaments that have bigger buy-ins than you're comfortable with, you're handicapping yourself right from the get-go. For example, some players who are accustomed to playing $100 buy-in tournaments think too much about their investment and overlook the potential return when they enter their first $500 tournament. They dwell on how much they've invested rather than concentrating on doing well in the tournament. Always remember that after you've paid your entry into a tournament, that money doesn't belong to you anymore. It belongs to the prize pool.

And if you're uncomfortable with the size of the buy-in, stay with the smaller events for a while longer. As you achieve success, your comfort zone will expand and you'll be able to play bigger buy-in events without feeling uneasy about the monetary risk.

Moving Up Another Notch

But enough talk about losing—winning is a lot more fun to talk about. Let's say that you have become successful at the $500 buy-in tournaments. You've placed high in several of them and have won one or two. Now you're ready to take your next step up the tournament ladder. There are very few tournaments on the circuit with buy-ins between $500 and $1,000, so your next step will probably be a $1,000 buy-in event. If you have been reserving a percentage of your medium buy-in tournament winnings in that envelope we mentioned earlier, you probably will have enough of a bankroll to get started. Also remember that the satellite system is a relatively inexpensive way to win a seat in higher buy-in tournaments. Virtually all casinos and online cardrooms run satellites around the clock for big buy-in tournaments. That's how they build those large tournament fields with such big payouts.

Don't be too surprised if you get smacked around a bit in your first few attempts at playing the $1,000 and higher buy-in tournaments. In the bigger buy-in events, you will be facing a lot of world-class players and until you become accustomed to competing against them, you can expect some reversals of fortune. Initial failure doesn't mean that you shouldn't play the bigger tournaments. Just don't expect instant success.

If you are not successful in your first few attempts at playing the big buy-in events, don't lose heart. Continue playing the medium buy-in tournaments where you know you're a success, while continuing to evaluate your play in the bigger events. Study why you were not successful and try to identify your mistakes. We encourage you to take notes on your opponents and on key hands that were played. What did the top professional players do that you weren't comfortable with? What moves did they make that were new to you? How did you and your opponents react to those moves? Record how you played your cards in critical situations—the good, the bad, and the ugly. You don't need to take notes at the table, do it when you get home, while everything is still fresh in your mind. Learning from your mistakes is of critical importance in poker, as it is in life.

Taking a Step Backward When You Need To

As we discussed earlier, it is sometimes necessary to take a step down to smaller buy-in tournaments if you find you are not comfortable with the stakes or the opponents in bigger buy-in events. But there are other reasons to drop down to smaller buy-in events occasionally.

Even top tournament players sometimes take a step down the ladder and play medium or small tournaments for a while. Some of them want to take a breather from the pressure of playing big tournaments in which they do not have as big an edge over the competition as they do in smaller events. But the most common reason why expert players occasionally move down a notch is—you guessed it—monetary necessity. Playing the big buy-in tournament circuit is expensive, to say the least. We estimate that playing several of the WSOP events, plus the WPT tournaments and a few other major events, costs over $300,000. That's big bucks by anyone's standards! Only a few elite tournament players have a big enough bankroll to be a solo act, and most top pros have backers who pay their tournament expenses in return for 50 percent of the win. Many of the excellent players who are approaching pro status have to foot their own bills without the protection of a backer. When their bankrolls get short, they often take a step back and play medium or small buy-in events until their bankrolls recover from the constant pounding of big buy-ins.

A third reason for taking a step in the opposite direction is experimentation. Lower buy-in tournaments are great venues for trying out different styles of tournament play. You can experiment with various styles and evaluate the merits of different plays without putting yourself at significant financial risk.

"I'll enter a $20 or $50 tournament just to try out some plays and determine what might happen if I try Play A as opposed to Play B," Don says. "I don't expect to win the tournament, I'm simply investing a few bucks to experiment with different plays that I plan to execute in bigger buy-in events. I find out first-hand what works and what doesn't work against aggressive players, tight players, novices, and people I haven't played with before."

Here's another advantage of occasionally stepping back and playing a relative small buy-in event: You can gain valuable experience by playing against large fields of inexperienced players. With so many new players venturing into no-limit hold'em tournaments these days, having this kind of experience can be invaluable when you enter a bigger buy-in, large-field tournament with a lot of money at stake.

Pros vs. Novices

Interestingly, many world-class players do not perform as well at the lower-limit tournaments playing against weaker competition. Part of the reason is that they don't understand the thinking of novice players. Further, they don't know how to play against a large number of inexperienced players.

Some pro players have even expressed genuine concern about—and in some cases, fear of—the amount of newcomers playing in the World Series of Poker. Many of these inexperienced players win their seats on the internet for a very small investment. They have nothing to lose, they have no fear, and they are very difficult to read. Professional players who take pride in correctly timing their bluffs find that opponents call their bluffs far more frequently than in higher-stakes tournaments. Therefore they can't maneuver as much as they would like and have to show down a hand more often. This disrupts their sense of rhythm and play.

"I play extensively on the internet, primarily at PokerStars, where I am a host," Tom says. "I already have a pretty good idea about how the pros play the game, so I am more concerned about how the less experienced players play, because they are the ones that I have a difficult time reading and adjusting to. For years, I have been a tournament target, especially among amateur players who want to brag that they beat me in a hand. They'll come after me with cards they probably shouldn't be playing, and sometimes they get lucky. There's very little that I can do about that except remain patient, read them as best I can, and wait for the best hand. Occasionally they're going to beat me when they've put their chips into the pot with the worst of it. But eventually, they will make mistakes."

In the long run, the players who make the fewest mistakes are the winners at any game—golf, tennis, backgammon, poker.

TOP TIPS FOR WINNING HIGHER-STAKES TOURNAMENTS

The several following tips on playing higher stakes tournaments are intended to help you play mistake-free in tournaments.

The Player Mix Is Different in the Big Ones

More new players are entering tournaments these days than ever before. Get to know the players at your table as soon as possible. Many of them will be cash-game players who want to take a stab at the huge prize pools no-limit hold'em tournaments are offering—especially televised events. These players often begin their tournament careers by playing in the medium buy-in $500 tournaments. Because they are seasoned cash-game players, they can be quite dangerous to play against. In the mid-level tournaments, you will also be playing against tournament novices, small buy-in tournament players, medium buy-in tournament specialists, and big buy-in tournament players.

If you recognize any of the players at your table, try to remember what you know about their play. Then find out about the players you don't recognize. As soon as the first hand is dealt, concentrate on how your opponents play various types of hands. Are they playing a timid game? Are they playing aggressively? What cards are they playing and from what position? How much do they usually raise? You know the drill.

In the higher buy-in tournaments that cost $1,000 or more to enter, you will be playing against an interesting combination of players that you don't often find in the medium buy-in tournaments, a combination of famous world-class players, celebrities, successful businesspeople, and high-stakes recreational players.

Playing against Celebrities

Expect the press and the gallery to focus a lot of attention on your table if you're playing with celebrity players. Screen stars such as Ben Affleck, James Woods, and Toby McGuire will be the focal points of an army of photographers and the center of attention for the spectators. Celebs are usually outgoing and talkative because they have a public image to uphold. Unfortunately, they will not be paying attention to you, but that can be a good thing, too. Don't let their presence distract you. Stay focused and concentrate on the job at hand. Think of them as opponents that you need to conquer.

Famous people often play cautiously because they don't want to make a mistake for the whole world to see. If you notice this happening, take advantage of it and bluff them more often.

Playing against Well-Off Recreational Players

Many top businesspeople relish going up against celebrities and famous pros, sometimes throwing caution to the wind by mixing it up and gambling. Don't expect to bluff these players too easily. Value-bet more and snap off their bluffs when you can. Keep in mind that well-heeled recreational players usually are not intimidated by the specter of losing and, therefore, are often unpredictable in their play.

Playing against Seasoned Professionals

Seasoned professional tournament players are more difficult opponents than wannabe pros, serious amateurs, celebrities, and recreational high-stakes players. Famous tournament pros are top-flight players who deserve respect. This does not mean that you should play like a wimp or become intimidated by them. Study the pros closely, learn from them, and try to play mistake-free against them. Remember that anybody can be beaten on a given day.

Keep in mind that most tournament professionals play a solid and aggressive style of poker. When they are in position, they'll sometimes see flops with marginal hands. They believe, often quite correctly, that they can outplay their opponents after the flop, even if they don't start with the best hand. You can combat this tendency of theirs by using the check-raise to slow them down. Remember that your advanced moves will be successful more often against strong players than they will be against weak players. And keep in mind that you know who the top pros are—you've probably seen them on television—but they most likely won't know who you are or how you play. Therefore, they may tend to underestimate the caliber of your play initially.

Nobody is unbeatable. All players, no matter how skilled or famous, make mistakes. The main difference between the great players and the lesser talents is that great players make fewer mistakes. And when they do, they strive to erase them from their game. Eliminating mistakes in your play should be your goal when competing against anyone, especially world-class players.

"For me, poker is about learning, and there is still so much to learn," world-class player Jennifer Harman stated in *Poker Aces* by Ron Rose. "I make mistakes, but as long as I learn something from those mistakes, they can actually be good for me."

Take her advice: "Be patient, watch, listen, and learn."

Playing against Satellite Players

Be on the alert for satellite players. Do not assume that just because they won their entry into a big event on the internet or in a casino that they are weak players. Assume they know what they are doing until their play proves otherwise. Some of them are weak players who simply got lucky, while others are powerful players who can challenge the top pros. Just look at the 2003 and 2004 World Champions, Chris Moneymaker and Greg Raymer.

Both were internet players who won online satellites at PokerStars to gain entry into the championship event at the World Series of Poker.

Play Straightforward Poker Early in the Tournament

No matter what style of tournament play you prefer—aggressive, solid, or conservative—we suggest that you play a straightforward game until you get a good line on your opponents' skill level and style of play. Play very solid poker, being careful to choose the hands you play according to your position.

Don't try to get fancy with check-raises or trap plays early on, because in intermediate tournaments there are many new players who will not respond in the way you want them to, simply because they do not understand what you're trying to do. Mike Caro calls making too many advanced moves the "fancy play syndrome." When you're up against players that you don't know much about, or players that you suspect are new to no-limit hold'em, you don't want to get too cute. A fancy play that may work against a pro will not necessarily work against an amateur.

Strong tournament players are more likely to recognize your sophisticated plays and will respond in one of two ways:

1. They'll think you're out of line and come after you, or
2. They'll believe you have them beaten and lay down their hands.

Play a Solid-Aggressive Game

Doyle Brunson hit the nail on the head when he defined solid play: "A solid player is a player who's tight about entering a pot in the first place, but after he enters the pot, he becomes aggressive." Selectively aggressive is the term we use to describe the style of play that we advocate in tournaments. Since you will be very selective about the hands you play, you won't be playing a lot of pots—but when you do play a hand, you will play it aggressively.

Some people think that playing solid poker means playing in a very predictable fashion, but that is a misconception. Playing solid does not mean playing like a robot or a rock. It means playing smart, choosing the right hand or the right time to play aggressively, and varying your play just enough to take advantage of opportunities when they come your way. After you have developed a feel for your opponents' styles of play and have accumulated some chips, you can further open up. Take it from Brunson: "Most good players are solid."

Take Your Time and Play Your Game

In higher buy-in tournaments, the rounds are longer and the number of chips you start with is much larger. For example, at the World Series of Poker $1,500 no-limit tournament, you receive $1,500 in chips, the blinds start at $25/$25, and the rounds last one hour. It always amazes us that in these big tournaments, we see players eliminated in the first 15 minutes!

Think of the long rounds and big starting stacks as power tools that you can use to implement your tournament strategy. You do not have to play as fast as you do in the lower stakes events that give you fewer chips to work with and shorter levels of play in which to maneuver. In the bigger events, you have plenty of chips and lots of time so you can play solid poker without feeling pressed into playing marginal hands.

Some players have trouble adjusting their tournament strategy for the longer rounds and bigger chip stacks found in bigger events. They start to panic when they aren't dealt playable starting hands for long stretches of time, and they try to force the action by playing mediocre cards. You can combat this tendency by exercising patience and discipline. Even if you've been sitting dormant with dead cards during the first three rounds or so, you still haven't lost a lot of chips because the blinds are small in comparison to your starting stack. On the plus side, you've established a tight image so that when you come into a pot with a raise, your opponents will show you some respect. They haven't seen you play a hand, so they will assume that you have a big hand—and hopefully, they will be right.

Keep the faith; the cards will come your way in due time. Don't fall into the trap of limping or raising from early position with chip burners such as A-J or K-Q. By playing a patient and disciplined game, you will survive the early rounds with plenty of ammunition to work with.

We suggest playing selectively aggressive when you're starting out, and then adapting your style of play to the changing conditions as necessary. There are many successful styles of play that will win the money. Great players are able to adapt and change their game when they need to.

Develop a style that you are comfortable with, concentrate on your game, and ignore the other distractions. If you are fortunate enough to be at a table that is being televised, tune out the cameras and the audience. Focus squarely on your game and the players at your table. Don't worry about the cameras catching you in a mistake—play the way you think you should and forget about what impression you might be making on the audience.

Play your cards in position and save more advanced or fancy plays for a little later in the tournament. Just play your own game using the style of play and strategies that have proven their worth for you in other tournaments.

Adjust Your Play When the Antes Kick In

At the start of the fourth level of play in $1,000 and higher buy-in tournaments, all players are required to post an ante on every hand. For example, in the Bellagio $1,000 buy-in events run by ace tournament director Jack McClelland, you start with $2,000 in chips and each level lasts for one hour. The blind structure escalates like this:

1. Level 1, $25/$50 blinds;
2. Level 2, $50/$100 blinds;
3. Level 3, $100/$200 blinds;
4. Level 4, $100/$200 blinds plus a $25 ante.

Note that in Level 3, with $100/$200 blinds, it will cost you $300 to play in a nine-handed game, but in Level 4, with the same blinds, it will cost you $525. The antes have increased the cost of playing a round by 75 percent.

In our opinion, when the antes kick in, the tournament kicks off. The late Stu Ungar, probably the greatest no-limit hold'em tournament player ever, said that when the antes started, that's when he started to play. With all that extra money in the pot, you can start playing more aggressively on the backside when you are the first one to enter the pot. You want to put pressure on the blinds by raising to steal

197

the pot, all so that you can maintain and build your chips position.

If you have followed our earlier advice, you've established a solid-aggressive image. Now you can begin to open up your game and capitalize on that image. Players have been eliminated and chip stacks are becoming defined. Your goal is to build your stack during Levels 4 through 6, the early-middle stage of the tournament, so that you will be in position to do the most damage to your opponents during Levels 7 through 9, the late-middle stage. If you can do that, you will be in a highly competitive position going into the late stage of the tournament—Level 10 onward.

Keep in mind that tournaments are not won in the early rounds. "I believe you 'win' a tournament during the middle stages," Don says. He believes that, in order to get to the money, you must continually increase your chip stack after the antes kick in at the beginning of the early-middle stage of a tournament. If you can accomplish that goal, as the blinds and antes continue to increase, you will be in a position to play your winning style of poker during the late-middle rounds.

Getting into the money and then to the final table is your goal—that's why we play tournaments. You build your chips in the early rounds and increase your chips during the early middle stage. From Level 7 onward, you want to inflict maximum damage to your opponents so that when you reach Levels 9 and 10, you are in the money, moving toward the final table. In summary, you build the foundation for your potential win during the middle rounds after the antes come into play.

Manage Your Stack Size with Proven Strategies

As the tournament progresses, your chip count in relation to the amounts of the blinds and antes becomes more of a factor in the way you play your hands. Your goal should be to have a minimum of thirty times the big blind at all times. If you can maintain this ratio through skillful play, good judgment, and some luck at the right time, your chip stack will not be in jeopardy.

If you have a short stack that is less than ten times the size of the big blind, you must begin to play aggressively in order to build your chips. Look for hands or situations where you can raise in order to try and win the blinds and antes. If you can win the blinds and antes two times per round, you can go from being a short stack to being a medium stack. If you raise once a round and are able to pick up the blinds and antes, you will at least be able to maintain your chips and hopefully find a hand that you can double up with in the upcoming round.

If you allow your chips to fall so low that you could be blinded and anted out shortly, you must find a hand to play right away. If you are sitting in a late position and can be the first player in the pot, move all-in. Sometimes you will win the blinds and antes simply because your opponents do not want to double you up if you have a hand. Other times someone will call you and, hopefully, the upcards will come to your rescue. But in any case, find a hand and take a stand before your chip stack gets so low that you no longer pose a threat to your opponents.

A medium stack probably is the most difficult to play. Decisions are all the more important when you have a medium stack because you can become short-stacked if you make a mistake in judgment. On the other hand, if you play correctly and bet your chips in the right spot, you can become a big stack. Medium chip stacks require the most careful decision making in tournament play. Think—and then think again—before you act.

If you are fortunate enough to have accumulated a big stack, your primary goal is to maintain your status. Your chip power will instill fear in your opponents. Most players do not want to play against a big stack because if they lose, they are out of the tournament.

Use your arsenal of chips as a weapon of mass destruction, but be wary if the target fires back at you. If you have been bullying your table by raising a lot of pots and an opponent plays back at you, be very careful—90 percent of the time, your opponent has a hand and is hoping to double through you. Before you raise, consider the chip stacks of your opponents. If you're up against a very short stack, your raise will force him to take a stand and move in with all his chips. Opponents with hands such as A-x, K-10, Q-10, K-9, and even K-8 will play against you. We suggest that you not raise with small connectors because you do not want to have to draw to the hand. Our advice is to raise with decent hands only. In other words, do not raise just because you are the big stack.

For example Tom was playing in an online tournament when everyone passed to the small blind, who had a sizeable stack. The big blind had a short stack with one-third of his chips already in the pot. This meant that he would have to defend his blind with a wide range of hands, especially heads-up against the small blind. Sure enough, the small blind raised and the big blind called with all his chips. The small blind had J-6 offsuit and the big blind had K-2 offsuit. The all-in big blind was the favorite, of course, and doubled his chips when he won the pot.

If you ever are tempted to make a similar play, ask yourself, "Why should I raise with a weak hand when I know that the short stack is going to have to call me?" Take a lesson from the small blind in this example. He lost a healthy percentage of his chips because, without thinking, he put a lot of chips at risk in a situation where his opponent would almost certainly call the raise with almost any hand.

When you have the biggest stack at the final table, don't be in a rush to pick on the shortest stacks unless you have a good hand. Pick on the medium stacks. They will respect you and lay down a hand against a raise because they don't absolutely have to play.

You Need Less Strength in Shorthanded Play

When only two or three tables are left in the tournament, they will often be shorthanded. The fewer the number of players at your table, the less strength you need to play a hand, because so few cards are out.

Since you need less hand strength in shorthanded play, any hand with an ace becomes a strong hand. Any pocket pair, including deuces, is very playable in three-handed action. All the troubles hands—such as K-J, Q-10, J-10, and 10-9—gain value and actually become raising hands, especially when you are the first player to enter the pot. For example, suppose you're in the big blind and the small blind just limps into the pot. If you have a hand such as Q-10, you might raise, figuring that it probably is a better hand than the small blind has. If he reraises, you can reevaluate the situation.

When you're playing shorthanded no-limit hold'em, you need less strength to attack the blinds. You constantly have to try to pick up the blinds in order to maintain your chip position and, hopefully, go on to victory. Look for situations in which you can attack when you're the first one to enter the pot. Also, since the blinds are much higher in the final stages of the tournament, you can't afford to just sit there and let the blinds gobble up your chips.

Normally when the tournament gets down to three- or four-handed play, the blinds and antes are so high that winning the blinds two out of three times will increase your chips throughout the round. And if you can do that, you will eventually win the tournament.

"I was coaching a player during a recent online tournament," Tom says. "Twelve players were sitting at two six-handed tables, trying to make the final ten-handed table. My student was in first position with pocket threes. I advised him to move in because the blinds were very high—$1,500/$3,000—and he only had $16,000 in chips. Going through the blinds once more was going to cost him one-third of his stack, so I thought it was the worth the risk. He needed to win some chips and build his stack enough that he would be able to sit through another round or two even if he didn't catch any cards. He moved in and won the hand.

"Then he made another positional play, moving in when he was on the button with an A-3. Getting picked off worried him, but I assured him that that's the chance you take in shorthanded play. There's always some risk involved when you move in with a hand like that, but he survived again.

"The point is that when you're at a shorthanded table late in the tournament and the blinds are high, you can't sit quietly while your chips get blinded off into oblivion."

But keep in mind, of course, that you can't win the tournament until you get to the championship table. To get there, you have to hang in long enough to give yourself a chance to get lucky—and you're going to have to take some risks along the way. Most of the time, you won't have the luxury of a big stack, so you'll have to be creative in your play.

Naturally, if you are fortunate enough to have built a big stack, you can be very selective and possibly cruise on in. Your primary goal is to maintain your big stack by playing very solid and being aggressive when you come into a pot. Your game plan is to make it to the point where only three or four players are left in action. That's where the big money is up for grabs!

Play a Strategically Sound Game at the Final Table

If you have the biggest stack at the start of play at the final table, don't be in a rush to pick on the shortest stacks unless you have a good hand. Pick on the medium stacks. Opponents with medium stacks usually will lay down a hand against a raise because they won't feel forced to play a hand. They will respect your raise more than a short stack will. Why? Because the medium stacks have the most to lose. The short stacks are quite often forced to play with you because they have no better options. The blinds are high and they have to play something soon. Therefore if you have a strong stack and a weak hand, you would be far better off playing against a medium stack than a short stack.

Three- and Four-Handed Play

When only three or four players are left at the final table, you can win the tournament by choosing the right situations and picking on the right opponents. Don't always wait for somebody to get knocked out so that you can move up a spot. Look to put yourself in position to win, or in a position to discuss a deal. Because of the large amount of money at stake in big buy-in tournaments, the final three or four players often discuss making a deal and splitting the prize money according to chip counts. The tournament is then played out for the trophy alone, or some money may be left in the prize pool for the winner.

When the action is four-handed, you must post a blind two out of every four hands. If it's three-handed, you have to post a blind in two out of three hands you're dealt. With all those blinds to post, you must play very aggressively to prevent the gradual erosion of your stack. If you have a large stack, keep putting pressure on your opponents. However, don't underestimate the strength that you need to raise with and start putting on the pressure with hopeless hands. Even though you need less strength to raise shorthanded, and even though you have a big stack, you still must have at least some semblance of a real hand. The most dangerous thing you can do is double-up the short stacks by playing weak hands aggressively.

Heads-Up Play

Now let's say that you have used sound final-table strategy and are heads-up for the championship. The first-place prize money, the title, and the bragging rights are up for grabs. You don't want to make a deal so you decide to play it out. Good for you! But now what do you do?

First, you will play more hands than you'll fold—otherwise, your stack is headed for destruction. And you'll play hands that you wouldn't normally play because you will be in the blind every single hand. Big hands aren't dealt as often heads-up. In fact, you seldom see two really big starting hands such as aces against kings in heads-up play, so you'll be forced to make moves against your opponent with lesser hands than normal. This is when you really have to get inside your opponent's head.

You must make a lot of decisions based not only on your knowledge of your opponent, but also on the size of your stack relative to his. If you have 60 percent of the chips and he has 40 percent, you're pretty close. You have an edge, yes, but you have to be very careful because if you lose a hand and double-up your opponent, he will have 80 percent of the chips and you'll be on the short end of the stick. Also remember that if your opponent has a 3 to 1 edge over you in the chip count, you're still only two hands away from winning the tournament. If you double-up once, you will have half of the chips; if you double up again, you've won the whole enchilada. Don't give up just because you're trailing, and don't get too cocky or overconfident if you have the lead. You have to use good judgment and keep things in perspective.

In heads-up play, the small blind is on the button, so he will act first before the flop and last after the flop. Quite often, it is correct to just call—match the size of the big blind—when you have the small blind in heads-up play. It's okay to see a lot of flops for half a bet. For example, suppose I have a Q-6 suited. I don't want to raise with the hand, but I may want to see the flop for half a bet.

And when you do have a premium hand, you might be able to trap the big blind by just calling. Since you've called a number of times before, he cannot be sure about the strength of your hand. Therefore, don't always be in a rush to raise with your good hands.

Conversely, when you're the big blind and the small blind limps, don't be afraid to see a free flop. If I'm in the big blind with a weak hand and my opponent has limped, I'm not going to raise. I'm going to take the flop for free and see what develops. Don't think that you have to raise every single time just because your opponent has shown some apparent weakness. Sometimes he may be slow-playing a good hand to try to trap you. Or he may have a medium-strength hand and decide to play with you if you raise. Since the big blind is the first to act after the flop in heads-up play, if you raise and the small blind calls, you will be at a disadvantage in position from the flop onward.

Keep the Big Picture in Mind

You can't win it if you're not in it, so you've got to make the final table. Understand that everyone wants to (a) get into the money, and (b) make the final table. When you get to the final table, first gauge the number of chips you have versus the chip stacks of your opponents. If you have the smallest stack, look for a hand and take a stand. An opponent may come after you, of course, but if you can double-up, you'll be in a better position to win the tournament. Usually the difference between ninth- and tenth-place money is so small, that it doesn't pay to sit patiently, hoping to hang on and move up one rung on the ladder. What's the point of trying to move up just one rung if, in the process, you give up any chance of winning the tournament?

The big money is always in the first three places, so moving up a notch becomes significant when the action gets down to three or four players—especially in a big buy-in tournament. We hope that by using the tips in this chapter, you will climb the ladder to the very top.

Tournament Talk

Don's Top 10 Tips for Winning No-Limit Hold'em Tournaments **By Don Vines**

1. Avoid playing small and medium pairs from early position. If you raise with them and get reraised you are almost always in trouble and will probably have to fold. If you decide to play them, just call the amount of the big blind. If a player raises any significant amount after you have entered the pot for the minimum bet, fold.

2. People misplay A-K more than any other hand in hold'em. Remember that A-K is a drawing hand and that you will only flop a pair to Big Slick 30 percent of the time. It is almost always a mistake to go all in with A-K before the flop in the early stage of a tournament.

3. As a general rule, small pairs and suited connectors should only be played in late position for the minimum bet. Ideally, two or more players—in addition to the blinds—will have entered the pot for the minimum bet. If somebody reraises any significant amount before the flop, it is better to fold, even if you have already called the minimum opening bet.

4. Avoid playing trouble hands if somebody raises the pot. Hands that can get you into serious trouble are A-J, K-Q, A-10 suited, and often A-Q. Pocket jacks and lower pairs are hands that players often go broke with. Avoid playing big pots with these hands in the early stages of a tournament, because you are usually already beaten or drawing very slim.

5. Remember that no-limit hold'em is a bettor's game. If you are constantly calling other players' bets instead of doing the raising yourself, you are vulnerable. Selective aggression is the key to survival. You should not play a lot of hands, but when you do play, you should usually be the raiser, not the caller. You want to put your opponents on the defensive, making them react to you. This is how you take command of the game.

6. Pairs are a slight favorite over two overcards. In the late stages of a tournament, many players with a pair put their money in against two overcards. These hands are coin-flip situations because they are very close to even money. You should avoid playing coin flips if at all possible, especially in the early stages of a tournament. But in the late stages, when the blinds and antes are high, you will often have to take a stand with either the pair or the overcards in order to survive.

7. Slow-playing big hands is a viable strategy in no-limit hold'em. If you flop a big hand that is the nuts or close to it, you should often check and then just call an opponent's bet. The idea is to trap your opponent on a later betting round for as many of his chips as possible. Strong hands like trips or a nut flush are examples of hands you might slow-play after the flop. You want action with your made hands, and many times, the only way to get action is to disguise the strength of your hand by slow-playing it.

8. If you limp in with a big pair like aces or kings before the flop, do not allow yourself to get broke with your pair. The idea of limping in with a big pair is to get somebody to raise so you can reraise them. If you limp in and several other players also enter the pot without raising, it is quite likely that someone will flop a good enough hand to beat your aces or kings. Therefore do not put a lot of money into an unraised pot after the flop if you think someone has out-flopped you. You played it cheap before the flop, so get away from it cheap.

9. Bluffing is a big part of the game, but you must time your bluffs correctly. Inexperienced players will often bluff at the wrong times and go broke. There is no disgrace in getting caught in a bluff, but good timing will help avoid this disaster. In televised tournaments, players frequently make big bluffs at each other, especially in final table action when the blinds are very high. In this situation, you aren't going to be dealt very many premium hands, so you must take some risks in order to survive. But in the early stages of a tournament when the pots are much smaller, you don't risk too much trying to bluff at a small pot.

10. Get to know your opponents by constantly studying how they play. Observing their play is easier when you are not involved in a pot. Try to figure out what hands they are betting and calling with. Determine who is likely to bluff and which players are the easiest to bluff. Be aware which players get very upset when they lose a pot and start playing a lot more hands. If a player is raising way more than you would reasonably expect, you know that he does not always have a premium hand. If you think your opponent is weak and your hand is good enough, take advantage of him by reraising.

The No-Limit Hold'em Playbook

"In poker there is a moment when there seems to be a harmony of perfection where everything is working."

–James Woods, actor and poker player

INTRODUCTION

As in all sports, no-limit hold'em is a game in which you can use certain standard plays to gain the advantage over your opponents. In this chapter, we will identify several types of plays and show you how and when to use them.

THE POWER PLAY

The power play is almost always either a big bet, a big raise, or a reraise, the purpose of which is to win the pot by shutting out opponents who may be on drawing hands that could beat you on a later street. You can use the power play at any time during a hand—before the flop, on the flop, on the turn, or on the river—whenever you want to win the pot right on the spot, without having to continue any further with the hand. And if you don't win the pot then and there, you at least want to narrow the field down considerably, usually to heads-up play. First, let's take a look at an example of a power play before the flop.

A Power Play with Pocket Aces

Let's say the blinds are $50/$100, and you are sitting in the cutoff seat and look down to find the A♠-A♥. Three players have called the minimum bet and now the action is up to you. You definitely do not want to play your aces against multiple opponents because big pairs play best against one or two opponents at the most. You decide to try to win the pot before the flop so that you will not have to risk getting drawn out on by multiple opponents. This is when you can use the big raise as a power play. With $450 already in the pot—the three callers at $100 each, the small blind at $50, and the big blind at $100—we suggest raising to at least $800. A big raise like this should knock out all the marginal hands. If one player calls, that's fine since your goal in making the big raise was to either win the pot before the flop or play the hand heads-up. Sometimes a player with a small pocket pair or a hand like K-Q suited will call, and occasionally a player who puts you on a steal will do the same. This is good news for you, because you are a 4 to 1 favorite from the start.

Against one caller, be prepared to make a heavy bet on the flop. In low buy-in tournaments, you might need to put in 50 percent or even all your chips when you make a power play. In the bigger events you receive more starting chips in relation to the big blind, so you should adjust the amount of chips you bet, raise, or reraise. In the same situation in a big buy-in event, you might not bet more than 15 to 20 percent of your chips.

If your opponent calls your big bet on the flop and a non-scare card comes on the turn, be prepared to make another big bet, or even put the balance of your chips in the pot. If a scare card comes on the turn, you have to decide how to proceed based on your knowledge of your opponent and whether you are the first or last to act.

Suppose you have been called before the flop, on the flop, and on the turn. Now you're at the river and must decide whether to bet or check. If you are confident that your pocket rockets are still the best hand, tailor your bet to the amount that you believe your opponent will call.

For example, suppose you have $2,500 in chips, your opponent has $2,300, and the blinds are $25/$50. Before the flop, you bet $175 with your pocket aces, and your opponent calls. The flop comes K♥-8♣-2♦ rainbow. You bet $300 on the flop and your opponent calls. The turn card is the 5♠, so no flush draw is possible. Now you bet $600 and again he calls. The river card is the 10♣, so the board is now showing K♥-8♣-2♦-5♠-10♣. At this point, you have bet $175 plus $300 plus $600 for a total of $1,075. Since you started with $2,500 in chips, you have $1,425 left. Your opponent has $2,300 minus $1,075 for a total of $1,225. You have put your opponent on a big king, probably a K-Q, and are confident that your read is correct. How much should you bet?

If you move all-in, you will make it easier for him to fold a hand such as K-Q or K-J because he may suspect that you have him out-kicked with an A-K. But if you bet a lesser amount—in this case, we suggest $800—your opponent may be more inclined to call, and perhaps even move all-in. The point is that you want him to call, so you should bet an amount that you believe will induce him to do so, and therefore pay you off for your good hand.

A Power Play with Pocket Kings

Now let's take a look at another scenario. Suppose you have pocket kings and made a big bet before the flop. One player called your raise. Now the flop comes J♥-10♣-4♥. You do not want drawing hands in the pot, so if your opponent called your big raise with an A-K or A-Q, you want to drive him out of the pot right now. With this flop, he might have picked up a flush draw, a straight draw, or even a gut-shot straight draw. You do not want him to call your bet, so you must make a large enough bet that he will not have the right odds to call.

If there is $1,000 in the pot before the flop, you must bet a minimum of $1,500-$2,000 on the flop in order for your opponent to realize that he should fold based upon the pot odds he's getting to outdraw you. If your opponent has A-Q or A-K, he is drawing to three aces and a gutshot straight for a total of 14 outs—7 outs multiplied by 2 drawing opportunities, the turn and the river. If you do not make a big enough bet, he might have the correct odds to make the call. With $1,000 in the pot, that $1,500-$2,000 will take away his pot odds. If he calls, he has way overpaid for the privilege of drawing and is taking by far the worst of it.

But what if your opponent has called on the flop with a J-10? Oops! Even though he made a horrible play by calling your big raise before the flop with that hand, you can still draw out on his two pair. Look at the bright side: If he has a pocket pair such as 8-8 or 9-9 and has put you on an A-K, you're in a great spot to pick up a lot of chips.

When and How to Use the Power Play

On television we see a number of power plays, most of which are made shorthanded because only the final six players are in action during most televised tournaments. The execution of the power play is almost always the same, whether the table is full or shorthanded. How you use it stays the same, but when you use it might vary depending on the number of players at the table.

When the table is shorthanded, players normally make their power plays on the flop. For example, say a player raises and is called in one spot. The flop comes down, and the initial raiser makes a big-bet power play on the flop.

When used before the flop, the power play is used as a reraise. For instance, say Player A raises and Player B, with a medium pocket pair, decides that the initial raiser has A-K or A-Q and he wants to win the pot right there. So Player B makes a power play by reraising. If his read on his opponent is correct, he hopes that Player A will release his hand. If he gets called and the flop comes with small cards—no aces, kings, or queens—the initial raiser is in trouble. If he checks and Player B bets, he will normally give up his hand. If Player A check-raises, Player B must decide whether Player A is making a play at the pot or actually has a hand. In most cases, if Player A has a high pair such as J-J or Q-Q and he thinks Player B reraised before the flop with A-K, he will bet because he doesn't want Player B to get a free card.

The power play can be attempted at any stage of the tournament—early stage, middle stage, late stage, and the final table. At a shorthanded table or at the final table with only a few players left, you are more likely to be called when you make a power play, especially by an opponent who has you way out-chipped, or by a player who has so few chips that he is forced to commit the balance of his stack in order to play the hand.

THE CHECK-RAISE

The check-raise is one of the most valuable tools in no-limit hold'em. Your opponents will put you on an extremely strong hand when you check, they bet, and then you raise them. It definitely gets their attention. In most cases, your opponents will respect a check-raise and fold. If anybody calls after you have check-raised, check again on the turn if you think you can induce another bet. Otherwise, come out betting.

Check-raise bets quite often earn a lot more respect than a normal big bet at the pot. When you check-raise someone, you're telling them, "You may have a hand, but I have a better one and I'm gonna force you to put a lot more chips in the pot if you want to play with me."

Not only are you showing a lot of strength when you make this move, you also are aggravating your opponents. Even though check-raising is just a part of the game, some people have a strange attitude toward check-raising and many of them seem to take it personally when you use it against them. The check-raise can put your opponents on tilt, and it's always to your advantage when an opponent becomes upset. Some players dislike this move so much, they do not allow it in their home games, because they think it is unethical. That is not true, of course.

Using the Check-Raise as a Semi-Bluff

At times, you check-raise when you don't have a hand because you don't think the other guy has anything either. If you think your opponent is on a steal, you are actually re-stealing with the check-raise tactic. Even if you get called, at least you usually have outs. As a general rule, unless you're positive that your opponent has nothing, using this kind of a play to re-steal is usually what we call a semi-bluff. In other words, if your opponent has a better hand than you anticipated, you still have something to draw to that can become the best hand.

For example, suppose you have a 10-8 in the big blind in an unraised pot with one or two callers. The flop comes K-9-7 so you have an open-end straight draw. You check and one of your opponents bets. If he gets called by the second player, or if the second player folds, you can put in a check-raise. We suggest that your check-raise be three times the size of the original bet, and your goal is to win the pot immediately.

If your opponent calls and you hit your straight on the turn, make a modest bet of about one-half the amount of the check-raise.

Conversely, if you do not hit your hand, you have the option of either betting or checking. If the turn card is a blank and you think that it did not help any of your opponents' hands, we suggest that you bet the same amount as your check-raise, again, hoping to win the pot right there. The other option is to check and hope that your opponents check behind you, giving you a free card. This play is actually quite weak because if you check and get a free card that does not help your hand, your opponents will call you at the river. We prefer betting the turn because a bet shows strength and often, your opponents will respect your bet and fold if they think they are beaten.

If they call and you do not complete your hand on the river—and if the river card is not scary—the right play is to bet a substantial amount in order to make your opponent believe that you have a big hand. This type of play works best in big buy-in tournaments with a large amount of chips to play with. In smaller buy-in events where you have fewer chips to work with, you might not have enough ammunition to make this play.

Check-Raising Against Aggressive Players Behind You

The check-raise can be very effective when the players sitting to your left are aggressive and you think that they will bet the hand for you. For example, say you are in middle to late position and you limp in with an A-J suited. Two aggressive players come in behind you. The flop comes J♠-6♥-2♣, and it is checked to you. Here, you also check, hoping that one of the aggressive players will bet at the flop and give you the opportunity to check-raise. If the first bettor was trying to steal, then he will fold and you will pick up his bet. However if the player has K-J, Q-J, J-10, or a jack with an even worse kicker, he may call your check-raise. In that case, you can bet again on the turn and hope that you get called. If that happens, you can bet again at the river.

Many players cannot lay down a K-J or a Q-J and will give you their chips, but be careful if the turn or the river comes with a scare card, such as a king or queen. The ideal scenario would be for the board to pair its bottom card. For example, say the flop comes J♠-6♥-2♣, the turn card is the 7♦, and the river the 2♠. With a board that reads J♠-6♥-2♣-7♦-2♠, players often will call your bet with K-J or Q-J, and you will win a nice pot.

Check-Raising with A-A and K-K

Say you are in middle position with A-A or K-K. You limp in, hoping that an aggressive player behind you will raise or maybe even bring other players into the hand. It comes back to you and you re-raise. Your goal is to win the pot right then or get it heads-up—especially if you have K-K—because if you have been raised by an A-Q, A-J or ace-anything, you do not particularly want to see the flop. Why? Well, suppose an ace comes on the flop. If you bet and your opponent raises, or if you check and your opponent bets, then your kings head for the muck.

Now say you have A-A and have limped into the pot. If an aggressive player raises, you have two options:

> 1. You can reraise and try to win the pot right there; or
> 2. You can call the raise and see the flop.

Suppose you just call and the flop comes down K♥-9♣-3♠. Now you can check in the hope that your aggressive opponent will fire in a bet. Once again you have two choices:

> 1. You can smooth-call in the hope of trapping your opponent on the turn; or
> 2. You can check-raise in the hope of getting called or even winning the hand right then.

It all depends on your read of your aggressive opponent. Will he fire another bet on the turn if a non-scare card comes out—the 6♦, for example? With a board of K♥-9♣-3♠-6♦, you check the turn and hope that your opponent will fire at you. If he does, you might check-raise about twice the amount of his bet. If your opponent bets $400, you might check-raise to $1,000-$1,200. If he lays the hand down, that is fine; and if he calls, that's okay, because you can bet at the river. Hopefully he hasn't made two pair and you will win a substantial pot.

Check-Raising with A-10 Suited

Suppose you have called on the backside with an A-10 suited and the flop comes 10-high with two of your suit. You check to the player on the button. If he bets into you, you can check-raise a substantial amount. If you are called and the turn is any card under a 10, but you have not made your flush, then you can bet into the pot with the expectation of winning it right then.

If you are called after your check-raise, your options at the river depend on whether or not the river card is higher or lower than a 10 and whether or not you make your flush:

1. If the river card is lower than a 10 and you do not make your flush, you can value-bet the hand.
2. If the river card is higher than a 10, you bet again, or just check and call. We prefer betting again here, because if your opponent has not made two pair, he might call you.
3. If you make your flush, then we suggest a small bet of about twice the size of the big blind. You are hoping that the aggressive player will raise you, pretending that he has made a big flush—and now you can win a very substantial pot. Of course, if he really has made a flush, you are in great position to win all of your opponent's chips.

THE BLUFF

The bluff play works best against one opponent. Bluffing into two other players is possible, but bluffing into more than two is generally suicide. Bluffs usually occur on the river, when all the cards are out, and if you're heads-up with another player, you can bluff at the pot from either position, first or last to act. You should have studied your opponent and believe that he will muck his hand when you make the bluff bet. If your opponent is timid player or a straightforward rock, a bluff should work, and you'll win the pot.

This is a situation where you really have to know your opponent. Almost all the top players use the bluff quite extensively in scenarios like this one. In fact, some of the best players bluff so often that even when they get called and lose, it works to their advantage on later hands. Since their opponents have seen them bluff so often, they can value-bet a lot of other hands, including their strong hands, and get good action. Therefore even if you get caught attempting a bluff, you can reap residual advantages.

Quite often, when you're in the big blind in the early or middle stage of a tournament, five or six callers will already be in the pot for the minimum bet. If this is the case you might put in a raise that is big enough to make everybody lay their hands down. Many times, if the first player folds, the other players will fall like dominoes. People know that some players will slow-play their better starting hands by limping into the pot with a big pair. Therefore, if the first limper folds after you raise, they will know that he didn't have a big hand. And there's a very good chance that the rest of them will follow suit because they will have to give you credit for having a big hand. If you can get past the first limper, you're usually home free.

Here's an example from a tournament at the Bellagio in Las Vegas. Six players had already limped into the pot for the minimum bet when Don looked down at an A-K offsuit in the big blind. He simply pushed his entire stack into the pot. The first limper showed his hand, pocket nines, and mucked them. Everybody folded around to the button, who was not a good player and didn't think before he pushed all his chips into the pot with pocket fives. He caught a five on the flop to win the pot, but thankfully, Don had more chips than his opponent had.

"The Best Bluff That Didn't Work"

"I have been playing no-limit hold'em tournaments for many years," Don says, "and the following is a story about the best bluff I've ever seen that didn't work. We were playing the $2,000 buy-in no-limit hold'em tournament at the 2004 World Series of Poker and were down to 125 players. I got moved to a table in the four-seat and immediately recognized a strong player—Mike Laing, who is a world-class no-limit tournament player—sitting on my left in the nine-seat. Laing is a great reader and has an uncanny ability to win without cards.

"'Well,' I said to myself, 'this should be a fun table to play,' because whenever Laing is at the table, you can expect great action and play.

"With blinds of $200/$400 and a $50 ante, I was the first to act and mucked my hand. Another strong player on my left had about $15,000 in chips and made a raise to $2,000. It was folded around to the player in the eight-seat, who called. Now it was Laing's turn to act. Without any pause or hesitation, he announced 'All-in!' and pushed $14,000 into the pot. Now it was time for the player in the five-seat to act. He studied and studied, asked for a chip count, and then tried to talk to Mike, which is never a problem. Finally, after about seven minutes, he said to Mike, 'I have laid down so many good hands to you over the years, A-K, pocket jacks, and pocket queens.' And very reluctantly, he pushed his chips into the pot. The other player mucked. Opening his hand, he showed pocket queens.

"Mike looked at him and said, 'You're in trouble!' and opened his hand—9-2 unsuited, the great Montana Banana hand! We all gasped and started to laugh. Mike lost the hand and was eliminated from action.

"About one hour later, I spoke to Mike and asked him why he had made that play. He told me that he was totally confident that the player who called would lay down any hand except aces and kings and probably queens, so he was trying to pick up the $5,050 that was in the pot. He thought he had a 90 percent chance of winning the pot right there and was willing to put his tournament life on the line.

"'You made a great bluff,' I told him. 'It took balls of iron to make that play!'

This is one characteristic of great no-limit hold'em players—they are willing to bet all their chips with nothing in order to win a pot.

THE INTUITIVE PLAY

In a no-limit hold'em tournament there are situations that come up from time to time that require you to use your gut instincts, which will become more accurate as you play more tournaments. Say you have studied the play of a hand, you know the players, and now you must decide whether to raise, call, or fold. There is no clear-cut answer. This is when your intuition comes into play.

"Go with your first impression," says T.J. Cloutier, who says his instincts are better than 75 percent accurate.

An Example of an Intuitive Play

"At a no-limit hold'em tournament during the 2004 World Series of Poker," Tom says, "I was dealt the K♠-K♣. I raised the pot and was called by one player. When the flop came A♦-7♥-6♣, I checked and my opponent bet a large amount of chips. I studied the situation and was tempted to fold, but my initial reaction was to call or raise, since my intuition was telling me that my opponent did not have an ace. I thought for about two more minutes. Just as I was about to fold, a little voice—my gut instinct—told me once again to raise. I raised and won the pot immediately.

"Later in the same tournament I was faced with the same situation. I raised and my opponent immediately reraised enough to put me all-in. This time, I folded and the other player showed me an A-Q. Sometimes you're right and sometimes you're wrong, but the more no-limit hold'em tournaments you play the better your initial reactions will be."

THE SLOW PLAY

The purpose of the slow play is to get full value for extremely strong hands. You want to disguise the strength of your hand in the hope of trapping your opponents. This can be accomplished by checking, just betting the minimum, or simply calling an opponent's bet rather than raising.

The slow play is often used before the flop. In fact players almost always slow-play pocket aces or pocket kings to try to lure other people into the pot. Or if you're heads-up, you might just call your opponent's pre-flop raise and try to trap him either on the flop or on a later street with what you figure is the best hand. You can slow-play from any position but it usually works best when there are callers behind you.

For example, suppose you flop the nut flush and someone makes a bet in front of you. You may decide to just call his bet, especially if one or two other players have yet to act. You slow-play the nut hand to try to lure the other players into the pot. Then if the first player bets into you on the turn, you just call again. Hopefully, he will bet into you again at the river, and that's when you show the true strength of your hand by firing in a raise.

But what if your opponent checks on fourth street? In that case, if you have a hand that you are confident is the best hand and you don't believe he has very many outs, you bet an amount of chips that you think your opponent will call.

Slow-Playing from the Blind

Let's say that you're in the big blind with pocket eights, and the pot has been raised a normal amount, say three to four times the big blind. Three players have called, so you also call the raise. Your goal is to flop a set in order to win a big pot. And if the pot has not been raised, that's even better, because you get to see the flop for just your posted big blind.

The flop comes A♠-8♦-2♣. You have two options: bet or check. If I am playing at an aggressive table, I might make an average bet in the hope of getting raised or just called. If I get raised, then I will call the raise and check the turn, in an attempt to induce a bet from the raiser. As long as the turn card is not a scare card, like a suited card or a straight card, I will check, hoping that the initial bettor will bet and give me the option of check-raising him or just calling.

A scare card on fourth street is one that might allow your opponent to draw out on you, such as a flush card or a card that could give your opponent a straight draw. For example, suppose you have the same pocket eights, and your opponent has the A♣-5♣. The turn card is the 4♣, making the board A♠-8♦-2♣-4♣. Now your opponent is drawing to an inside straight and a flush. Against this type of board, I would make a big bet on the turn so that my opponent will not be getting favorable pot odds to draw. If my opponent raises, I will reraise a large amount. But if he just calls, then I will bet the same amount on the river, hoping to get called again.

My goal is to win as many chips as possible with this hand in this scenario, and a check-raise is not always the right move, as many players will give up their hands to a check-raise if they are sure that they are beaten. The best time to check-raise is at the river; however, you should be confident that your opponent will bet the river.

Slow-Playing vs. Check-Raising

The slow play works best when you flop middle set or low set because you can check when you know that an aggressive player sitting behind you will bet at this pot. He probably will bet the flop and the turn, but don't count on him to bet at the river. You should bet the river because if you check, your opponent might check behind you and you will lose a bet.

You can also use the check-raise on the turn if you are heads-up or three-handed. You do not have to raise a large amount to be successful. You want opponents to pay you off at the river, so you should bet an amount on the turn that you believe they will call. If you bet too much, they may throw their hands away unless they have two pair. In many cases, if they call your check-raise on the turn and you bet the same amount at the river, you will get paid off for your good hand.

Slow-Playing the Nuts from the Big Blind

"In a recent no-limit hold'em weekly tournament with a $500 buy-in," Don says, "the following hand came up at the second limit with blinds of $50/$100. I had managed to build my starting stack of chips from $2,000 to $4,400 and was in the big blind with the A♠-J♠ when a player went all-in for $875. A player sitting two seats to the right called. He had been playing a lot of hands and had accumulated about $8,000 in chips. The rest of the players folded, and it was my turn to act. The initial raiser had been raising with weak hands such as K-Q and A-x, and the first caller had been showing a lot of marginal hands, so I decided to call. The flop came 10♠-8♠-3♠. I had flopped the nut flush!

"I checked and the player who had called the all-in raise went all-in for $7,125. Of course, I beat him into the pot. We opened our hands and the all-in raiser had a K-Q unsuited; the other player had 3♦-3♣. The board did not pair and I more than doubled up. If I had bet into this pot in a normal fashion, the other caller probably would have folded, and I would have won a decent pot. However, when I checked and slow-played my nut flush, the player who flopped a set of threes decided to make an all-in bet. He did not stop to consider that I might have a flush, he just wanted to freeze me out of the pot. By slow-playing the nuts, I was able to accumulate a lot of chips early in the tournament."

Slow-Playing the Nuts from Late Position

Suppose you have the A♠-J♠ on the button with three or four callers in the pot, and you also call. The flop comes with 9♠-5♠-2♠ and a player bets into you. In this situation, you should just call. Slow-play your nut flush because if your opponent also has a flush, he most likely will bet the turn, especially if the turn card is not a spade. On the turn, you have to decide whether to raise or once again just call, in the hope that your opponent bets at the river.

"I like to wait until the river to raise," Don says, "because if I raise on the turn, my opponent may muck the hand."

If no spade shows on the river, your opponent might bet again. Now you can raise and hope that he has a flush or another hand that is strong enough for him to call your raise. If your opponent checks the river, bet an amount that you want him to call, say one and a half times the amount of the bet on the turn. By slow-playing your nut flush from last position, you will be able to win the most chips.

THE DECEPTIVE PLAY

Any time you disguise the strength of your hand by checking, flat-calling, or betting less than the standard amount, you are playing deceptively.

One type of deceptive play is the underbet. Like the slow play, the purpose of the underbet is to disguise the strength of a powerful hand in order to get some action. For example, suppose you've made the nut straight on fourth street. You are the first to act and you check, then your opponent checks behind you. When a blank comes off at the river, you're thinking that your opponent probably has some kind of a pair. Knowing that you have the best hand possible, the only question is, "How much can I bet and still get this guy to call?" In this case, you can disguise the strength of your hand by under-betting the pot. A bet of one-half to two-thirds the size of the pot might induce your opponent to call. And keep in mind that if the hand has been checked on fourth street, your opponent will often call you at the showdown, thinking that you're bluffing, on a draw, or holding a weaker hand than his.

Here's another example of a deceptive play that will help you get full value for your hand: Suppose four limpers are in the pot, you're in the big blind with pocket fours, and the flop comes A-9-4 with two suited cards. Here, you might make a small bet at the pot, knowing that someone most likely has an ace, or even a nine, and will raise you. You don't mind that because, with two suited cards on the board, you can reraise to try to thin out the field. Or if you see that the action will be heads-up, you might just call the raise on the flop and then check to the raiser on fourth street to give him the chance to bet into you.

THE FINESSE PLAY

Suppose you're in middle position with the A♦-10♦. Boom, three diamonds flop! You've made the nuts. Two or three people are yet to act behind you, including one or two other limpers and the blinds. You're in a big multiway, unraised pot, and an aggressive player leads with a pot-sized bet. You think he might have flopped a flush and be willing to put in the rest of his chips if you raise. But remember that other people have yet to act behind you. Since the original bettor is known for his aggressive tactics, you may just want to just call his bet in order not to tip off the strength of your hand, which will hopefully lure other players into the pot. Your opponents might have flopped a set, a lower flush, or two pair, and believe they have the best hand. They will come in for a reraise and might even move all their chips into the pot. You've totally fooled them about the strength of your hand by not putting in any kind of a raise.

If you're the last person to act, you have the nut flush, and everyone has checked to you, you can make a small bet and likely get one or two callers. They probably won't put you on a flush since your last action seemed to be a positional bet, an attempt to pick up the pot. If someone has been slow-playing a lesser flush, he might think you're trying to steal the pot and raise you. Now the betting has been driven back into you, and you have all the options in the world at your disposal.

"I usually think of making a finesse play when I have the stone nuts on the river," Don says. "I'll make a small bet because I want players to call me, or maybe even raise. This play is usually made from either early position or very late position."

Second-Hand Low

T.J. Cloutier calls our next type of finesse play, playing second-hand low. Holding a big pair and with several people yet to act behind you, you call someone else's initial bet or raise, hoping to get someone to come into the pot for a reraise. Ideally, the betting will get back around to you and then you can put in another raise.

Here's a specific example: A player opens for a standard raise in early position, and you are next to act with pocket rockets. You have several aggressive players to act behind you, so you smooth-call the raise, planning to reraise if one of those aggressive players comes over the top of the initial raise. Even if nobody raises behind you, you have cleverly disguised the strength of your hand by not reraising to begin with, and hopefully, you'll be able to trap at least the initial raiser after the flop.

"I only would attempt this play," Tom adds, "if I have very aggressive players to act behind me who are very likely to make an aggressive reraise."

If that's not the case—say, if you're in the big blind and the first raiser has driven everybody out of the pot—you might just call with pocket aces. Then you check on the flop and let him bet into you in order to get more money into the pot. Most of the time, your aces will hold up against just one opponent.

THE BUTTON PLAY

The button play involves raising with a medium-strength hand—or maybe even a fairly weak hand—against opponents that you think will fold their blinds. Against super-aggressive, liberal blind defenders, this play usually won't work, but there is another play that you can make against those opponents.

"Against that type of player," Tom says, "I love opening the pot with a big pair, because a lot of times they won't give me credit for it on the button. They might come after me with a far lesser hand, so I often make a very standard raise in this situation.

"Other times, if I'm up against players who are not very experienced, I may just slip into the pot with a fairly strong hand—almost always a big pair—by flat-calling to try and get some action. My opponents might not suspect that I am trying to trap them, especially if they are novices."

If you're on the button, everybody checks to you, and you think you can win the hand right there by simply betting, always fire in a bet. You can do this on any street. For example, suppose you raised before the flop on the button with a Q-10 or a 9-8 suited, say, and one player called. If he checks to you on the flop, you can often represent whatever's out there by following up with a bet on the flop, whether you've improved your hand or not. Be wary, however, of the check-raise. Sometimes an opponent will check to you on the flop in the hope of inducing a bet so that he can raise. If you're up against a tricky, deceptive opponent, do not make this type of play.

The button plays that we have mentioned are always based on your knowledge of how the blinds play, and your prediction about what they're going to do in response to your action.

THE POWERLESS PLAY YOU DON'T WANT TO MAKE!

Some players don't take time to analyze the situation correctly and make what we call reflexive plays. They put their chips in first and either think about it later or don't think about it all. If you watch good no-limit hold'em players, you will notice that they seldom act quickly. They sit there, count their chips, and think. What are they thinking about? The type of hand you might have, how much they should raise, and whether they should fold or just call.

The reflexive player does just the opposite. He has no idea what you might have, never even gives it a thought. He only looks at his two cards—if he likes them, he's going to put his chips in the pot, no matter what. Be wary of this type of player. If you're playing against someone like this, you had better have a hand, because these players are virtually bluff-proof. This is one more reason why you need to carefully study the opposition so that you know which players think before they act, and which ones act before they think.

Remember that whenever you make a bet, you might be risking your entire stack. You will often have to put more chips into the pot by either betting again or calling an opponent's bet. So always think through the possible consequences of your actions rather than making mindless plays that can lead to your destruction.

Here is an example of a mindless play. Several limpers already are in the pot, and the next player to act raises for exactly double the size of the big blind. This is absolutely mindless, as it simply reopens the betting. All it does is make the pot slightly bigger without driving anyone out of it. If you have a small pair, an ace-small suited, or suited connectors, you want a lot of callers, so why bother to raise? Why put in any more money when you can take a cheap flop? And if you have a big pair when several limpers already are in the pot, you're not raising enough to drive people out, which is what you really want to do. With a big pair, you want to thin the field, pare it down to one or two opponents, at the most.

Here's another type of mindless bet that Tom observed during a $2,500 buy-in super satellite that awarded seats in the $25,000 World Poker Tour championship event at the Bellagio. In a heads-up pot, the flop came Q-10-8. The first player, who was holding a J-9 and had flopped a straight, bet on the flop, and the second player called him with the A♣-7♣. With a Q-10-8 on the board, the second player had called on the flop with a bare ace and a three-flush. On the turn, he picked up a flush draw when the 9♣ came down. The player who had made the straight on the flop bet again on the turn, and the second player raised—in a situation where he couldn't possibly have the best hand. The first player, fearful that his opponent might have made the nut straight with a K-J, just called the raise. When a blank came at the river, the player with the made straight checked, and his opponent moved in with the rest of his chips with absolutely nothing! It was obvious to everybody at the table that the first player had a made straight and was not going to fold. The second player made a mindless play and it broke him, and he'd actually had a fair amount of chips when the hand began. What he was thinking about escapes us.

Always think before you act. Ask yourself:

1. What does my opponent have?
2. What is he trying to accomplish with his bet?
3. What do I want to accomplish?
4. And how can I best accomplish it?

The best players have several levels in their thinking processes and that's why, when they have to make key decisions, they think it through, even when they're 80 or 90 percent sure about what they're going to do. They still want to analyze the big picture, including their opponent's action, before they act. Follow their example and eliminate powerless plays that can only get you into trouble.

Tournament Talk

Tom's Tournament Quiz **By Tom McEvoy**

1. You have the A♦-J♦ on the button. A very conservative player opens the pot for a raise about four times the size of the big blind. Everyone passes and it's up to you. What is your best play: (A) Call, (B) Fold, or (C) Reraise?

(B) Fold. A-J is always a trouble hand when someone raises from early position, especially if the raiser is a tight player.

2. You are dealt the 4♥-4♣ in second position. With several aggressive players sitting behind you, what is your best play: (A) Call, (B) Fold, or (C) Raise?

(B) Fold. Small pairs played in early position cannot take any heat. If you bet with aggressive players in the game, it is likely that you will get raised and be forced to fold.

3. You are dealt A-K in early position and make a standard raise of three times the size of the big blind. You get three callers, including the big blind. The flop comes 10♥-9♣-3♠. The big blind checks, and it's your turn to act. What is your best play: (A) Make a pot sized bet, (B) Check and fold if someone bets, or (C) Check and call if someone bets?

242

(B) Check and fold if someone bets. If someone bets when you have nothing but two overcards and no draw and three other players are in the pot, you are better off folding.

4. Two players have limped into the pot for the minimum bet. You are in middle position with the 9♣-8♣. You decide to call as well. Two more players sitting behind you call, as do both blinds, making a total of seven players in the pot. The flop is the 9♦-8♠-2♦. You have flopped the top two pair. The blinds check, the first limper makes a pot-sized bet, and the second limper calls the bet. Now the action is up to you, and you still have two players to act after you. What is your best play (A) Call, (B) Fold, or (C) Make a big reraise?

(C) Make a big reraise. You probably have the best hand right now, but with the possibility of several straight and flush draws being out against you, you need to protect your hand by forcing your opponents to call a very big bet in order to continue playing.

5. You are in the big blind with an A-K. A player in middle position makes a standard raise and is called by two players. The small blind folds, and now the action is up to you. What is your best play: (A) Call, (B) Fold, or (C) Raise?

(B) Call. You are out of position, and it is best not to risk a reraise with that many players already in the pot. See the flop and then decide what to do.

6. You are dealt the A♦-J♦ in late position. Two other players have limped into the pot and you decide to limp also. The small blind calls and the big blind checks. The flop comes with the 9♦-7♦-4♦. You have flopped the nuts! Both blinds check, the first limper bets about half the size of the pot, and the second limper folds. Now it is up to you. What is your best play: (A) Call, (B) Fold, or (C) Raise?

(A) Call. You are hoping that by just calling, at least one of the blinds will also call. You are also disguising the strength of your hand and putting yourself in position to possibly trap the bettor for a lot of chips on a later betting round.

7. You are on the button with the A♦-5♦. Two players have limped into the pot in front of you. You also limp, and so do both of the blinds. The flop comes with the A♣-9♥-2♣. The small blind checks, the big blind bets the size of the pot, and the other two players fold to you. What is your best play: (A) Call, (B) Fold, or (C) Raise?

(B) Fold. When a player bets into several players he usually has a made hand, not a draw. If he has an ace in his hand, your ace is almost certainly out-kicked. Furthermore, the big blind could easily have flopped two pair in this unraised pot.

8. You are in the cutoff seat with the 10♣-9♣, and everybody has passed to you. The player on the button is fairly conservative, as are both players in the blinds. What is your best play: (A) Call, (B) Fold, or (C) Raise?

(C) Raise. This is a good opportunity to try to steal the blinds. If someone raises you back, you know they have a strong hand and you can fold. If someone calls, you might out-flop them or bluff them out on the flop since you have superior position.

9. With two limpers already in the pot, you look down at pocket deuces on the button. You decide to limp as well, both blinds check, and you are able to see the flop cheaply. The flop comes down with the K♥-7♣-2♦. You have flopped bottom set. Both blinds and the first limper check, and the second limper bets about half the size of the pot. The action is up to you. What is your best play: (A) Call, (B) Fold, or (C) Raise?

(A) Call. The pot is still fairly small, and you should be in great shape with this type of flop. The only hands that can beat you are pocket kings or pocket sevens. You want to entice one or more of the other players into the pot, and you don't want to scare off the bettor. You want to try to win a much bigger pot, so wait to bet or raise on a later street.

10. You are in early position and raise with the A♦-A♠. Much to your surprise, you get three callers. The flop comes K♦-Q♦-6♦, and you decide to bet about the size of the pot. Your first opponent calls, the second one folds, and the third one raises twice the size of your bet. Both of your remaining opponents are known for their loose play. What is your best play: (A) Call, (B) Fold, or (C) Raise?

(C) Raise. There is the possibilty that you are beaten at the moment, or up against another drawing hand. But since your opponents are known for their loose play, you must protect your hand. Put in a substantial reraise, possibly even moving all-in. Even if you are beaten, you still have the nut flush to draw to. And if you aren't beaten, you want to make it mighty expensive for them to draw against you.

Tournament Hands in Action

by Don Vines

INTRODUCTION

The following hands are from actual no-limit hold'em tournaments that I've played. The buy-ins ranged from $100 to $2,500, and the fields were of various sizes. As you read my analysis of each hand, think about how you might have played it.

POT-COMMITTED AT THE BELLAGIO

I've played at a lot of tough tournament tables, but this one might've been the strongest set of opponents I've ever had to face. With only twelve players left in action out of a starting field of over three hundred, we were playing six-handed at two tables during the Festa al Lago $2,500 no-limit hold'em tournament at the Bellagio. On my immediate right sat "The Professor of Poker," Howard Lederer, who had the chip lead. On my left was the legendary Bobby Hoff, one of the greatest no-limit players in the world. Two seats to my right sat my friend and poker guru, T.J. Cloutier, who has won more no-limit hold'em tournaments than anybody else on the circuit.

With $98,000 in chips sitting in front of me, my chip position was slightly above-average. The blinds were $4,000/$8,000 with a $1,000 ante, and I was in the big blind with the 4♥-4♠. Everyone passed to T.J., who had approximately $115,000 in chips. T.J. raised the pot to $25,000, and I had a gut feeling that he was raising with a big ace rather than a pair. I reraised to $75,000, and he went all in. Since I was pot committed—I had 74 percent of my stack already invested in the hand—I called. We opened our hands. T.J. had the A♠-K♠ against my pocket fours—a classic coin-flip situation in which neither of us had much of an edge over the other. Here's what happened:

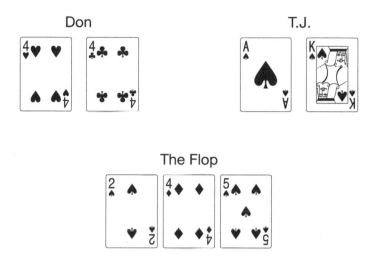

Don   T.J.

The Flop

When I flopped a set of fours, it looked like my plan to win a big pot and put myself into position to win the tournament had worked. But T.J. had a lot of outs to the hand—he flopped the nut flush draw and an inside-straight draw—so I knew my set wasn't a cinch to win the pot. He had twenty-two outs—eight spades and three threes twice, meaning that he had two draws to the cards that would win the hand for him.

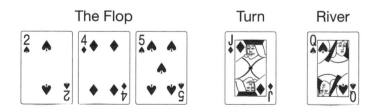

The Flop   Turn   River

When the Q♠ floated onto the board at the river to give T.J. the winning flush, I was eliminated in 12th place and took home $12,500 for my valor in the field of battle. T.J. went on to finish second in the event for an $88,000 payday.

I believe that both T.J. and I played this hand incorrectly. The best I could expect from my hand was a coin flip, and T.J. should have known that the least I could have in this situation was a pocket pair. Furthermore, I played the hand incorrectly by calling his raise, and then compounded my error by reraising.

My best play would have been to fold against T.J.'s raise, since I knew that between the two tables, at least five stacks were shorter than mine. If I played more conservatively, I would probably have made it to the final table. T.J. surprised me with his play; he was willing to put his tournament life on the line in a coin-flip situation. When I asked him why, he said that he had put me on a big ace or a small pair and that he was willing to gamble with his suited A-K.

What did I learn from this hand? Plenty! In a nutshell, after you have made the money and are very close to the final table, be very selective about the hands that you call a raise or reraise with. You are much better off being the raiser than the caller!

FEAR FREEZES A WEAK ACE

At the final table of the one-rebuy, $100 no-limit hold'em tournament at the Orleans Casino in Las Vegas, the action was down to the last seven survivors from a starting field of around one hundred players. The blinds were $1,000/$2,000 with $500 antes. Everyone passed to me in the cutoff seat, and with the 3♠-3♥ in the hole, I raised to $10,000. Only the big blind called.

On the flop, the big blind checked and I checked. On the turn, we both checked again. I made a set at the river when the 3♣ showed up. For a third time, the blind checked. This time I bet $10,000—and he called. What hand do you think he had?

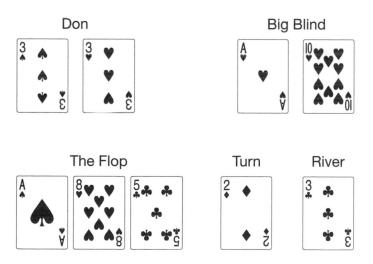

Don	Big Blind

The Flop	Turn	River

He showed the A♥-10♥, the better hand on the flop and the turn!

I won the pot, and went on to win the tournament for a nice $7,500 payday. My conservative opponent was so concerned about having a weak kicker for his ace—and was further intimidated by my previously aggressive play— that he thought I might raise him, and he froze. Instead of playing like a statue, he should have checked the flop and bet the turn. By not doing that, he cost himself a second or third place finish in the tournament.

The lesson: When you flop top pair and your opponent checks after you have checked on the flop, go ahead and bet the turn, especially if a blank hits the table.

WRONG PLAY – RIGHT RESULT

Usually when you make the wrong play in a tournament, you suffer the consequences. But occasionally you'll make the wrong play and still get good results by hitting a lucky flop. When one of your opponents plays bad but gets lucky, he can put a brutal beat on you. Take a look at this hand that was played at the Orleans Casino and you'll see what I mean.

In a $100 no-limit hold'em tournament with one rebuy, we were at the final table with six players remaining. I was in third chip position and the two chip leaders were

Warren Karp, an excellent no-limit player, and a Brit who was playing rather fast. The Englishman raised in early position to $18,000. Warren responded to his aggression by shoving his chips all-in, and the Brit practically beat him into the pot.

As is customary in heads-up play at the final table, when one player goes all-in and only one opponent calls, the two hands are turned face up before the flop. Looking at their hands from the sidelines, I tried not to show my shock at seeing the Brit turn over such weak cards in an all-in pot. Here's what they had:

The Brit got super lucky at the river when the 10♠ came to complete his straight and eliminate Warren in sixth place. His initial raise was bad enough, but his all-in call was even worse. In shorthanded play, K-Q on the backside is a raising hand. But if you play K-Q from up front and get called or reraised, you can be sure that you are almost always beaten. Showing some class, Warren said something like, "Nice hand," and split for some high-stakes side action.

PLAYING A DRAWING HAND OUT OF POSITION

The following hand came up in a $2,000 freezeout no-limit hold'em tournament at the Bellagio, when the blinds were $200/$400 with a $50 ante. Two players limped into the pot in front of me, which surprised me, and the small blind called the minimum bet. Sitting in the big blind, with the 6♣-6♦, I said "Let there be a flop!" And lo, it came:

Don | Small Blind

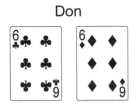

The Flop

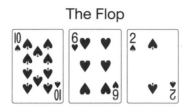

I had flopped a set! On the flop, the small blind moved all-in for $6,800. I thought for a while and then decided that he had either an A-10 or a flush draw. I moved in for all my chips, $7,500. My other two opponents folded, so the small blind and I opened our hands. When I saw his hand and realized that he was a dog to make his flush, and needed runner-runner A-J to make a straight, I was relieved. He didn't catch either one:

The Flop   Turn   River

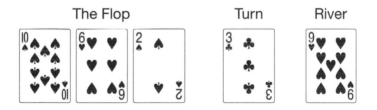

Then I had to listen for ten minutes while he told me and everybody else in the Bellagio how unlucky he was. But was he? Actually, he was a dog from the start. I do not like to bet flush draws without also having the top pair, so I would have played his hand more conservatively by checking the flop. He didn't have the nut flush draw, nor did he have a pair, but he put all his chips at risk when he did not have to.

Playing drawing hands in no-limit hold'em will cost you chips in the long run. Of course, if you are short on chips and have to make a stand, that is a different story. But the player in this scenario had plenty of chips to play with and didn't need to take any unnecessary risks at that stage of the tournament. A good player would have gotten away from this hand without losing his entire stack.

POCKET QUEENS PUT MONEY IN MY POCKET

During the 2004 World Poker Challenge at the Reno Hilton, Poker Pages sponsored one of its popular Poker School online tournaments, a $300 buy-in no-limit hold'em event. This tournament was one of many during the month leading up to the $5,000 World Poker Tour championship tournament. After plunking my buy-in bucks on the table, I joined 192 other players vying for the top prize, which included a buy-in for the prestigious WPT championship event.

Six tables were still in action when I was moved to a new table, where I sat down with $12,000 in chips. I knew only one player at the table—I'll call him "John"—so I took some time to get to know my other opponents. John had about $16,000 in chips, and I knew that he liked to gamble. I was sitting in a middle position when the following hand came up.

With blinds at $300/$600 and a $75 ante, I was dealt the Q♣-Q♥. I raised to $2,400, two players folded, the next player, Rick, reraised all-in, and then John also went all-in. Since I had the initial reraiser, Rick, covered and thought that John the gambler had a weaker hand than mine, I went ahead and called. When we opened our hands, I thought, "Oops, I'm in trouble!" But even I get lucky sometimes. Here's how the boardcards came off the deck:

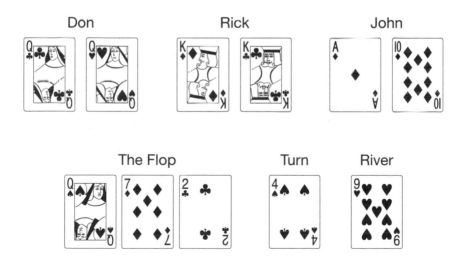

I flopped a set of queens, won a huge pot, and cruised to the final table. However, I played the hand incorrectly! Against a raise and a reraise, I should have mucked my pocket queens because I clearly was beaten in one spot and maybe even both. As my poker mentors T.J. and Tom have written in their many books, pocket queens should be mucked in situations like this.

Certainly I got very lucky on this key hand, but I would like to think that my tournament skills played a major role later in the tournament. I went on to win the tournament and some bragging rights, plus $13,000 and a seat in the $5,000 main event.

PLAYING A SMALL HAND IN THE SMALL BLIND LEADS TO BIG TROUBLE

On the second day of a $10,000 no-limit hold'em World Poker Tour championship event, when the blinds were $800/$1600 with a $200 ante, a hand came up that involved a friend of mine, who I will call "Sam." Here's how he describes it:

"I had $31,000 in chips in the small blind, and two limpers had entered the pot for the minimum bet. With the 7♥-5♦, I was looking to play a multiway pot, so I also limped by putting in another $800. The big blind just called by tapping the table. This was the situation:

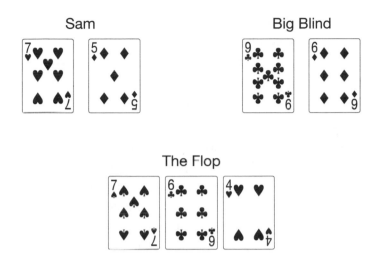

"I bet $5,000 with top pair and a straight draw, but to my surprise, the big blind, who had more chips than I had, moved all-in. The other hands folded, I called with the rest of my stack, and the big blind and I turned over our cards. And here's how it turned out:

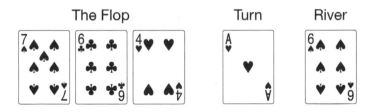

"The big blind's trip sixes knocked me out of the tournament."

I know all the details of this story because Sam immediately called me, crying about his bad beat.

"What bad beat?" I answered, showing deep sympathy. "You made a mistake and got punished for it. You never should've played the hand in the first place; it belonged in the muck before the flop."

I also advised him that after calling the half-bet before the flop, he could have simply checked his hand when the flop hit the felt, in order to get a feel for his opponents' reactions to the board. Instead, he led with a drawing hand from the weakest position at the table and went broke.

Sam had no viable reason to put his tournament life in jeopardy at this point in the tournament. Small connectors are very tricky hands to play under any conditions. If the big blind had held 8-5 and flopped a straight, the best that Sam could hope for was a split pot if an 8 hit the board on the turn or river. If Sam had been on the button with a 7-5 suited, he could have played the hand with two limpers already in the pot and superior position over them. Then he could have decided the best way to play his hand on the flop after his opponents had acted in front of him. Position, position, position!

Tournament Talk

Seven Secrets to Success in Tournament Poker

By Don Vines

1. Pay attention from the moment you sit down. Start reading the players at your table immediately. Stay at the table—don't wander off to smoke or chat. Time away from the table will cost you valuable information that you can use later on.

2. Learn how to survive in the early rounds. Rebuy tournaments do not really start until the rebuy period ends; freezeouts begin when antes start.

3. Chips are precious. Chips are power. Chips that you lose recklessly will come back to haunt you. Suppose you start with $1,000 in chips and fritter away $200, then luckily pick up A-A and double-up. Instead of having $2,000, you have only $1600. Those chips you wasted earlier cost you $400. Protect your chips and always have a logical reason to put them in the pot.

4. Do not be overly protective of your blinds. Once you post a blind, those chips do not belong to you; they belong to the pot. Too many players lose pots and get busted out of tournaments by playing hands from the blinds instead of folding.

5. Rocks do not usually make the final table. They will survive and go fairly deep in a tournament and sometimes make the money—but they don't win tournaments.

6. Tailor the plays you make to the caliber of your opponents. Bluffing new tournament players and low-level players is a recipe for disaster. They are more interested in the quality of their own hands than the cards you might have, so they call more often than they should.

7. When a player goes all-in, be careful about the hands you call with. Suppose a player raises all-in and you call with pocket sixes. Why? At best, you are a small favorite when he has two overcards; at worst, you're a huge dog if he has a pocket pair higher than yours. Doubling-up an all-in player is the last thing you want to do. It will come back and bite you on the ass. Be the player who goes all-in, not the player that calls an all-in bet without having a premium hand.

11

Adjusting Your Tournament Strategy

"I've gone from playing perfect to having more holes in my game than a golf course. It's at times like these that I need a little luck to carry me through."

–Tournament ace Kenna James in *Bluff* magazine

INTRODUCTION

Tournaments come in a Heinz 57 variety of structures and a wide range of sizes. Some have short incremental rounds, in which the blinds escalate every twenty minutes; others have medium-length rounds of forty minutes; and a few have long rounds of an hour or more. Some events draw fields of one hundred or fewer entrants, others have three hundred-player fields, and a few have fields that number one thousand or more players. In this chapter, we'll help you adjust your tournament strategy depending on what type of tournament you're taking on.

In addition, the ability to adjust your game to the current conditions at your table is of critical importance if you want to become a successful tournament player. If you've been watching your opponents carefully and have read your table correctly, you'll know who has been playing what types of hands. You simply have to adjust your play to the types of opponents that are in the hand at the moment. You cannot expect your opponents to play a style of poker that you're comfortable with. You need to be very flexible and switch gears by going from tight to loose and vice versa.

ADJUSTING BASED UPON THE LENGTH OF THE ROUNDS

The length of the betting rounds should have an impact on your tournament strategy. The shorter the rounds, the faster you need to play; the longer the rounds, the more solid you can play. And as a rule, the higher the tournament buy-in, the longer the betting rounds.

Most low-stakes tournaments are what we refer to as "fast-action events," which means that the tournament is designed with short rounds, so that the event will end as quickly as possible. The rounds in fast-action tournaments generally last for twenty minutes or less, although some casinos allow for thirty-minute rounds. Medium buy-in tournaments that cost $500 to enter usually have rounds of forty minutes to an hour, depending on the buy-in, and tournaments with entry fees of $1,000 and more usually last an hour or longer. By way of comparison, the World Poker Tour tournaments have ninety-minute rounds, and the 2004 World Series of Poker championship event began with ninety-minute rounds on day one, then progressed to two-hour rounds on day two. Time-wise, the longest tournament rounds on the circuit today are the two-hour rounds at the WSOP.

So while there are a lot of variations within each category, in this chapter, we will assume that the rounds in **fast-action** tournaments last 20 minutes or less; the rounds in **medium-action** events last 30 to 45 minutes; and the rounds in **slow-action** tournaments last 50 minutes and longer.

Fast-Action Tournaments
(Rounds of Twenty Minutes)

The play in fast-action events is fast and furious, especially if rebuys are allowed. Most of these tournaments allow rebuys during the first three rounds—that is, for the first hour, which will cause people to play all types of hands, play very fast and aggressively, and gamble like crazy with hands they normally wouldn't play in order to accumulate chips. Quite often, these players expect to make several rebuys.

"What I like to do in fast-action events," Don says, "is find a hand that I can double-up with in the first pot I play. Once I've done that, I have a little time to sit back and pick the hands that I want to play, because my chip stack isn't in immediate jeopardy. However if I have lost one or two hands and my chips are low, I will rebuy. If it isn't a rebuy event, I just have to gamble with a few hands to try to win some chips. Otherwise, I'll get eliminated from the tournament."

You have to be willing to mix up your play and do some gambling in a fast-action rebuy tournament. If you are not prepared to make one or two rebuys, plus an add-on, you probably should not play this type of event.

With some good judgment and a little bit of luck, rebuys allow you to accumulate chips. And since many fast-action rebuy events allow a single or double add-on, this gives you one last opportunity to build your chip stack. So if you're ready to put in multiple buy-ins, you should be able to accumulate chips one way or the other.

"When I play a fast-action tournament," Don says, "I assume that by the end of the rebuy period, every one will have made at least two or three rebuys. This allows me to judge the size of the average chip stack. Then I use that information to decide whether or not to add on." You also can eyeball the stacks at the other tables to estimate where you stand in the chip position.

If the tournament offers a premium of chips when you add on—in other words, if you get $400 in chips rather than the usual $200—then it is almost always correct to make the add-on. When deciding whether or not to add on, ask yourself, "Can I increase my stack by one-third or more if I buy an add-on?" As a general rule, if you can increase your stack by that much, take the add-on. If you're a little uncertain about what to do, it is better to err on the side of additional chips. In fast-action rebuy events you must be ready to get into the action, mix it up, play hands strongly, and risk going broke.

Once the rebuy period is over, you will sometimes see dramatic changes in the way people play their hands. You won't see the craziness you saw during the rebuy period, when players were calling raises and getting involved in big, multiway pots with hands like 4-2 suited, when players were playing any two suited cards or any pair for multiple raises before the flop. That type of wild play stops when players realize that they cannot add to their stack if they lose a lot of chips with marginal hands. The reality sets in: If I lose all my chips, I'm out of the tournament!

In these events, it is not uncommon for a large percentage of the field to be entry-level players who are new to tournaments. They've watched no-limit hold'em on television and they're ready to throw their hats into the tournament ring for $40, $60, or maybe $100. And they are going to play! In fact if you watch them very carefully, you'll see them playing any two cards from any position. These players can be dangerous to your bankroll. Treat them like you would a stick of dynamite—you never know when or why they're going to explode!

Even when the rebuy period is over, you can expect some bizarre plays if a lot of novice tournament players are still in action. In a situation like that, your results may seesaw. You may run into a series of bad beats and wonder what you've been doing wrong, when, actually, you haven't been doing anything wrong. You've simply run into players who don't respect bets and raises and therefore stick around longer with hands they shouldn't be playing. If enough players do this, they're going to draw out on your good hand frequently.

The flip side of the coin is that many times, when your good hands hold up in pots where you get more action than you should, you will accumulate a vast amount of chips, far more than your hand would normally warrant, which will give you an excellent chance to go the distance in the tournament. So many times, the players that you go home talking to yourself about because of the bad beats they put on you are the same ones that contribute the most to your financial success in the long run.

Medium-Action Tournaments
(Rounds of Thirty to Forty-Five Minutes)

Most of these tournaments do not allow rebuys, but there are a few that allow one. In medium-action events, you should play straightforward poker without getting too tricky. Your goal is to increase your chip position each round as quickly, yet as safely, as possible.

You will have a lot more play from the get-go in medium-action tournaments than in fast-action events, meaning that players will be more advanced and will think through hands more seriously. More play and better opponents are a result of the higher buy-ins.

Try to get a line on how your opponents play as quickly as you can. Entry-level players will make plenty of mistakes against you, so you just have to be patient and wait them out. Use good judgment in hand selection, and don't jeopardize your chips any more than you have to by gambling too much on speculative hands.

Be careful about the hands you play from late position, especially those that contain an ace. For example, if you are sitting on the backside and no one has raised the pot in front of you, you might think that a hand such as A-7 is good and decide to come into the pot with a raise. Trust us, that is not a good idea. In the medium-action events, it is not unusual for players in middle position to just call with hands like A-10 or A-J. Your weak ace won't fare well against a stronger ace unless you happen to get lucky and catch your kicker to make two pair.

Also be prepared to dump a lot of hands that you might normally play. If the pot has been raised in front of you, you probably should fold hands such as K-Q, A-J, or A-10 suited. These hands can be very dangerous in raised pots, even against inexperienced players. Even the weakest of players recognize strong hands such as aces, kings, or A-K when they are dealt them, so give them some respect when they raise—unless of course, they are unpredictable in their betting patterns or loose-aggressive maniacs.

Most of the time you will be playing solid poker, selecting your hands carefully, and playing them in position. By being selectively aggressive and using good judgment, you should meet with success in medium-action tournaments.

One final word: Don't go on tilt if someone puts a beat on you. As in all tournament play, never give up the ship.

Slow-Action Tournaments (Rounds of 60 to 90 Minutes or More)

These tournaments usually cost $1,000 or more to enter. When you play a slow-action event, you can truly play your game. You have a lot of time and plenty of starting chips, so you don't need to push any panic buttons. You can wait for quality hands in position to try to accumulate chips.

In slow-action tournaments, you will usually start with 40- to 50-times the size of the big blind. For example, with starting blinds of $5/$15 or $10/$15, you'll probably start with $1,000 in chips. This type of structure gives you plenty of play.

In the $10,000 buy-in championship event at the World Series of Poker, you begin with $10,000 in chips with blinds of $25/$50. That is an enormous amount of chips in relation to the size of the blinds.

The longer the tournament rounds and the more starting chips you receive in relation to the size of the blinds, the more likely it is that skill will prevail over luck. Skilled players rise to the occasion in these slow-action events because they have plenty of time to outmaneuver the opposition and less reason to fear the luck factor.

In a slow-action tournament, you'll have enough chips to play, even if you don't get any cards and nothing happens for a round or two. You're not in trouble, so remain patient and play your game. You can sit through the first two hours of play without ever playing a hand and still have probably 80 percent of your stack. Be patient and don't try to force it if things aren't going right. Don't rush into anything or push your panic button. The cards will come.

Because the rounds are long, you will have plenty of opportunities to learn your opponents' styles of play and develop a feel for who are the most aggressive players and who are the passive ones. Just remember that in big buy-in tournaments, nobody wants to go out first, so most players are playing their A-games when they first sit down. This usually means that they are playing more conservatively or even tight. However after about an hour has passed, you can expect people to loosen up a tad and revert to their normal styles of play.

Ideally, you should be playing your A-game all the time, but a lot of players don't have the discipline, patience, or stamina to continue playing their best game indefinitely. At some point, they will begin loosening up their play, especially when things aren't going right for them. You'll see them become impatient and get sloppy about the starting hands they play. The flip side is that if one of your opponents gets lucky in the early minutes of the tournament, he may believe that he is bulletproof and get overly aggressive. Be aware of these tendencies in your opponents and adjust your play accordingly.

Your aim should be to increase your chip stack by about 20 to 25 percent during each round, which is a reasonable goal. If you do that, you will probably make it to the championship table, perhaps with the chip lead. Sometimes you will get lucky and double-up early; other times you will lose a little bit along the way. But your overall goal remains the same: Increase your stack of chips at each level. When T.J. Cloutier finished second in the 2000 WSOP championship event, he told us that throughout the entire tournament, he had increased his chips "some" during every single level. That's really all you have to do to get there. Increasing your chips 50 percent would be terrific, but even if you only gain 10 percent each round, you will be in good shape to go the distance in the tournament.

If you are fortunate enough to double-up early in the tournament, don't make the mistake of playing too loosely afterwards. Treat your chips with proper respect, keeping in mind that a big stack is worth protecting. If the cards go dead and you aren't being dealt any playable hands, you still have plenty of time and chips to just sit on your stack and wait for better cards to come to you.

This is one of the biggest mistakes we see tournament players make. When things are going well for them and they have accumulated a lot of chips—maybe they got lucky by playing a marginal hand, hitting a big flop, and cracking a much better starting hand—they continue gambling and wind up blowing their chips off to their opponents, rather than tightening up their play and protecting their big stacks. Sometimes they even blow themselves out of the tournament before they make the money by playing the same loose, gambling style of game that brought them the chips in the first place. If they had simply played a bit more conservatively and had used better judgment after accumulating a big stack, they would have done far better, possibly making the final table or at least finishing in the money.

Your goal in tournament poker is always two-fold: First, make the money; second, make it to the final table. Tip of the century: You can't win a tournament until you get to the final table. You cannot win it in the first round, the second round, or any other round except the last one. Always keep in mind that even though you can't win the tournament in the early rounds, you can certainly lose it.

ADJUSTING BASED UPON THE SIZE OF THE FIELD

The more players in a tournament, the longer it takes to reach the final table and complete the event. Some players think it's just as easy to get there in a five-hundred-player tournament as it is in a one-hundred-player event. "All you have to do is beat your own table, one table at a time," is what these people say.

We disagree with that notion. While it is true that you can't beat players who are sitting at other tables, you do have to survive a lot more tables in medium- or big-field tournaments in order to make it to the final table. Of course the reward is much greater in big-field events than it is in smaller ones. In addition, more players make the money because larger events pay more places than just the last nine or ten. And if you're fortunate enough to make it one of the last three spots, the payoff will be far more rewarding than in a small tournament.

Small-Field Tournaments (Fewer than One Hundred Entries)

Small-field tournaments of about one hundred players pay the final table only, and if the number of entrants is much smaller than that, the tournament might pay only five places. The major difference between small-field tournaments and the rest is that you will reach the final table in less time. If you start with blinds of $10/$15 and a starting stack of $1,000 in chips, the championship table will probably begin play at around the seventh level, when the blinds are still small, say $200/$400. If the rounds are thirty minutes long, the final table will usually commence play in less than four hours.

Some players like these tournaments because they don't want to spend more than four or five hours playing before they reach the last table. With a smaller field, they feel as though they can see the light at the end of the tunnel.

Regardless of whether or not you agree with this, play solid tournament strategy, try to build your chip stack at each level of play, and you'll do just fine.

The number of rounds it takes to finish the tournament depends on two things:

1. The number of entrants, and
2. The rate at which the blinds increase.

Some tournaments double the blinds almost every round. Other tournaments have slower increases, such as 50 percent or less. Obviously the bigger the field and the smaller the increases, the longer it takes to finish the tournament. Some tournaments with one hundred or fewer entrants may end by the ninth or tenth level of play, whereas the same type of tournament with two hundred to three hundred entrants may last fourteen or fifteen rounds.

Big-Field Tournaments
(Four Hundred to Six Hundred Entrants)

Not every player who enters a big-field tournament is a skilled tournament player—even if the event has a big buy-in. A lot of them are entry-level players who have won their seats on the internet or in a casino satellite. In other words, big numbers do not equate to strong players.

Your goal—as always—is to increase your chip count during every level. Don't push the panic button if you have to coast for a round or two because you aren't catching good cards. Try not to be overwhelmed by the size of the field, and don't get discouraged if things don't go your way in every hand. Focus on the pot of gold at the end of the rainbow.

Concentrate on playing successfully against the people at your table. It's true that the more players in the field, the longer it takes to get to the final table and the harder it is to get there. But keep in mind that the reward is enormous. If you can conquer a big-field tournament by finishing in one of the top three places, the prize money will quite possibly support your tournament buy-ins for the remainder of the year.

"All I'm interested in," Don says, "is how many chips I have in relation to the rest of the field and how long the rounds last."

Use the tournament clock to evaluate your chip position in the tournament at any given moment. If you have an average number of chips, you will be in the top 30 to 40 percent of the field, because there are always a few huge stacks and a lot of small stacks. For this reason, an average stack is actually a pretty good spot to be in, and even a somewhat below-average stack isn't all that bad.

Even if you are short-stacked, keep in mind that in no-limit hold'em, things can turn around very quickly for you, especially with a lot of players in the field. Unfortunately, they can turn in both directions—you can rebuild a short stack by winning a big pot, or demolish a big stack by losing a monster pot. This is all the more reason to protect a big stack.

As a general guideline, you have a short stack when your stack is less than or equal to 50 percent of the average stack. And if you're far away from a money payout, you must be willing to take a few more risks with a small stack in a big-field event. Any time you have only enough chips to successfully go through the blinds two or three more times without playing a hand, you're in a situation where you have to take a stand sooner rather than later.

Another thing to remember is that more entries means more tables are paid. Just winning a payout at the fourth or third table will often earn a decent profit. A lot of players in big-field events think, "I don't have a chance to win the tournament, but I think I have a good chance of cashing if I get lucky." They aren't really trying to win it, they're just trying to hang on long enough to cash. A lot of times they will actually announce this out loud. Playing against people with this mindset is to your advantage because, although you want to get to the money, your goal is to eventually make it to the last table and give yourself a chance to win the whole shebang. You must have enough confidence and ability to win it, and you have to truly believe that you can. If you don't feel that you have a chance to at least cash and maybe make it to the last table and win it, reevaluate whether you should be playing tournament poker at all.

Make every effort to maintain a reasonable number of chips. If you can do that, you will be in a position to win the tournament, no matter how many chips the chip leader has when you get down to one or two tables away from the money. By that time, you'll know which players you can bully simply because they have tightened up their play, hoping just to finish in the money. When you're one or two tables away from the money, play will tighten up dramatically. A lot of players will go into a shell, which makes them easy to maneuver off a hand and bluff. If you're willing to take a few risks at this point—willing to risk getting broke, even—you will have a great opportunity to pick up a lot of chips.

Huge-Field Tournament
(One Thousand or More Players)

Be sure to pencil in two days of play on your calendar when you enter a tournament that has a huge field of players. These days, tournament directors structure the event so that you play until around 2:00 a.m. on the first day and return the next day to complete the tournament. Normally when the fields are huge, and especially if the rounds are an hour long, you will play twelve rounds on the first day. By the time you're done for the day, over 90 percent of the field will have been eliminated.

The day-one survivors are usually in the money already, or close to it. If you make it though the first day, you can come back a little bit fresher on the second day, knowing that you're still in the hunt. You should have plenty of time to build your chips in an orderly fashion and move up the food chain. Even with a short stack, you're still in it—and anything can happen in no-limit hold'em.

"At a recent tournament at the Wildhorse Casino in Pendleton, Oregon," Tom says. "We started with $1,000 in chips. The blinds were at $50/$100, and I had had no playable hands. I was forced to wait until I was in the big blind to put my last lonely $100 chip in the pot. Luckily I won that hand. Then I picked my spots carefully and continued to win.

"By the time I made it to the final table, I was the chip leader. At one point I had $90,000 in chips in front of me. Yes,

279

I got lucky to survive, but it shows you what can happen if you never give up. The last five players of the tournament ended up making a deal, so I had a nice payday—all because I never quit and got lucky at the right time."

MAKING A DEAL AT THE FINAL TABLE

At the final table of most no-limit hold'em tournaments, the last few players decide to divide the remaining prize money among themselves in a way that is different from the payout schedule posted by the tournament sponsor. In poker lingo, they "make a deal." Although most deals are made between the final two, three, or four players, some can include five or more players and, occasionally, even the entire championship table. Usually the chip leader or the second-chip leader proposes the idea and the players still in action discuss the possibility.

While the discussion is in progress, the dealer pauses and the tournament director sits at the table. The tournament director must be included in the process to ensure that everyone involved in the split approves it, and so that he can adjust the payout accordingly.

The tournament clock will usually display the amount of money that each remaining player would receive if an even split were accepted. But the "let's split it down the middle and head for home" type of deal is rarely accepted unless all the remaining players have roughly the same number of chips. We believe that deals should be based on the amount of chips that each remaining player has left.

Below are some guidelines for making an equitable settlement at the next final table you play. Let's say that with $375,000 remaining in the prize pool, the final four players agree to a deal.

The payouts posted by the tournament sponsor are:

1. $200,000 for 1st Place
2. $100,000 for 2nd Place
3. $50,000 for 3rd Place
4. $25,000 for 4th Place

The chip totals are as follows:

1. Player A: 380,000
2. Player B: 260,000
3. Player C: 200,000
4. Player D: 160,000

Based on chip count, here is how the deal might look: First, each player receives 4th place money, 25,000 in this example. That $100,000 is subtracted from the prize money, and the balance ($275,000) is divided by the total amount of chips in play (1,000,000). The resulting amount ($0.275) is what each remaining player is paid per chip.

Using this system, here is what the final payouts would be:

1. Player A: $129,500 ($25,000 4th Place payout, plus 380,000 x $0.275)
2. Player B: $96,500 ($25,000 4th Place payout, plus 260,000 x $0.275)
3. Player C: $80,000 ($25,000 4th Place payout, plus 200,000 x $0.275)
4. Player D $69,000 ($25,000 4th Place payout, plus 160,000 x $0.275)

If all four players agree to make this deal, the tournament ends and the chip leader is declared the winner, unless the remaining players agree to play on and see who actually wins. Money-wise, it makes no difference; only the trophy and the bragging rights are at stake. In some deals, players decide to leave money on the table so there's something to play for in addition to the trophy. In any case, this chip-count format is the fairest way we know to make an equitable deal, and it can be used for any number of players.

Tournament Talk

Making History at the 1983 World Series of Poker
By Tom McEvoy

At the 2003 World Series of Poker, 838 of my closest friends and I played in the championship event. Six of us—Rod Peate, Doyle Brunson, Carl McKelvey, Robbie Geers, Donn O'Dea, and me—celebrated a reunion of sorts. We had played together at the final table of the WSOP twenty years earlier, when Rod and I made history as the first two satellite winners ever to place first and second in the championship event.

In 2003 only sixty-three players paid the $10,000 entry fee out of their own pockets—the rest of the players in the race for the bracelet and the $2.5 million prize won their seats via satellites at the Horseshoe and poker rooms across the globe. About fifty won satellites sponsored by online casinos. PokerStars.com alone sent thirty-seven players to the Series, including the eventual winner, Chris Moneymaker.

Things were a lot different two decades ago. During the 1983 WSOP, all the hotel rooms in downtown Vegas were fully booked and business was booming. The Horseshoe didn't have its own cardroom at that time, so some of the preliminary events were held downstairs in the Sombrero Room, where the coffee shop is located today. They closed the restaurant and put in poker tables, and they took some slot machines on the main floor out so they could set up a few more tables. Even though the Series was much smaller then than it is today, the Shoe didn't have enough room for all the WSOP action, so it had to use tables from adjacent casinos that had poker rooms, like the Nugget, Queens, and Fremont. They didn't just borrow tables, either; some of the tournament games were actually played in the cardrooms of the rival casinos. We made jokes about "making the final casino." For example, the limit hold'em tournament had 234 players, and because of the Shoe's lack of space, some people had to play at the Nugget. As players busted out and a tables were broken down, remaining players would be transferred to the Horseshoe and they'd simply carry their chips with them across the street. But for the main event, they squeezed twelve nine-handed tables into the Horseshoe.

I used to play all my cash games ($10/$20) at the Golden Nugget, and many of my colleagues stayed in the gallery throughout the tournament to cheer me on. A lot of them were also rooting for Rod—we were two of their own who "got there." Rod and I were just a couple of $10/$20 dark horses that they could all identify with, two of their regular friends who just happened to place first-second in the championship event at the World Series.

The legendary Doyle Brunson finished in third place. He had already won back-to-back championships in '76 and '77, and in 1980 he came in second against the rookie Stu Ungar. With the possible exception of Amarillo Slim, Doyle was the most famous poker player in the world.

When the final table got down to the three of us, Rod raised on the button with pocket nines. I folded, and Doyle called with the J♦-9♦ in the small blind The flop came 9-high with two diamonds, giving Doyle top pair and a flush draw—

which looked pretty good on the surface—but he was up against Rod's set of nines. On the flop he checked and Rod bet about $15,000. Doyle moved all-in with over a quarter of a million in chips. He over-bet the pot, apparently trying to run over Rod, but Rod had made it something like $9,000 before the flop, and $15,000 to go on the flop, so he wasn't about to relinquish the hand. He called Doyle's all-in bet and sent the legend to the rail.

The fourth-place finisher was Carl McKelvey, a road gambler who travels all over the country playing pot-limit and no-limit games wherever he can find them. Carl had practically no chance to finish any higher than fourth because by the time it got down to four-handed, he had only $50,000 in chips while everybody else had $300,000 or more. In fact, I was the leader four-handed, but when it got to heads-up, Rod had a 3 to 2 chip lead on me after busting Doyle.

Robbie Geers, who finished in fifth place, had also won a satellite. He got broke when he was finally dealt a big hand, a pair of kings, and decided to slow-play them against Peate, who had suited connectors. Geers flopped a set and Peate flopped a flush draw. Geers checked, Peate moved in on him, and Geers called. Peate made the flush to beat him.

Donn O'Dea, who was the best player in Ireland at the time, finished in sixth place. He was also the runner-up to me in the limit hold'em event a few days before the championship tournament. Interestingly, after that second-place finish in the limit hold'em tournament, it took him seventeen years to win a gold bracelet at the WSOP—in pot-limit Omaha. He said he blamed me for how long it took!

I realize how fortunate I was to win the championship, and to make poker history as the first satellite winner. I have built upon that win by writing poker books and magazine columns, giving poker lessons, and conducting seminars. Since poker has added so much to my life, giving something back is the least I can do. As always, I'm hoping to make it to the championship table at the WSOP again, where I hope to meet you sometime soon.

12

Tips for Winning Online Tournaments

"Online you have to be a lot more aggressive. In live play you have time to contemplate your moves, and you get to pick up physical tells and betting tells."

–Chris Moneymaker, 2003 World Champion of Poker, in an ESPN.com Timeout Chat Show

INTRODUCTION

Welcome to the wide world of online poker where you can play tournaments and cash games around the clock at home in your pajamas! Internet tournaments are great places to start your tournament career. Many online sites offer free games where you can practice the basics before you begin playing for real money. From the free games, you can move up to small tournaments with buy-ins as low as

$5 and gradually progress to events with higher buy-ins. Young tournament ace and *Card Player* magazine columnist Scott Fischman credits playing online tournaments with improving his game and helping him develop "a great feel for the technical aspects of poker tournaments."

"Playing a few online tournaments per day," Scott says, "can provide you years of experience in a short span of time."

The first decision you have to make is what type of online tournament you wish to enter. Sites offer an enormous variety of tournaments in almost all forms of poker with buy-ins ranging from zero to $1,000. PokerStars, the online site for which Tom is a spokesman and where he regularly plays, spreads tournaments around the clock for virtually every poker game in the book, although the emphasis is on no-limit hold'em events. Now that no-limit hold'em has captured the imagination of players around the globe, everyone seems to want to play the exciting game where they can push all their chips into the pot anytime they feel like it. For this reason, no-limit hold'em tournaments draw the biggest fields of players.

Once you have decided what game you want to play, you need to find a tournament with a buy-in that fits your budget and level of experience. We suggest playing small buy-in events until you've cut your baby teeth. Once you start getting good results and feel you can afford it, start playing the bigger buy-in events. You might want to start with something in the range of $50 plus juice, and then move up to an event that costs $100 or more to enter. Each site posts a list of daily events with the buy-in, type of game, and starting time.

Don't start out by playing tournaments with buy-ins that make you nervous or uncomfortable. Play within your comfort zone. However, if you wish to improve your skills as a poker player, you must eventually move up to the bigger buy-in events where you will face tougher players, and where the prize money is much larger.

Be sure you understand the rules for the internet tournament you are playing. Some online casinos protect a player if he gets disconnected and allow him to be declared all-in. This means that he can win the chips that are in the pot at the time of his loss of connection, assuming that he has the best hand at the showdown. Any bets placed after a player has been disconnected will be placed in a side pot among the remaining players. Not all internet cardrooms allow this safety net. Some make you forfeit the hand if you get disconnected, so be sure you understand the rules of the online site. If you have all-in protection and have been forced to use it, make sure to request a new all-in protection option. Most online casinos will provide you with one upon request.

Here are a few more tips to help you get the most out of your internet poker experience and help you win online tournaments. Some of these suggestions appeared in *Beat Texas Hold'em*, the book Tom co-authored with Shane Smith.

TOM'S TIPS FOR WINNING ONLINE TOURNAMENTS

Schedule Your Tournament Play

Before you begin, you should find out how much time it will take to play the tournament through to its conclusion. You can determine that by examining the length of the rounds, the number of starting chips, and the approximate number of players that will be in the event. Pick tournaments that work with your schedule. It makes no sense to play in an event that will take about four hours to complete if you have to be somewhere else in two hours. You cannot possibly do a good job if you feel like you have another obligation to take care of before the tournament concludes.

PokerStars and several other sites schedule events twenty-four hours per day, seven days a week, but other sites have fewer tournaments with fewer numbers of players, which can be a consideration when you have limited time. It's always easier to wade through a field of two hundred players than it is to face one thousand or more, and it usually takes less time. If you make a thorough search, you can find a site that has the type of tournament you want to play and a time frame that is suitable for your schedule.

Determine the Size of Tournament Field You Want to Play

The size of the tournament field should be a major factor when you're deciding whether or not you want to enter an event. Some online tournaments that feature small buy-ins attract thousands of players, and even though the levels increase at a faster rate than they do in bigger buy-in events, it still takes a lot of time, luck, and expert play to get through that many players. Other tournaments may have fewer than one hundred players and won't take as long to complete, but they might still offer a large enough prize pool to make it worthwhile to play.

Naturally, the bigger the number of starting players and the longer each round lasts, the more time it will take to complete the tournament. In big-field events, you must have patience by the bushel. If you get restless when you aren't catching any good cards, you might be tempted to force the action with a marginal hand. Don't do it. You cannot magically pull good cards out of a hat. Wait for a good starting hand or good position against weak opponents before you decide to make a move at the pot.

My bottom-line suggestion: If you are a patient player with plenty of endurance, play big-field tournaments. If you aren't particularly patient and don't like having to concentrate on one thing for hours at a time, or if you have only a limited amount of time to devote to the event, play tournaments with smaller fields.

Play Small Buy-in Tournaments First

If you're a tournament junkie like me, I suggest that you begin your online tournament career by playing one of the numerous small buy-in online tournaments that are available around the clock. Why? To create a comfort zone for yourself as a fledgling tournament aficionado. If you consistently do well in the smaller buy-in tournaments against weaker opponents, your confidence will steadily increase. If you are successful in tournaments and learn to love them as I do, you can gradually increase the parameters of your comfort zone and play bigger buy-in events.

You can enter some tournaments for as little as $1 or as much as $530 on a regular basis, with all sorts of buy-ins between those numbers. Some sites, like PokerStars, even offer freeroll tournaments in which all the prize money is put up by the site. I have seen as many as 5,000 players playing in tournaments like these. Whew! Just try conquering that size field some time! Poker has a way of teaching all of us humility.

All online tournaments and satellites, except those that specifically state that they allow rebuys, are freezeout events. If you lose all your chips, you're out of the tournament. Freezeout events limit the amount of your investment and prevent you from spending more money than you planned on, as we all sometimes do in rebuy tournaments.

Playing a small buy-in, one-table tournament, often called a "Sit-and-Go," can be a great learning experience for new tournament players. For a limited investment, you can get a good idea about what kinds of hands people play and how they perform in different situations. Sit-and-go events are not scheduled to begin at a specific time. As soon as ten players "sit" down to play, they "go." Clever, huh?

Once you arrive at the championship table, the object is to win the tournament. In order to do that, you must know how to play at a table where the number of opponents is gradually reduced until eventually you are playing heads-up against one final opponent. One-table tournaments and satellites can give you valuable experience playing shorthanded, so that when you make it to the final table of a multi-table tournament, you will have a much better feel for what to do.

Avoid Playing Too Loose in Online Tournaments

One thing you will soon discover when you're playing low buy-in no limit tournaments online, is that most players see too many flops and play too many hands. In other words, they play loose as a goose, especially if rebuys are allowed. One reason is that many of the players in these low buy-in tournaments are new to the game, and they want to play a lot of hands. It's fun and they love the action. They aren't there to fold—they came to play!

Just remember that it isn't how many pots you play that counts; what's important is how many pots you win. But how do you win against the kamikazes you so often face in small no-limit hold'em online events? The way to beat these super-loose players is to play tighter than they do, meaning you might have to play fewer hands than you would like. Avoid playing weak and marginal hands when you are in early position, or when the pot has been raised in front of you.

You also need to avoid bluffing very often, especially in the early stages of a low buy-in tournament that allows rebuys. Some players have a tendency to bluff too much, probably because they see the superstars bluff so often in televised tournaments. But that's not the way to beat small buy-in online tournaments. You will get called more often than not, so you'd better have the goods. Remember this cardinal rule for playing in the early stages of big-field, low buy-in tournaments: Tight is Right!

Concentrate on Playing Strong Starting Hands in Position

Strong starting hands such as pocket aces, kings, queens, and jacks, as well as A-K, can usually be played from any position at the table. Big pairs and A-K fare much better when fewer players are in the pot, so you usually raise or reraise with these hands, trying to eliminate as many players from the pot as possible. Often these big hands can stand up without improvement against only one or two players, but against three or more opponents, your chances of winning go down. The more players that are in the pot, the more likely it is that someone will hit a flop and beat you. Even if your opponents are only on a draw, and you still have the best hand on the flop, you are in serious danger of getting beaten by the end of the hand if lots of players are drawing against you.

What do we do about position in online play? The later you have to act in the betting sequence, the bigger your advantage over your opponents. This does not mean that you should play extremely weak starting hands just because you have the button. But you can play a few more hands in late position than you would if you had to act from an earlier one.

At the risk of being too repetitive, allow me to review why position is so important in no-limit hold'em tournaments. The earlier—or worse—your position, the stronger starting hand you need in order to enter the pot, because you run the risk of being raised by players acting after you. And when you are sitting in the small or big blind, you'll have the worst position of all after the flop. Keep this in mind when deciding whether or not to defend your blind when somebody raises.

For example, suppose you have that marginal 8-7 suited. You can play this hand in late position for one bet and even for a small raise when several other players have already entered the pot. But it is not playable from very early position because it isn't strong enough to call a raise. To justify calling a raise from either the small or big blind, several other callers must already be in the pot, and the raise has to be fairly small. Because you are in one of the blinds and will have the worst position from the flop onward, you will not know what your opponents have on their minds after the flop. Always remember, he who acts last, acts with the most information.

Adjust to the Speed of the Game

You will soon discover that online games move along much faster than casino games. In a typical casino hold'em game, thirty to thirty-five hands are dealt per hour. In online games, that number is around fifty to fifty-five hands per hour, and sometimes more depending on the speed of the players. There are two reasons for this. First, the cyber dealer deals the cards much faster than a human dealer. Second, players cannot deliberate at length when it is their turn to act. Online poker rooms have a time clock with a very annoying beep that reminds players who have delayed too long that they must act on their hands. If the player fails to act on his hand in time, he is automatically folded.

With a little practice and experience you can adjust to this faster pace and learn to like it, as I do. One thing to remember is that if you do need a little extra time to make a really tough decision, most sites offer you the option of requesting an additional sixty seconds or so.

Take Notes While You're Playing

Most online poker rooms offer a box or window for jotting down notes about your opponents and each hand. Taking notes will help you determine the quality of your play and give you a better idea of what the opposition is up to. Players often play in the same tournaments on a regular basis, and if you've been taking notes, you'll have a good read on how they play when you face them in the future.

Just typing a few quick thoughts, such as "Margie just played A-4 offsuit in early position," can help you get a better idea about how your opponents play and the types of hands they enter the pot with. The more you know about your opponents, the better your chances of beating them.

Look for Online Tells

When playing online, you can't see your opponents like you can when playing face-to-face in a real casino, but there are tells to be discovered online. Let's take a look at a few of them.

Most sites have what are called "advance action buttons" that allow you to predetermine your action on any given hand. These buttons include options such as "Fold to any bet," "Automatic check," or even "Check and fold." So if you make top pair with a weak kicker on the flop and you are uncertain whether or not you have the best hand, you might decide to check. If all the players who act after you rapidly check, that's a sign that they have hit the automatic check button. This usually means they did not flop much of a hand, and that your pair is probably the best hand. Therefore, you can consider betting it on the next round.

Other online players take a long time to act on their hands, and then come out betting or raising. If you pay attention to the hands they show down when they do this, you can figure out whether or not they always hesitate with a strong hand. If it always indicates a strong hand at the showdown, play accordingly. If it doesn't always mean strength, then don't put too much stock in it.

Many people who play online often do other things at the same time, such as read or answer email, chat with the other players, run to the bathroom, or watch television. Pay close attention so you can better decide whether your opponents' delays have real meaning or are purely the result of their lack of focus.

One final tip: Don't be one of these distracted players while you're playing an online tournament. You can answer your email, watch TV, or play with your dog later. Focus on winning the tournament by keeping your eyes and brain on the game. That's the winning ticket!

Fatal Flaws and How to Fix Them

"A lot of tournament players play their A-games for an hour or so—until they can't stand it any longer."

–Tom McEvoy in *Championship No-Limit & Pot-Limit Hold'em*

INTRODUCTION

T.J. Cloutier followed Tom's quote above with: "There are a lot of players in tournaments who don't have an A-game. In the long run, the weaker players are going to make calls and plays that are so far out of line that they don't have a chance to win the tournament."

In other words, the player who makes the fewest mistakes in no-limit Texas hold'em is the one who makes the most money. All the top pros understand that playing mistake-free poker is their ticket to the top. Sometimes, however, we all have lapses in concentration or make errors in judgment. Our mistakes can become fatal flaws, especially in freezeout tournaments. In tournament play, it is particularly important that you recognize leaks in your game and correct them as completely and quickly as possible. Here is a list of fatal flaws to look out for, and our suggestions for how to fix them before they put you in a terrible fix at the table.

BLUFFING AT THE WRONG TIME

Pulling off a successful bluff is one of the most exciting and gratifying plays you can make in no-limit Texas hold'em. But for everything, there is a season and a reason. Don't commit the fatal error of bluffing when you shouldn't.

You need to know your opponents very well before you try a bluff. Who is most likely to fold if you bet? Who is more likely to call?

Do not attempt to bluff a calling station, a player who hates to fold a hand and calls far more often than optimal strategy indicates. Because so many new people are experimenting with no-limit hold'em these days, you often will run into a gang of calling stations in low-limit tournaments. We repeat, don't bluff if you think you're going to get called.

BETTING THE WRONG AMOUNT

A lot of your success in no-limit hold'em is based on how you bet or how you raise. When deciding what amount to raise, always ask yourself, "What is the purpose of my bet?" If you have a marginal hand that you think might be the best hand, consider over-betting the pot in order to shut out your opponents. In other words, if you have a good hand and somebody bets into you with two flush cards on the board, you might want to raise four times the size of his bet in order to drive all the drawing hands out of the pot.

"The minimum I would raise in a situation like this," Tom says, "is double the size of my opponent's bet. Say that my opponent bets $100 and there is $100 in the pot. I want to make it at least $300 to go, because I want to force all the drawing hands out of the pot. My reraise also reopens the betting and the players sitting behind me will realize that even if they call my raise, the original bettor may decide to reraise, which would make it too expensive for them to continue. And even if the original bettor doesn't reraise, I have still managed to isolate him. I have position over the original bettor and depending on how I bet the hand, he might pay me off."

Sometimes by betting too much, you'll make your opponents suspicious. "There's only $100 in the pot," they might think, "and he's betting $1,000. Why is he betting so much?"

Many times, a player in late position will grossly over-bet the pot with a hand such as pocket sevens, hoping everybody will fold. The problem with that type of play is that there are only two likely outcomes:

> 1. Everybody folds and he wins a small pot, or
> 2. He gets called and loses a very big pot.

Over-betting and under-betting are signs of an inexperienced player. If you raise the pot the same amount every time you are first to act, your opponents will have difficulty putting you on a hand. If you decide to play a hand, we suggest raising three to four times the size of the big blind, no matter what cards you are holding.

Betting More Than Your Opponents Will Call

When you think you have the best hand, try to bet an amount that you think your opponents will call. Why make a big bet that might force everyone out of the pot? If you bet more than they are willing to call, what have you accomplished?

For example, suppose you start with pocket aces, make a pot-sized raise and get some action on the hand. The flop comes A-9-2. Bingo! You've flopped the absolute nuts. Now you bet two or three times the size of the pot, and guess what? Nobody can call you, and you might have just cost yourself a few more bets.

And keep in mind that when you make a big bet at the pot in a situation where your hand might not be the best out there, the only players who are going to call are the ones who can beat you.

If you have been studying your opponents, you will have picked up some clues about how much to bet. A pot-sized bet or slightly less usually will reward you with callers.

Betting Too Little

Suppose you are playing in a medium-limit tournament and the blinds are $50/$100. A player comes into the pot for $200, exactly twice the size of the big blind. Your first reaction might be, "Uh oh, a limit hold'em player." Or if you know the raiser is a seasoned no-limit hold'em tournament player, you might think, "He wants me to play. He has a big hand and wants some action on it." Most of the time, however, a double-the-big-blind bet simply indicates that the bettor is a novice and doesn't know any better. This is another good reason to get to know your opponents as early and as well as you can.

One of the worst plays made by inexperienced or low-limit online players is this: Two or three players have entered the pot for the minimum bet and the novice raises to exactly double the size of the big blind. A raise that size will not drive anybody out of the pot. All it will do is reopen the betting for anybody at the table who wants to reraise. If someone has slow-played or "sandbagged" a strong hand or if he believes the raiser's hand is a bit weak, he will often make a big reraise and take the pot away from the original raiser right there. The original raiser has not accomplished anything with his double bet except losing money on the hand.

Raise three to four times the size of the big blind. If callers are already in the pot, add one increment for each caller up to three. For example if three players are in the pot, raise six to seven times the big blind.

By betting too little, you also allow the drawing hands into the pot too cheaply. Players that make bets that size have a limit hold'em mentality. Suppose you have an A-J, and the flop comes J-10-3 with two diamonds. You probably have the best hand, but this is a coordinated flop. If there's $100 in the pot and you decide to bet $20 or $30, you're making it profitable for anybody with any kind of reasonable draw, including an inside straight draw with an overcard, to call the bet and take off a card.

If you believe that you have been betting too little in no-limit hold'em tournaments, here's how to fix the flaw:

"Depending on the size of the pot," Tom advises, "I will make a pot-sized bet. I don't want to over-bet because occasionally I'll run into a bigger hand. But I want to make it costly enough that the marginal hands will leave."

If you always bet the size of the pot when you think you have the best hand on the flop and want to protect it or when you're on a bluff, and did no other type of betting, you probably would be right about 90 percent of the time.

PLAYING TOO MANY HANDS

You're in a tournament, you're in early position, and you pick up an A-6 suited. You think, "Gee, this is a pretty good hand if I flop a flush to it," so you play the hand. If this sounds like you, you're playing too many hands. And you're probably also playing way too many hands out of position. You're playing hands such as suited connectors and small pairs out of position and often calling raises with them. You should not do this; these hands are chip burners.

This is a common error that many novice players commit. No-limit hold'em is a backside game, meaning that the power is in late position. If you are patient and disciplined and pay close attention to your table position, you can erase the flaw of playing hands out of position.

Pocket Pairs and Suited Connectors

"I don't mind playing pocket pairs from any position if I can enter the pot for only one bet," Don says. The problem comes when you're out of position and you limp in with a small pocket pair such as fours, an opponent raises five to six times the size of the big blind, and you call. It is rarely profitable to call a raise in situations like this. You shouldn't do it unless a lot of other players have called in front of you, and you have a ton of chips. But normally, you would not make this call with a small pocket pair and certainly not with suited connectors. Small pairs are easier to play after the flop than connectors, because if you don't flop a set to your pair, you simply fold the hand.

"If I'm playing at a table where there's a lot of raising," Don says, "I won't play small pocket pairs from up front. I just throw them away."

This is a good rule of thumb. The aggressiveness of your opponents should help you determine which hands to enter the pot with from early position. So if you're at a passive table, it isn't terrible to play the small pocket pairs from up front. But if you're up against several very aggressive players, limping will be seen as a sign of weakness, so don't get involved.

We suggest not playing suited connectors from an early position because if you flop a draw to your hand, it can get expensive to continue playing. You might make an exception with K-Q suited, but smaller suited connectors are chip burners. For example, suppose you have 8-7 suited and the flop comes 8-4-2. You're in trouble! You have flopped top pair, but you don't have a decent kicker. If you bet and get raised, you will have to muck the hand.

Early Rounds vs. Late Rounds

During the early rounds of a tournament, players have a tendency to play a lot more hands than they play in the later stages, especially in rebuy events. They will come into pots with a wide variety of marginal hands, hands they will not play once the rebuy period ends. Early in the tournament, many players play too many hands out of position and too many marginal hands in position.

"My philosophy is the opposite," Don states. "I prefer to play fewer hands early in the tournament, and later on in the event, I play more hands from the backside that might be considered slightly marginal. I do this because I will usually have fewer callers later in the tournament, and since I am in late position with these marginal hands, I might be able to take the pot away from my opponents if nobody flops anything."

When the rebuy period ends and the blinds get bigger, or when the antes kick in, players tend to tighten up. This is when you can take advantage of that tendency.

Stu Ungar's philosophy on early play in major no-limit hold'em tournaments was not to play any big pots before the antes started, which usually happens around the fourth round. The ante prevents somewhat conservative players from just sitting there, waiting for the nuts. Since the blinds are relatively small in relation to your starting stack in the early rounds, why take big risks for relatively small rewards?

NOT PLAYING ENOUGH HANDS

Many players play too tight during the opening stages of a tournament because they want to survive. They wait until the cows come home for pocket aces, kings, or queens, or A-K. These too-tight players are not playing true no-limit hold'em, because they are afraid to get involved in a hand, lose it, and get eliminated from the tournament. They have no heart.

Against observant opponents who notice a layer of dust on top of a rock's chips, players like this won't get any action on their good hands. So they finally wake up with aces or kings, raise the pot, and everybody folds. What have they gained? The blinds.

It is almost impossible for a very tight player to win a no-limit hold'em tournament, or any other type of tournament, because nobody gets dealt that many premium hands over the course of an event. And when the rock does get a premium hand, he doesn't get enough action and doesn't win enough chips to become a contender. Position, chip power, and good timing are often more important than cards in no-limit hold'em.

"I have won many tournaments," Don says, "when the biggest hand I held during the entire event might have been pocket nines, followed closely by A-Q offsuit."

T.J. Cloutier is very adept at accumulating a lot of chips without having a hand. "He has told me many times," Tom says, "that even with hands no better than a pair of tens or an A-K, he can triple his chip count in three or four rounds of play."

How does he do it, you ask? By picking his spots, stealing some pots, knowing when to play a marginal hand, when to push it if he flops something to it, and analyzing his opponents. In other words, he can win with no cards.

Don't Let Fear Freeze Your Play

If you play scared, you're beaten before the first card is dealt. You have no chance whatsoever of winning if:

1. You're intimidated by the opposition or the size of the field;
2. You're uncomfortable with the stakes;
3. You're afraid that you will lose if you bluff and get called; or
4. You think that your hand isn't good enough, so you freeze up and either under-bet the pot or fold to somebody else's bet.

You've got to occasionally try to steal the blinds or make a move without the best hand, because there are only so many good hands that you'll catch. At some point, you have to be willing to take a shot at the pot without the nuts. If you're afraid to execute, if you freeze up, your chances of success are almost nonexistent.

If you get caught but you don't lose all your chips on the play, slow down and play very solid poker. But if you are successful, try another move a little later on. If you lose all your chips, at least you can go home knowing that you did the best you could. You made a move, trying to put yourself in a position to win the tournament, and it didn't work—that's the end of it.

People who don't gamble enough are usually afraid of getting knocked out of the tournament, but there is another way to look at things.

"It makes no difference whether I get knocked out first or one place out of the money," Don says. "The result is the same. Actually I'd rather go out early than late, because then I can go and do something else."

Throughout the entire tournament, you must play to win and try to accumulate chips so that you can make the money. Don't freeze up, and don't worry about getting knocked out. Play to win or don't play at all.

"I've been knocked out of big buy-in tournaments on the first hand that was dealt, almost always when I had a big hand that got beaten by a lesser hand," Tom recalls. "Early in 2004 during the PokerStars.com World Poker Tour tournament, I was dealt pocket aces on the very first hand. Two people at my starting table hadn't even taken their seats yet. My hand got cracked by a player with pocket kings. I went broke on the very first hand! Did I feel bad? You bet! But do I think that I made the wrong play? No. As Max Stern, my co-author for Championship Stud, wrote, 'You must be willing to die in order to live.'"

"I was playing a World Series tournament, a $1,000 no-limit hold'em event with rebuys, and on the very first hand I was dealt pocket aces," Don adds. "With blinds of $25/$25, I raised to $75. Chip Jett came over the top of me with pocket jacks, and we got all the money in. The first card off the deck was a jack. And the tournament wasn't even a minute old! Good news for Chip, bad news for me. Stuff happens, as the saying goes."

If you believe you have the best of it and you put your chips in the middle, play the best you can to give yourself a chance to win. If that means you get broke early or you get knocked out late, so be it. Remember that in order to win, you've got to have every chip in play.

As T.J. Cloutier always says, "You want to get your money in with the best of it. If you get it all-in with the best hand and they beat you, that's just the way it goes—that's poker."

Unlike limit poker in which you have to win a series of pots and show down a lot of hands, you only need to win a few pots in no-limit hold'em, so you don't have to show down as many hands. You can often win with a bet.

Don't Get Caught Up in a Betting Frenzy

In the 2004 WSOP, the two chip leaders at the end of day one had around $120,000 each in chips, and both were eliminated on day two. How did that happen? We believe it was the result of getting caught up in a betting frenzy. They played too many hands and made too many marginal calls during the second day.

If you are fortunate enough to accumulate a lot of chips early in the tournament through aggressive play, you do not need to continue using the same strategy. As we discussed earlier, you need to protect a big stack, so be willing to change gears, depending on the circumstances and the chip count. Above all, if you're at a table with several loose, aggressive players, don't get so caught up in the action that you start playing like they do and squander your big stack. This lack of discipline can take you from the penthouse to the outhouse in a hurry.

PLAYING MARGINAL HANDS OUT OF POSITION

Here is a list of marginal hands that you should avoid playing when you are in an early position:

A-J, A-10, K-Q, K-J, K-10, K-9, Q-J, Q-10, Q-9, J-10, J-9, and J-8.

Don't play small suited connectors, either. If most of the players at your table are loose and passive, you might play any pocket pair, but only for one bet. If several of your opponents are aggressive, you might play pocket eights and higher, but if you get raised, be prepared to fold.

"I don't like playing many hands from an early position," Don says. "If I'm in late position, I will loosen up my starting requirements. Sometimes I am tempted to play a Q-J, K-J, or K-10 suited from up-front, but I force myself to throw them away. And usually, I'm glad I did. The flop may come king-high and I'm thinking, 'Gee, I had a king.' And then somebody shows down an A-K or a K-Q."

It's not so terrible to occasionally raise with a marginal hand when you're the first one in the pot, but you have to be able to get away from it when necessary. If somebody has already entered the pot, you should only get involved with a marginal hand if you are in late position and the pot has not been raised.

"A player in the Four Queens Classic raised under the gun with K-Q suited," Tom says. "I was sitting on the button with two aces and simply doubled his bet. He was the type of player that I knew could be trapped for all his chips if he called my raise, so I raised just enough to lure him into the pot. The flop came Q-8-8. Now he thinks he has the best hand, and he leads at the pot. He is committed to the pot, so I put in the rest of my chips and he was forced to call— with only two outs. When he missed, he said, 'I knew you had a big hand.' And yet he still lost one-half of his stack to me! A while later he again raised with K-Q. A player in the big blind with a J-10 suited made a loose call, and the flop came K-10-10. The blind checked, the raiser moved in, and the blind called. Déjà vu, he lost again."

In no-limit hold'em, if anyone has shown any strength from an early position, K-Q is a trap hand, as is A-Q. In other words, if someone raises the pot from an early position, these are not the kinds of hands you want to call with.

313

These same hands can be played for a raise from the backside if you can be the first player in the pot. But you have to be able to fold these hands if someone comes over the top. You must have the discipline to fold when you know you should.

INCORRECTLY EVALUATING YOUR OPPONENTS

People have a tendency to overrate their own play and underrate that of their opponents. Too often players attribute their opponents' success to luck rather than skill. A lot of times players base their judgments on their opponents' physical appearances. Some men still believe that they can run over female poker players with aggressive play at the poker table. With so many talented women playing poker these days, male chauvinists are in for a rude awakening.

Don't underestimate your opponents. When you first sit down at a tournament table and begin evaluating your opponents, err on the side of caution until you have played with them for more than one round. In a sense, everybody is innocent of being a bad poker player until proven guilty!

"I make the assumption that everybody knows what they're doing," Tom says. "I pretend they are all world-class players until they prove differently. I try not to give any loose action to my opponents until I have learned how they play. I would rather give my opponents credit than cash."

Err on the side of caution, but be careful not overestimate your opponents' abilities either. Don't assume that they are geniuses at the poker table just because you've heard people say they are. Not every great player brings his A-game to the table every time he sits down.

Some players become automatically intimidated by their tablemates. Sometimes their opponents are legitimate world-class players like T.J.; other times they may simply have an imposing aura about them. But remember that just because your opponents have strong personalities, that doesn't necessarily mean they are strong players.

"In my case," Tom admits, "I can sometimes get away with a few moves just because I have a reputation for being a conservative player. Even though I may not have a strong hand, my opponents will sometimes give me more credit than I deserve just because they have overestimated the strength of my cards."

Do not misjudge your own ability either. You might be a great player, but do not let your ego get in the way of your decisions. How often have you heard someone say, "The players in that $4/$8 game can't play a lick!" as he walks away from the table broke? Or, "They're so bad, I can't beat 'em!"

MISREADING OPPONENTS

Players often misjudge the strength of their opponents' hands early in the tournament when the limits are low. Therefore, their misreads do not do a great deal of damage to their stacks. If you make a similar error in judgment, reevaluate your opinion of that opponent. If you realize during a hand that you have misjudged your opponent's hand, don't allow yourself to get stuck by refusing to adjust your opinion and strategy. For example, if you think your hand is only strong enough to beat one or two others at the showdown, don't put your opponent on one of those hands for the sole purpose of justifying a call. Misjudging the strength of their opponents' cards and then refusing to reevaluate that judgment is often the downfall of mediocre players.

You can fix this problem by being flexible enough to reevaluate the situation. Good players take their time before they make a major decision that could put their chips in jeopardy. It isn't that they are unsure as to what to do; they are replaying the hand in their minds and trying to make the best decision possible. Sometimes they go with their first instincts and other times they reevaluate, but before they act they pause long enough to analyze things thoroughly.

It is also possible to misread your opponents' betting actions. If you have been playing against an opponent long enough, you should know whether his tendency is to over-bet the pot, under-bet the pot, or be afraid to bet altogether. Try to recall his betting pattern.

"I played a tournament in Las Vegas in which the young daughter of a well-known septuagenarian poker player was sitting at my table," Tom relates. "She had only one play— all-in. She didn't do it with marginal hands, however. She folded most of her hands, and then she'd suddenly push all her chips into the pot. Knowing this, I folded pocket sevens against her all-in raise, but another player called with a K-Q offsuit. The young poker maven showed A-K suited to win the pot. Her opponent lost a bundle because he had not been paying attention to her betting pattern."

By the way, your best defense against someone like this is a very strong hand. Don't leave home without one, so to speak. The move-in artist will eventually go all-in one time too often.

PLAYING TOO AGGRESSIVELY

Certain players enjoy taking command of the table right from the get-go. They might force the action early on, especially when the blinds are small in relation to the starting chips, and end up winning four or five pots in a row. But if they get out of line one too many times, they'll often lose one-half or more of their stack on one hand.

There is a fine line between playing selectively aggressive and being overly aggressive. Overly aggressive players constantly over-bet the pot, play too many hands, and get more deeply involved with hands than they should.

What is the point of being overly aggressive in the early stages of a tournament, when you have far more to lose than you have to gain? You cannot win the tournament during the first few rounds, but you can certainly lose it. The fastest route to the exit in the early rounds is to play too fast. Sooner or later somebody with a superior starting hand will pick you off.

Here's what poker pro Annie Duke says about controlled aggression:

"To be great, you need more than an 'on' button. Being aggressive in a vacuum might get a player a few wins, but not consistent results. My brother [poker pro Howard Lederer] and I understand why we choose aggression at any given moment. If aggression is not warranted, we aren't aggressive."

RAISING WHEN YOU SHOULDN'T

Before you slide your chips into the pot with a raise, ask yourself, "What is the purpose of this raise?" Raise for one of two reasons:

1. You want to win the hand immediately, or
2. You believe you have the best hand and want to build the pot so that you can maximize your win.

If an opponent has shown some obvious strength by raising in front you, you should not raise unless you have a big pair. For example, say that player with the layer of dust on his chips wakes up with a hand and raises from early position. You have the A-K offsuit and, thinking it's a big hand, you fire in a reraise. Big mistake! You almost always will be taking the worst of it against a tight player who has raised from up front.

Here's another scenario: You call a raise from late position with a K-J offsuit. The flop comes K 8 4. A player bets into you and you call. The next card off the deck is a blank, he bets again, and now you raise. If he calls your raise or reraises you, you're beaten nine times out of ten. If you have limped in or called a standard raise with a marginal hand, don't go crazy when you flop something to it. Always remember that having a good kicker is very important. This is a good example of a player overplaying his hand and getting broke in a no-limit hold'em tournament.

Finally, suppose you're in the big blind, the pot has not been raised, and you have an A-6 offsuit. The flop comes A-7-3. You bet, and two opponents call. When a blank comes on the turn, you check and one of your opponents puts in a pot-sized bet. You're probably beaten. But we have seen players grit their teeth, decide to commit their stack to the hand, and raise all-in with their weak ace. Almost always, they are drawing to only three outs—one of the three sixes left in the deck—if that. If you have top pair with a weak kicker and your opponent fires in a big bet, don't be unwilling to fold.

NOT RAISING WHEN YOU SHOULD

You should never be afraid to raise when you think you have the best hand. As we said in the previous section, you should raise either to thin the field before the flop, or because you want to build the pot. You should also raise if:

1. You have either an overpair to the flop or top pair with top kicker,
2. You are 90 percent certain you have the best hand, and
3. There are a lot of drawing possibilities out against you.

And you should raise enough to take the pot odds away from your opponents. Any time you take a pot when you don't have the nuts and drawing hands are out against you, it's a sweet win.

When a loose-aggressive player bets into you, don't make the mistake of just calling or merely raising the minimum, as that won't be enough to drive anybody out of the pot. As long as you think you have the best hand, you want to force the drawing hands out of the pot rather than letting them have a cheap draw to beat you, so raise enough to eliminate them. If you take a passive approach, you are inviting disaster. Even if you have the best hand, if several people are in the pot drawing against you, one of them inevitably seems to get there.

If you flop bottom or middle set and somebody bets in front of you, don't be afraid to put in a small raise. They're not going to go away, and you might be able to trap somebody behind you. If drawing hands are out against you and the flop is coordinated, there are two good reasons to put in a raise:

1. To get more money in the pot, and
2. To isolate a single opponent.

It's important to isolate, because with a lot of players in the pot and a straight or flush possibility on board, it's more likely that someone will draw out against you. And if that happens, it's very hard to get away from a set. You'll have to play catch-up, hoping the board pairs so you can make a full house. Bottom line: You let them in too cheap.

TRYING TO OUTFOX THE FOX

When you are facing an established tournament star, your game plan should not be "How can I outplay him?" It should be "How can I avoid him?" You can duck having to make tricky decisions against top tournament players by not playing marginal starting hands. Play strong starting hands in position whenever possible. Even the best no-limit hold'em players will have a difficult time trying to outplay a superior starting hand.

Avoiding strong players is not always possible, of course, so how should you play when you're up against one? Try betting or raising enough chips, either before or after the flop, to put your crafty opponent to the test. Force him to make a major decision, even if it means moving in on him. When you bet most or all of your chips, you put the pressure on your opponent. Your commitment to the pot will narrow his options considerably. If your opponent does not think he can outplay you, he'll have to believe that he has the best hand before putting his chips in the pot. Many times he will fold fairly strong hands against you in this situation, believing that you have him beat.

Many times, you and your opponent will have nearly the same odds of winning the hand. Top tournament players try to avoid these coin toss situations whenever possible. They prefer to either outplay the opposition or wait for a more favorable situation. But for you, a coin toss might be the preferred option against a tournament star.

For example, suppose you have pocket eights, and you feel reasonably certain that your opponent has two overcards, such as A-K or A-Q. Even if you think there is a good chance he will call you, it is often the right play to put your chips in and hope for the best. That way you don't have to worry that your famous opponent will find a way to outplay you after the flop, especially if one or more overcards come on the board.

The bottom line is that you should avoid playing marginal hands against strong competition, especially when you are out of position. You want to force them to have to react to you instead of you having to react to them, so put the pressure on them whenever possible, even in a coin-toss situation.

ACTING ON REFLEX RATHER THAN REFLECTION

Acting before you think things through is the kingpin of fatal flaws. Too often, new players push chips into the pot before their brain kicks into action. Don't make the same mistake; always take time to think through the situation before you act on your hand.

All top-level no-limit hold'em players constantly analyze the play of a hand and take ample time to decide their best move. Any time you have to make a serious decision, especially if someone raises you, don't automatically throw your hand away—but don't automatically call either. First, review each player's betting action. Then think about what happened beforehand. Many times your final decision will be based on your gut instinct, but you still need to stop, think, and analyze.

For example, suppose you're sitting two seats to the right of the button, and you want to win the blinds.

"In that situation, I raise with any two cards," Don advises. "The cutoff seat folds, the button folds, and the small blind folds. Then the big blind reraises. Now what do I do? I don't automatically throw my 7-2 away; I sit there for maybe twenty seconds apparently thinking it over. Then I say, 'Okay, I think you have me,' and fold my hand. I don't want my opponent to think I'm a chicken who gives up against a raise, nor do I want him to think that I have absolutely nothing."

"I played an evening tournament with a $200 buy-in during the Four Queens Classic," Tom says, "and pulled the same type of move with a 7-2 offsuit. A very loose-aggressive player moved in all his chips. I had shown down nothing except strong hands, and I had just beaten him in a big pot. My raise was strictly a positional play that I made from a late position. But this time, he moved in on me from the button. After the blinds folded, I sat there thinking, thinking, thinking about it. Finally I turned my cards face up so that the whole table could see them. 'Well, I think you've got me this time!' I joked as I folded. Everybody got a big laugh out of that.

"The reason I showed the hand was to get action on future hands. I wanted my opponents to know that I was capable of making that type of play. Of course I was very selective about the hands I played from then on."

Always think about your opponent's motives. There is a reason for everything they do, although you won't always see the logic in their reasons. Even if your opponent's actions go against proper, by-the-book strategy, in his mind it is the correct thing to do. Normally, your opponent is betting because he thinks he has the best hand. Or, if he's a good player, he might bet middle pair on the flop when he's in late position, hoping that he has the best hand. A good player might also bet if he thinks he can get you to fold— even if you think your hand is slightly better than his hand.

14

Managing Your Tournament Bankroll

"All of the world-class play is on a freezeout basis. This places a great emphasis upon money management. Money management is the name of the game!"

–Bobby Baldwin, 1978 World Champion of Poker, in *Tales Out of Tulsa*

INTRODUCTION

New business owners often underestimate expenses and do not properly plan for things that could go wrong. Before you create a new business, you need to be aware of two things:

1. Most new businesses fail within the first six months, and
2. The main reason they fail is that they don't have enough working capital to survive.

It's the same with your tournament bankroll. Most players don't get lucky just starting out on the tournament trail, so surviving those first few months, while you're still learning, is crucial to your success. If you are not a winning player from the get-go, you're going to have a tough time making a profit. You must be adequately financed in order to make it through some tough times and ultimately survive. You can't build your bankroll if you are out of action.

So, what do you need to do? Set aside enough money to ensure that you can stay in action long enough to guarantee profitable results. And don't risk too much of your bankroll in any one tournament. For example, if your tournament bankroll is $5,000, it would be foolish to risk $1,000 or $1,500 of it on one event. If you double your bankroll to $10,000, taking a shot at a higher buy-in is a more acceptable risk. Now let's take a look at bankroll requirements for small, medium, and big buy-in events.

BANKROLLING SMALL BUY-IN EVENTS

Most people who enter small buy-in tournaments that cost up to $100 also play live side games. Their goal is to win their tournament buy-ins in cash games, which makes playing tournaments something like a freeroll. Of course, there is a limit to how much you can realistically expect to win in a side game. If you double or even triple your initial buy-in, you've had a pretty good session. But if you invest some of your cash-game profits in a tournament, you have the opportunity to gain perhaps 50 to 100 times the size of your investment.

You can easily win a $100 tournament buy-in in a $3/$6, $4/$8, or $5/$10 cash game. If you are a good player, all it takes is some time and work, plus a little bit of luck. Some cash-game players do not have a firm grasp of tournament strategy—and vice versa. But as a general rule, if you're a successful side-action player, you should be able to build a tournament bankroll through your live play.

If you are playing small buy-in events, how big a bankroll do you need in order to stay in action? As is so often true in poker, it depends. Are you a winning tournament player? If you are, what is the average amount you invest per tournament? How many tournament losses can you sustain and still have enough money to play? The smaller your bankroll, the more likely you are to go broke, even if you are a winning player.

You need to play about thirty tournaments to get a good idea of what results you can expect to achieve over the long run. This means that you must have large enough bankroll to finance your entries into those thirty events. If your average tournament investment is $60, you would have to invest about $1,800 to play that many events. Therefore, you should have a tournament bankroll of approximately $3,000, so that in case you lose them all—which is possible—you won't be broke. Make sure you have a cushion, so you can fend off an initial losing streak.

If you are unsuccessful in your first few low buy-in tournaments, we suggest that you take a breather and play online to gain additional practice. You will be able to find plenty of these inexpensive online tournaments at sites such as PokerStars, some of which are freerolls for new players or cost as little as $5 or $10 to enter. Try playing two or three of these small tournaments a day if you have the time. When your results improve, return to playing tournaments with higher buy-ins, utilizing your online experience and the tips you have learned in this book.

BANKROLLING MEDIUM BUY-IN EVENTS

Even medium buy-in tournaments that cost $100 to $500 can be financed through your cash-game play. If you're a successful $10/$20, $15/$30, or $20/$40 player, you should be able to build a tournament bankroll from your profits. This doesn't mean that you will be playing a medium buy-in tournament every day with your side-game profit, but you may be able to play a tournament a week or maybe three events per month.

You want to maintain your bankroll without risking too much of it for tournament play. Set aside about 20 percent of your cash-game winnings for tournament buy-ins or to allow you to move up to higher-stakes cash games. That way, you will maintain your original bankroll, and still be able to use some of your profits for living expenses.

To stay in action for medium buy-in events, you need about thirty times the size of your average tournament buy-in, meaning you will probably need a bankroll of at least $10,000 bankroll—$15,000 would be even better—to play in medium buy-in tournaments. If you're not successful from the get-go in medium buy-in tournaments, you might only play an occasional tournament that size. In medium buy-in events, if you are broke or close to it after thirty tournaments, you should drop back and play the smaller buy-in events until you rebuild your bankroll. Then you can try the medium buy-in events again.

The greatest tournament players in the world started out by playing low-limit poker cash games. Johnny Chan, for example, used to play $3/$6 hold'em before he became one of the greatest tournament players of all time.

"When I first began my professional tournament career," Tom says, "I was playing $20 to $40 buy-in tournaments all around Las Vegas. Some of the legendary players were right there with me, learning their craft in small tournaments."

Another way to preserve your bankroll is to take advantage of the satellite system. Almost all casinos sponsor a number of pre-tournament satellites, in which you can win your way into the medium buy-in events. This inexpensive way to earn your way into tournaments will provide you with valuable experience playing at the medium levels. If you plan on taking this route, we strongly suggest that you learn how to play proper satellite strategy, which Tom and co-author Brad Daugherty cover in-depth in *How to Win Your Way into Big Money Hold'em Tournaments*.

BANKROLLING BIG BUY-IN TOURNAMENTS

Big buy-in events are commonplace on the tournament circuit. Today there are over three hundred tournaments per year worldwide and online with buy-ins in excess of $1,000. In the U.S. alone, there are around two hundred live tournaments of this size. If you want to play the big buy-in events, you should be either a very successful tournament player who plays professional-level poker, or have a backer with deep pockets that can carry you through the ups and downs of big-league tournaments.

Success in medium buy-in tournaments allows you to put money aside for playing big buy-in tournaments. If you are successful at the $1,000 level, we suggest setting aside 50 percent of your winnings for tournaments with buy-ins of $2,000, $3,000, $5,000, and $10,000.

To play the bigger buy-in events, you need a tournament bankroll of around $200,000, assuming that most of your buy-ins are below the $5,000 level. It would require a much larger bankroll—probably $500,000, including travel expenses—to play the World Poker Tour championship events and the bigger buy-in World Series of Poker tournaments.

As you can see, this is a considerable investment. Even winning tournament players have gone through negative swings and lost this kind of money in a single year. This is why many winning players secure some kind of backing. If you have a solid tournament track record, you'll usually be able to find a backer who is willing to invest in you. You can also sell shares of yourself, which will lessen your financial risk and still allow you to enter your preferred events. The 2004 World Poker champion Greg Raymer did exactly that, and his investors hit the poker lottery when he won the title and the $5,000,000 that went with it.

Taking Advantage of Satellites

Raymer won his seat for the championship event via an online satellite at PokerStars. Chris Moneymaker, the 2003 WSOP champion, was an obscure accountant from Tennessee who won his seat in a $40 PokerStars online satellite. Because of the magic of his Horatio Alger story, he probably is the best-known player in the poker world today. His success was not a fluke; Moneymaker's subsequent tournament success has proven that he is good—very good. And certainly he has the most recognized name in poker worldwide.

In fact, more than 50 percent of the entrants in big buy-in events earn their chance at millions by first winning a preliminary satellite. Before plunking down $5,000 or $10,000 on a big tournament, consider this option. If you are fortunate enough to win your way into a WSOP or WPT event via a satellite, the money can be truly life changing. We've seen it happen.

When you're planning to play a series of big buy-in events, it is very important to set up a tournament budget and stick to it. You don't want to play too big for your bankroll and get broke as the result—also know as gambler's ruin. Satellites are a good way to avoid that dismal fate. If you have been successful in a big buy-in tournament, you might take 50 percent of your win and earmark it for playing satellites, or for buying into the next tournament on your agenda. If you plan to play an event regardless of how you fare in the satellites, we suggest playing no more than two of them. If you decide that you'll play a big tournament only if you win a seat in the event through a satellite, you might play as many as three of them.

Scheduling

Tournament action goes year-round these days. You can enter a $5,000 to $10,000 tournament virtually every month. Cherry-pick the tournaments that you have the time and ability to play, and schedule them on your calendar. Many good publications and websites, such as *Card Player* magazine and PokerPages.com, run a complete tournament schedule one year in advance so that you can get a good idea of which events you want to enter.

Many players consider the World Series of Poker to be the start of their tournament year and plan their tournament schedule around the dates of the event. If you're a big buy-in tournament player, your success or failure may well depend on how well you do at the WSOP. If you do extremely well, doors to a lot of other events on the tournament circuit will be opened. If you don't do very well and lose a lot of money at the Series, that may put a crimp in your tournament bankroll until you can rebuild it. Whatever your budget or time constraints, there are tournaments available that will fit your desires.

Tournament Talk

Finding the Right Tournament **By Tom McEvoy**

In order to find a good investment and avoid a bad beat for your bankroll, you should shop around for right value as you would when you buy a new car. You want to pick a cherry rather than get stuck with a lemon. Obviously, good tournaments are well managed. They start on time, and the coordinator makes reasonable, fair, and quick decisions. What else should you look for in a tournament? Here are some guidelines to follow and questions to ask when deciding which tournaments to play.

1. What kind of overlay am I getting on my money and will money be added? Naturally, if money will be added to the tournament, so much the better. If not, determine how much return you will get on your investment if you win it. In my opinion, a tournament that promises a top prize of at least fifty times your original buy-in automatically is a good investment.

2. How tough is the field? Any tournament that has a starting field of rather weak, timid, or inexperienced players can be a very favorable event in which to participate. Tournaments with very large fields and what is referred to as a lot of "dead money" in them also are good values for experienced players. The championship event at Binion's World Series of Poker, which is often padded with recreational players is a good example of this type of tournament. Many of the amateur poker players won their way into the WSOP through a super satellite, which have fast structures. But these players lack the ability to put together a solid game for a weeklong run in the world championship event. In addition, the rule stating that players cannot transfer titles to the first seat they win for the championship event has helped to swell attendance in recent years. What all of this means is that that accomplished players enjoy a huge overlay on their money. The first no-limit hold'em event at the WSOP also offers a good overlay. A lot of people come to town for the very beginning of the Series, a large number of whom are only able to enter one event. Some of these players are hometown champions or amateurs who have won a satellite. They are not of the same caliber as many of the more seasoned tournament pros they must compete against, and they often enter this event. Conversely, watch out for tournaments with big buy-ins that have short and exceedingly tough fields. For example, suppose you put up $500 or $1,000 in a tournament that has attracted only sixty people, forty of which are professional-level players. You should avoid this type of short, tough field.

3. What is the time structure? If rounds last forty-five minutes to an hour or longer and there is a decent amount of prize money at stake, the situation is favorable. The longer the rounds are, the more they favor the better players because they'll have more time to outmaneuver the weaker opponents. One reader told me about a local tournament that began each day at noon and opened with ten-minute rounds to stimulate the action. Obviously, that time structure makes the tournament a total crapshoot.

4. How is the prize money distributed? In some older tournament formats, as much as 50 percent of the prize pool went to the winner, with 20 percent or less going to second place. But these days, I estimate that winning players make deals in 80 percent of tournaments in which they are able to do so. Since deals are made at the final table of the vast majority of tournaments, I think that having a more balanced distribution is favorable. Specifically, the top prize should pay out no more than 36 percent, while payouts for second place, third place, and fourth place should be around 19 percent, 9.5 percent, and 6 percent, respectively. Finally, avoid tournaments that cease play when it gets down to the final three players and award top prize to the person with the most chips.

5. What is the atmosphere like? A friendly atmosphere and a courteous staff that is willing to listen to the players and still run things in an orderly fashion can make a big difference in your enjoyment of the tournament. Being able to carry on intelligent conversations with your table companions—as opposed to constant bickering and complaining—is always a plus.

6. Rebuy tournaments that don't allow a lot of rebuys, or those that at least limited the rebuy period to one or two levels or the first hour, are preferable to tournaments that allow them for three rounds or three hours. The limited rebuy period gives players the opportunity to accumulate decent amounts of chips and swells the prize fund, all while keeping rebuys from getting out of hand. As long as the rebuys are within reason and I'll still receive fifty times my accumulated buy-ins if I am fortunate enough to win, I am getting a good tournament value. On the other hand, avoid rebuy tournaments in which you don't get the same value for your buy-in throughout the event. For example, say the tournament offers $300 in chips for your first rebuy, at the second level you get $500 in chips for the same amount of money, and then there is a 2 for 1 add-on. This policy can be unfavorable because there is no way to determine the total amount of prize money at stake relative to the amount of chips in play. I don't mind 2 for 1 add-ons as long as they are specified in the prize money breakdown. This can easily be done since about 85 percent of players take the add-on.

7. Are the starting limits too high in relationship to the amount of starting chips? For example, suppose you start with $200 in chips and blinds of $10/$20—that's only ten big bets. You'll usually want a better ratio than that, at least 15 to 1. So if the blinds start at $15/$30, you should have around $500 in chips to begin with, about 17 big bets. The one fault that I've found with World Series of Poker tournaments is that some of the early $1,500 events begin at $50/$100 limits, meaning you start with barely 15 big bets. And some of the pot-limit and no-limit hold'em events give you only $1,500 in chips with starting blinds of $25/$50. The $25/$50 blind structure has been used for the championship event at the WSOP for decades, but the big difference is that you get $10,000 in chips to start with, which is a very favorable ratio. That is why the WSOP is in a class by itself: You have a lot of days to play and a lot of ammunition with which to wage the good battle. This type of structure is what we call "player-friendly" because it favors skill over luck. But events that emphasize the luck factor—those that offer too few chips in relation to the starting limits—are poor tournament investments, even for a tournament junkie like me.

Successful Playing Styles

"My desire is to play each situation correctly. My goal is to play the perfect session of poker. I haven't gotten into that zip code yet."

–Annie Duke, WSOP Tournament of Champions $2 million winner, in *Card Player* magazine

INTRODUCTION

In this book, we have presented you with a solid-aggressive strategy for playing no-limit hold'em tournaments. Admittedly, we lean toward the conservative side in tournament strategy. Once you have grasped the basics of tournament play and have played enough events to get a handle on what it takes to win them, you will want to adjust your style of play to fit your personal traits and tastes.

A number of different styles of play are common in no-limit hold'em tournaments. In this section we'll discuss the characteristics of these various styles of play and some of the famous players who use them. Always bear in mind that all the best no-limit hold'em tournament players have the ability to change their style as the tournament progresses. By adapting some of their techniques to your game plan, you may find yourself in the winner's circle far sooner than you expected.

In this chapter we're sticking out our necks by providing our admittedly biased descriptions of the playing styles of today's tournament poker stars. The next time you watch them play in a televised tournament, try to decide whether or not you agree with our assessment. We'd also like to acknowledge T.J. Cloutier, our writing colleague and tournament guru, for his contributions to this chapter.

AGGRESSIVE STYLE OF PLAY

An aggressive player likes to raise with lots of different hands when he first enters the pot. He tries to take control of the table and will raise with marginal hands in many cases. If he gets called and thinks that he has the best hand after the flop, or if he feels the flop missed his opponents, he will bet the pot—with or without a hand. The idea, of course, is to get all his opponents to fold when they aren't holding much of anything.

The aggressive player will often call a bet after the flop if he thinks the bettor has missed the flop—even if he has nothing—in order to take the pot away from the bettor on the next round of betting. This can be a very dangerous play, however, requiring a correct read of his opponent.

Aggressive players are constantly trying to accumulate a lot of chips very early in the tournament. They will continue this style of play as long as it is successful. Often they will crash and burn early, but they can amass a ton of chips if they get away with their unflinching aggressive play.

What is the best strategy to use against this type of player? If you're sitting to his left, your best defense is to wait for a decent hand and reraise him before the flop. If he is on your left and gets to act after you do, your best strategy is to limp in with a strong hand. If he raises behind you, you can either reraise before the flop or check-raise him after the flop. Of course, what you do depends on the strength of your hand and how you evaluate the flop. Your assertive play will get his attention, and he will show you some respect.

Some top no-limit hold'em tournament players who use this style of play include Mike Laing, Huck Seed, and Amir Vahadi.

INITIALLY AGGRESSIVE STYLE OF PLAY

This is somewhat similar to the aggressive style, but with a few key differences. After accumulating chips, this player switches gears and plays a much more solid game. If this happens, you must change your defense against him as well. You need to be more selective in the hands you play against him. You can still use the check-raise and the reraise to defend with, but be aware that it's much more likely that he has a real hand than it was previously.

Greg Raymer, Phil Hellmuth, and Phil Ivey fit into this category.

SUPER-AGGRESSIVE STYLE OF PLAY

These guys have come to play! Often referred to as maniacs, super-aggressors will call, raise, and play just about any two cards from any position. They even call raises with hands as bad as 4-2 offsuit, and sometimes they will reraise with them!

You will frequently run into this type of player in low buy-in tournaments. Because of his limited tournament experience—or maybe because he just likes to gamble—the super-aggressor often won't have a clue about what he is doing. If he moves up to a medium or big buy-in tournament, he'll likely play the same way. You also will find a lot of super-aggressive no-limit hold'em players in online tournaments. Sometimes an internet player will win a seat into a big buy-in event and cause havoc among the pros. However the good players are usually licking their chops and waiting patiently for the right time to snap them off. Most of the time super-aggressors destroy themselves, usually sooner rather than later, and report to the rail to tell their bad-beat stories.

When you are playing behind this type of player, your best defense is to reraise and often go all-in. If you are sitting to the right of a maniac, just limp in with your premium hands, let him raise, and then reraise. If your good hand holds up, you can double through him. If the maniac gets lucky and beats you—oops! That's just part of the game.

In the history of the game, there is only one player who used this style of play against high-stakes competition and was able to consistently win with it. That player was the legendary Stu Ungar, three-time World Champion of Poker. It is said that in his lifetime, he played around thirty tournaments with buy-ins of $10,000 or more—and he won an unbelievable ten of them! Nobody—and we do mean nobody—got away with being as aggressive as Stuey.

SOLID-AGGRESSIVE STYLE OF PLAY

This is the style that we endorse and practice, because we believe that it will get you to the winner's circle. A solid-aggressive player plays the right cards in the right position. He knows where he is at in relation to chip stack, the size of the blinds, and the time left on the clock before the blinds and antes increase. A solid-aggressive player is an expert reader and uses this knowledge to steal blinds at the right time, re-steal when he thinks an opponent is out of line, and bluff when he thinks he can get away with it.

This player normally plays a conservative game during the first three or four levels of a tournament. He waits for someone to make a mistake against him so he can increase his stack size. He doesn't play very many hands, but he always knows where he is during a hand. A solid-aggressive player knows how to open up his game after the first three or four levels of play and has the ability to push all his chips into a pot with pocket deuces and other marginal hands if he thinks that an opponent is out of line.

Great solid-aggressive players have a tremendous feel for the game. They try to survive until they come upon the right situation to double-up and start accumulating chips. In most cases, solid-aggressives get their chips in with the best of it, and if the odds hold up, they will win. Often times their opponents will lay down hands out of respect or fear.

However, this style of play can make it difficult to accumulate a lot of chips early in the tournament because it requires a player to be in survival mode a lot of the time. The good news is that when a solid-aggressive player does get a lot of chips, he is a force to be reckoned with.

If you choose to use this style, be aware that playing a little too solid can be its one weakness. You occasionally need to open up your game a bit, especially in the late stages of the tournament, and gamble a little more than you might be comfortable doing.

Doyle Brunson, the world's premier living legend of poker, is a solid-aggressive player. He doesn't play as many tournaments as a lot of other pros on the circuit, but when he does, watch out! In 2004, at seventy-one years old, Doyle won a World Poker Tour championship event at the Bicycle Club that paid over $1,000,000. Against a huge field of over six hundred players—most of them younger— and in an event that lasted for several days, his win was phenomenal.

Brunson's reading ability is uncanny. We've seen him pick off hands where, no matter which two cards he held, Doyle knew the other player didn't have a hand and made him fold by moving in on him. Doyle once said that if he had the button on every hand, he could beat any hold'em game in the world without looking at his cards, as long as his opponents didn't know he hadn't seen his hole cards. We believe him. In fact we think he might be able to do it even without having the button on every hand!

Another solid-aggressive player who deserves mention is Dewey Tomko. Tom thinks that Dewey's style most closely resembles his own. Dewey has come in second twice in the World Series of Poker championship event, but could very well have won them both had it not been for the fickle finger of fate. He lost the title to Jack Straus in 1982 when a cruel river card beat him. In 2001, history repeated itself and Dewey had pocket aces but lost when the river card made a straight for Carlos Mortensen.

Other world-class solid-aggressive players who regularly appear in televised tournaments include: World Champions Chris Ferguson and Dan Harrington; Howard "The Professor" Lederer; world-renowned player Chip Reese; and the premier women of poker, Annie Duke and Jennifer Harman.

PROGRESSIVELY AGGRESSIVE STYLE OF PLAY

This style is somewhat similar to the solid-aggressive approach with a few modifications. The progressively aggressive player plans to survive the first four or five levels of the tournament, hopefully doubling-up but not playing a whole lot of hands. He is not pushing his hands as much as some of his opponents are willing to do. The idea is to make a few plays here and there in order to survive, but not to overdo it.

As soon as the blinds and antes start to get higher, the progressively aggressive player will open up his game and take more chances. This sudden switching of gears often takes his opponents by surprise and before you know it, he has picked up a few extra pots. If he has accumulated a lot of chips and established a strong table image, he'll be prepared to capitalize on that image. He will raise a lot more hands, and occasionally reraise to take hands away from his opponents.

If you are playing against a progressively aggressive opponent and you notice his change in play, don't fall into the trap of saying to yourself, "Wow, what a rush!" Just wait for the right moment to use his tactics against him by reraising or check-raising on the flop.

Be prepared to switch gears in order to react appropriately to your opponents' current styles. You want to make a progressively aggressive player revert to his normal game. Then you can step up your game and play more aggressively, and later you switch back to your normal style. As soon as you think your opponents have figured you out, change gears.

Remember that your goal is always to make the top three spots at the final table. Nobody gets all the cards they need to put them among the final three players in a tournament. You'll have to read your opponents properly and mix up your play.

T.J. Cloutier fits the profile of a progressively aggressive player to a tee. If he gets knocked out early, it is usually with a legitimate hand that he just got unlucky with. Sometimes his name alone wins some pots; players will lay down hands to T.J. because they don't want to go up against him. "Uh oh," they think, "here comes T.J. He must have a heckuva hand, and he probably has me beat." Because he is physically imposing, in addition to his tremendous tournament talent and record, T.J. can intimidate opponents with his physical attributes alone.

UNPREDICTABLE STYLE OF PLAY

This style of play can be used to win tournaments, no doubt about it. Three players in particular have had tremendous success with an unpredictable style of play: Gus Hansen, Daniel Negreanu, and David "Devilfish" Ulliott. They are all known for entering the pot with a wide variety of hands, an uncanny ability to put their opponents on the right hands, and disguising the strength of their own hands.

An unpredictable player will play a wide variety of hands, often out of position. His play might make you think he is a maniac, but put that thought aside—there is a method to his madness. Because Gus Hansen plays off the wall with unpredictable hands, he is virtually impossible to read. If he gets there with a weird hand, he'll often get paid off, in part because of his style of betting. To television audiences, it looks as though "The Great Dane" is unwilling to throw anything away. It appears as though Gus believes that he can outplay everybody—and he has often done exactly that.

In an interview with Allyn Shulman in *Card Player* magazine, Hansen said, "I am definitely more aggressive than most players, but I have a different philosophy about my game. My outlook is a little more from a mathematical perspective. Other players rely too much on their instincts and reading abilities. Sometimes they allow that to overshadow the mathematical truth. Usually I let the math do its thing. On TV, they show something I did that was unconventional, making it look like I always play like a wild man. But part of my success is that people always know I will call."

His success in WPT tournaments is a testament to his prowess as a player. He won the final hand of the 2004 PokerStars.com WPT championship event with a 7-3 offsuit, a hand that any "sane" player would not normally get involved with for even half a bet in the small blind.

Unpredictable players can seem to be super-aggressive, and often they are, but with several unpleasant twists to confuse the opposition. Daniel Negreanu is a super-aggressive and unpredictable player who is truly amazing to watch when he gets a lot of chips. With his unpredictable style, he can outplay and dominate the table like nobody else. Daniel also plays a medium and short stack very well late in the tournament. Even if he does not have superior chip position, he knows when to move his chips and when to use his survival skills. He calls a lot of raises from late position, and for good reason. If he thinks his opponent doesn't have a big pair, he will often be willing to play with him, no matter what cards show up on the flop. In 2004, Daniel Negreanu was the top-ranked tournament player in the world.

David "Devilfish" Ulliott is another unpredictable player who is absolutely fearless. When he is ready to gamble, he will put you to the test and make you gamble. This often forces the opposition to back down with anything less than a big pair before the flop. A lot of times, David will make a play on the flop with only a draw. He'll put his opponents all-in, which makes it very difficult for them to call unless they have made a big hand on the flop. When David gets a premium hand, he often gets played with because he gives so much action himself. He has an amazing ability to accumulate chips early and steamroll the competition.

One added comment: All three of these fine gentlemen often crash and burn early with their unpredictable and aggressive tactics. But once they get chips, watch out!

CONSERVATIVE STYLE OF PLAY

Conservative players are predictable in their tournament strategy. If you are playing against one of them, you'll notice that dust is gathering on his chips. Then all of a sudden, he raises and guess what? He has A-A, K-K, Q-Q, or A-K. If he gets a free flop in the big blind, the conservative player will seldom bet unless he has two pair or better. Conservative players are not there to gamble; they are simply hoping to get action on their big hands. And if they do get action, they can go deep into the tournament.

This type of player is often called a rock. Do not give a rock any action unless you have a very big hand yourself. You can steal a conservative player's blinds almost at will, and eventually he will be anted and blinded out of the tournament, because he won't catch enough big hands to stay alive. Even when he does catch a good run of cards, he won't get much action on them if his opponents are paying attention.

Tight players don't win tournaments. Occasionally they will make the money, and maybe even a final table, but don't look for them at the top of the money ladder.

CHARACTERISTICS OF GREAT NO-LIMIT HOLD'EM PLAYERS

People often ask us, "What makes a great no-limit hold'em player?" The following is a list of characteristics we believe great no-limit hold'em tournament players possess. Read this section carefully and practice these traits. They will help your tournament game immensely.

Hand Reading Ability

Great no-limit hold'em players spend many hours studying other players, fine-tuning their ability to put their opponents on a certain hand before flop. If necessary, they are flexible enough to change their initial read after the flop, on the turn, and on the river. Great players also know where they stand versus the opposition by carefully evaluating the boardcards. They keep close tabs on how each hand is played and who did what in which situations—whether they are in a hand or not.

Knowledge of Big-Bet Poker Mathematics

Being a great reader isn't enough. You have to know the math and how to apply it to different situations. Some expert players are formally trained mathematicians, while others have not received much if any formal education. But they all understand the odds and how to apply them when deciding whether to bet, call, or raise. Great players also know when to fold even the best starting hands when the pot odds are not in their favor.

A Feel for Betting

The best players know how much to bet when they want you to call, and they have a feel for how much to bet if they want you to lay down a hand. They are experts at increasing the probability of being called by value-betting.

354

When great players take their time before betting, they are reviewing the hand and deciding how much to bet. They are like topnotch salespeople—they know how to sell a hand.

Discipline

Great players don't go on tilt. They are even-tempered at the table and have the ability to shrug off bad beats without throwing their games off track. They don't beat themselves up if they misplay a hand. They might go for a walk to regain their composure or they may just laugh it off, but they get back into the great-player mode very quickly.

Ability to Adjust and Maneuver

Champions can adjust their play according to their chip position and the current table conditions at any time during a tournament. Their ultimate goal is to win the tournament, or at least to make it to the final three players because they know that's where the big money is.

Constant Self-Evaluation

Top players have the ability to recognize their own weaknesses and are willing to work on them in order to become even better players. They are true students of the game and are always open to learning new things.

"I enjoy the challenge of playing with the best," Jennifer Harman said in *Poker Aces*. "It's a constant learning experience. I make mistakes, but as long as I learn something from those mistakes, they can actually be good for me."

Class

True champions are gracious in victory or defeat. When they get lucky and put a beat on another player, they'll say something like, "I sure got lucky on that one." And if another player puts a beat on them, they don't bemoan their fate or go ballistic and berate their opponent's play. They are perfect ladies and gentlemen at the table, not exhibitionists.

Remember that when you win, someone else loses. Losers feel bad, especially when they lose a big pot at a crucial time in a tournament. It is our opinion that we all must act with proper decorum when we beat an opponent. Just a simple, "You played well" will do. Having class at the table will increase your stature in the poker community.

In a *Card Player* magazine interview with Allyn Shulman, Annie Duke had this to say about table demeanor in poker: "I have noticed that some of the less-experienced players … play up to the cameras in a way that is disrespectful to the other players. I can't stand excessive celebration. That loss by one player might cripple his tournament dream. It's not the first or last pot won or lost. At one time or another, everyone will be on the losing end of a pot. Excessive celebration is so inappropriate. A player who knocks out someone should be classy and shake the opponent's hand, and then celebrate. That's how you take care of business."

CONCLUSION

Now that we have presented you with the basic strategies for winning no-limit hold'em tournaments, we suggest that you adapt our advice to your own style of play. Maybe you'd prefer a slightly more aggressive version of our classic strategy, or perhaps you'd rather take it more slowly, sharpening your skills in low-limit tournaments.

Whatever your personal preference, we hope that you have gained enough valuable information from *How to Win No-Limit Texas Hold'em Tournaments* to attain your poker goals. If so, then we have done our job in this book. And, as Tom likes to say, we hope to meet you one day soon in the winner's circle.

Glossary

Add on— The final rebuy that you can make at the end of the rebuy period in rebuy tournaments. "I only add on when I think that it will make my stack more competitive."

All in— Betting all the chips or cash you have left in your stack. "When T.J. raised, I went all in with pocket kings. Unfortunately, he called my all-in bet with pocket aces and sent me to the rail."

Behind you (sitting)— Any player who can act after you do. "Sometimes, before you make a move to try to steal the pot, look to see who is sitting behind you."

Bluff— Betting with an inferior hand in the hope of stealing the pot. "The cowboy's bluff with nothing-cards drove Alto out of the pot at the championship table in 1984."

Bully— A player who raises a lot of pots in an effort to make other players fold their hands. "My opponents weren't going to be easily bullied, so I didn't want to do a lot of aggressive raising."

Buy-in— The amount of money it costs you to enter a tournament. Usually, the larger the buy-in, the tougher the competition. "I wanted to buy into the championship event, but the buy-in was about $9,000 more than I could afford."

Case (ace)— The last card of that rank in the deck. "When the case ace came on the river, Dana made a full house to beat Tom's nut flush."

Case chips— Your last chips. "It took my case chips to call Sexton's raise on the river."

Change gears— Shifting your level of aggressiveness from low gear all the way up to high gear, as though you were changing gears while driving a car. "I had to slow down and change gears in order to survive the late stage of the Four Queens Classic championship event."

Check— You choose not to bet. If someone sitting behind you bets, you must either call the bet, raise, or fold your cards. "When everybody checked the flop to Amir, he raised with a 7-6 offsuit. They all folded, and he scooped in the pot."

Check-raise— You check with a good hand in the hope of raising if someone bets. "After the flop, Daniel checked to Jeff, who made a modest bet. Daniel then check-raised him with pocket aces."

Chip status— A comparison of the amount of chips you have in relation to how many chips your opponents have. "At the start of the 2000 World Series of Poker championship table, T.J. was dead last in chip status. He moved up four spot to finish second to Chris Ferguson."

Cold call— Call a raise without having already put the initial bet into the pot. "When Jack cold called after Tuna reraised, Brad knew he was in trouble."

Come over the top— Raise or reraise an opponent's bet. "Some players like to come over the top to try to steal the pot."

Commit— Put in so many chips that you cannot turn back. You're going to play your hand to the river. "If I think the odds are in my favor, I will fully commit."

Counterfeit— The board pairs your key low card in Omaha high-low, demoting the value of your hand. "My A-2-6-Q got counterfeited when the board came 2-4-J."

Dog— Poker slang meaning that your hand is the underdog. "When I looked at Catherine's two kings at the showdown, I knew that my 10-9 offsuit was a big dog."

Double through— Going all-in against an opponent in order to double your stack if you win the hand. "I was so low on chips, I knew I had to double through somebody to build up my stack."

Flat call— Call an opponent's bet rather than raising. "Trying to trap Don, I just flat called the raise with my trip nines."

Get away from your hand— To decide it isn't worth it to play a hand and fold. "After Tight Ted reraised, I decided to get away from my hand."

Get full value— Betting, raising and reraising in order to manipulate the size of the pot so that you'll be getting maximum pot odds if you win the hand. "After raising on every round, I was able to get full value when my hand held up on the river."

Get the right price— The odds are mathematically favorable for calling. "After six players limped into the pot, Tom was getting the right price to call the extra $25 from the small blind."

Get there— Make your hand. "What happens when you don't get there, when you miss your hand? You cry a little."

Give action— Betting, calling, raising or reraising. Also, giving someone a gamble. "Be cautious about giving too much action if your kicker is weak."

Give up your hand— Fold. "I gave up my hand when he raised."

Gutshot— The card that completes an inside-straight draw. If you hold a 9-8 and the board is showing 10-6-2, you need a 7 to complete the straight. "In the small blind, I was all in with a 9-8. On the 10-6-2 flop, I had a gutshot draw at a straight. The 7 on the river made my day!"

Ignorant end— The low end of a straight. If you have a 6-5 in your hand and the board cards are showing 9-8-7, you have the lower of two possible straights. The common axiom in poker is to avoid drawing to a lower straight when a higher one also is possible. "I got punished by a higher straight when I drew to the ignorant end of it. Then I kicked myself for making such an elementary blunder."

In the dark— You don't look at your hole cards. "Tuna was so low on chips when he bet, Jack called him in the dark."

Kamikaze— A very aggressive player. Someone who seems to just close his eyes and shove his chips into the pot. "When the kamikaze in seat four capped the pot, my cards flew into the muck."

Key Card— The one card that will make your hand. "I knew I needed to catch a deuce, the key card I needed to win."

Key Hand— The hand in a tournament that proves to be a turning point, for better or worse. "There is usually one key hand which, if you make it, will win the tournament for you. Unfortunately, it also goes the other way."

Kicker— The sidecard you hold in hold'em, the strength of which often determines who wins in a showdown. "I had a gorgeous hand, an A-Q with an ace showing on the board. But my beauty turned into a beast when Dana showed her A-K at the river to beat me with a better kicker."

Lay down your hand— Fold. "Sometimes you have to lay down your hand because it gets too expensive to play it."

Lead— You are the first one to enter the pot. "Jack loves to lead into the raiser from the blind."

Level— In tournaments, the round that you are playing. A tournament level is defined by the size of the blinds. "At the $50-$100 level, I had only $800 in chips."

Limp (in)— Enter the pot for the minimum bet (the size of the big blind). "You might decide to just limp in with a pair of jacks and see the flop cheaply."

Limper— A player who enters a pot for the minimum bet. "With two limpers in the pot, a pair of jacks should be your minimum raising hand."

Make a move— Try to bluff. "When Phil made a move at the pot, Huck called him down."

Maniac— A very aggressive player who sometimes plays hands his more sensible or conservative opponents would not consider. "Maniacs sometimes crash and burn earlier than they should in tournament play."

Mini-raise— In no-limit hold'em, you raise the minimum amount allowed, which is double the size of the big blind. "When Nguyen made a mini-raise from up front, I wondered whether he was trying to disguise a big hand, or just wanted to get into the pot cheaply."

Nuts— The best possible hand. "Nani won the pot when the A♥ fell on the river, giving her the nut flush."

On-Land Tournament— A tournament that is played in a traditional land-based casino such as Foxwoods in Connecticut. "When online poker whiz Chris Moneymaker won the World Championship of Poker in 2003, it was the first time he had ever played in an on-land tournament."

Online Tournament— A tournament that is hosted by an Internet cardroom such as UltimateBet.com. "Yesterday I played a PartyPoker.com online tournament on my laptop while I was lounging poolside at the Golden Nugget."

Out(s)— Cards that will improve your hand. "When they turned their cards face up on the turn, Duane showed three kings and Peggy showed trip aces. 'I only have one out to win,' Duane lamented."

Overbet— You make a raise in no-limit hold'em that is larger than normal. "Some new players who don't understand how much to bet in no-limit hold'em often overbet the pot."

Payout— The prize distribution in a tournament. "The payout for first place was 38 percent of the prize pool."

Play back— Responding to an opponent's bet by either raising or reraising. "If a tight opponent plays back at you, you know he probably holds the nuts."

Play fast— Always betting or raising. "Many players play fast in the early rounds of rebuy tournaments to try to build their stacks."

Play with— Staying in the hand by betting, calling, raising, or reraising. "I wasn't sure exactly where he was at, so I decided to play with him on the turn."

Position (chip position)— How your chip stack compares to the stacks of your opponents. "Going into the final two tables, Brad was in tenth chip position. Then he went on a rush and wound up winning the whole enchilada."

Position (table position)— Where you are sitting in relation to the big blind. For example, if you are sitting one seat to the left of the big blind, you are in first position. "Eric was sitting in middle position with a K-J offsuit when Phil raised from a front position. Figuring Phil for a stronger hand than K-J, Eric wisely folded."

Position (have position on)— You can act after someone else acts. For example, if you are sitting on the button in a hold'em game, you have position on your opponents. "I limped into the pot because Mad Max had position on me and I didn't want to get into too much trouble in case he decided to raise."

Positional raise— A raise that is based more on a player's table position than on the value of his cards. "Sure, I admit that it was just a positional raise, but it seemed right at the time."

Pot-logged— You have so many of your chips already invested in the pot that you are committed to going to the river with your hand. "When I called Dewey's reraise, I knew I'd be going all the way with my hand. What else could I do? By then, I was pot-logged."

Rag (or blank)— A card that doesn't help you. "The next card was a 4, a total blank."

Ragged(y) flop— The cards in the flop are ones that do not appear to be able to help anyone's hand; i.e., there are no straight, flush, face cards, or pairs on board. "When the flop came raggedy with a 7-4-2, I knew Tight Ted didn't have any part of it."

Rail— The place from which spectators and losers watch the action. "When Brad made his flush at the river to beat my set of aces, I was forced to join the other losers on the rail."

Raise— Increase the bet. In limit hold'em, the amount that you can raise is prescribed, but in no-limit hold'em, you can raise any amount you want so long as you raise at least twice the size of the big blind. "When you get to the final table, you seldom just call. It's either raise or fold."

Read (your opponents)— You can determine what your opponent is holding, or the significance of his betting strategy. "His play was so erratic, it was hard to get a read on him."

Read (the board)— You have an understanding of how the board cards in hold'em relate to your hole cards. "You must be able to read the board well enough to tell whether you have the nuts or nothing at all, whether you have 16 outs or no outs."

Rebuy— In rebuy tournaments, you can add chips to your stack by rebuying during a specified time period. "Before the end of the rebuy period, I had made three rebuys."

Reraise— Raise the player who raised you. Sometimes there is more than one reraise during a hand. When the maximum number of reraises have been made, the pot has been capped. "Tom knew that Brad was trying to steal his blind by raising from the button, so he reraised him in defense."

Ring game— A cash game, not a tournament. "The side action ring games during tournaments can be lucrative."

Rise— A term that refers to the increase of the blinds at the start of a new round or level of a tournament. "I knew the blinds would rise in three minutes, so I played a marginal hand while they were still at the lower amounts."

Rock— A very conservative player who always waits for premium cards before he plays a hand. "Smith was playing like a rock, so when she bet into me, I knew she had me beat."

Round— Every time the button goes completely around the table. "I just sat through three dry rounds where I had to fold every hand."

Run over— Playing aggressively in an attempt to control the other players. "Everyone was playing scared trying to make the money, so it was easy for Daniel to run over them."

Rush— A winning streak during which you might win four out of six hands, for example. "Robert is one lucky so-and-so. If he hadn't gone on that rush at the final table, I would've busted him in eight place."

Satellite— A preliminary tournament in which you can win a seat for a more expensive tournament. "Brad won an $80 buy-in satellite online at PokerStars.com that awarded an entry into a $650 buy-in super satellite." To be continued: see "super satellite."

Semi-bluff— You bet with a hand that probably isn't the best one at the moment, but which has a chance of improving. If everyone folds, your semi-bluff wins the pot for you; if someone calls, you still have a decent chance of winning. "Don's semi-bluff bet with only two overcards to the flop paid off when he caught an ace on the turn."

Slow down— Discontinue playing aggressively. "If Maniac Mike doesn't slow down in the late stage and start playing more conservatively, he's probably going to lose all those tournament chips he won with his early, aggressive play."

Smooth-call— You call rather than raise an opponent's bet. "Herb smooth-called me on the flop, but raised on the turn with his trip jacks."

Solid (player)— A well-grounded player who has a thorough understanding of the game and plays it at a superior level. "You can depend on Knox to never get out of line. He's a solid player who always knows where he's at in a hand."

Splash around— Playing a lot of pots. "Loose Louie splashed around too much with a big chip lead and went broke."

Stack— All of your chips. "I just don't have the temperament to play no-limit hold'em," Timid Tony said. "I can't bear the thought of possibly losing my whole stack at one time."

Stage— A tournament term that refers to a particular period during a tournament. Players usually think of a tournament as having an early stage (the first three rounds), a middle stage (when about half the field has been eliminated), and a late stage, when only about three or four tables are left in action (out of a starting field of 40 tables, for example). "I caught three premium hands in the middle stage of the tournament, but I just couldn't hang onto them and bombed out in the late stage about three places out of the money."

Super Satellite— A preliminary tournament in which you can win a seat for a major tournament. Super satellites usually have 10 or more tables of players, and award as many seats into the main event as the satellite prize pool will cover. "After winning a smaller satellite, Brad won the big super satellite and was awarded a Caribbean cruise plus entry into the $8,000 main tournament on board ship. What a life!"

Survival (mode)— Fighting to say alive in a tournament when you are very shortstacked. "It was against my basic nature to shift into survival mode," Action Al said, "but I wanted to hang on long enough to give myself a chance to get lucky, as Tom McEvoy advised in his book, Championship Tournament Poker."

Take off a card— Calling a single bet in order to see one more card. "Tuna decided to take off a card to see if he could hit his inside-straight draw."

Tell— A playing habit or personal mannerism that a player consistently displays that enables his opponents to tell what he is holding or what he is likely to do during the play of a hand. "I noticed that every time Jake the Snake raised from early position with a weak hand, he sort of wobbled his chips into the pot, so I used his tell against him and reraised."

Throw away (a hand)— Fold. "If Action Al raises from middle position, you might call with a K-Q, but if Solid Sam raises, you're probably better off to throw your hand away."

Throwing a party— Several loose or amateur players are making significant monetary contributions to the game. "You have to stay in the game when they're throwing a party."

Trap— You play deceptively in order to induce an unwise response from your opponent(s). "When Devious David limped into the pot from first position, I could small a trap. Turns out I was right: Loose Louie raised and David come over the top for all his chips."

Wake up with a hand— You are dealt a hand with winning potential. "It looked to me like Daugherty woke up with a hand in the small blind."

Where you're at— You know the value of your hand compared to your opponent's hand. "Hamid may have raised just to find out where he was at."

World's fair— A very big hand. "Suppose the flop comes with 8-8-4 in different suits. You know you're either up against nothing or the world's fair."

POWERFUL POKER SIMULATIONS
A MUST FOR SERIOUS PLAYERS WITH A COMPUTER!
IBM compatibles CD ROM Win 95, 98, 2000, NT, ME, XP - Full Color Graphics

These incredible full color poker simulation programs are the absolute best method to improve your game. Computer opponents play like real players. All games let you set the limits and rake, have fully programmable players, adjustable lineup, stat tracking, and Hand Analyzer for starting hands. MIke Caro, the world's foremost poker theoretician says, "Amazing...a steal for under $500...get it, it's great." Includes free telephone support. "Smart Advisor" gives expert advice for every play in every game!

NEW!
Windows Versions
More Features!

1. TURBO TEXAS HOLD'EM FOR WINDOWS - $89.95 - Choose which players, how many, 2-10, you want to play, create loose/tight game, control check-raising, bluffing, position, sensitivity to pot odds, more! Also, instant replay, pop-up odds, Professional Advisor, keeps track of play statistics. Free bonus: Hold'em Hand Analyzer analyzes all 169 pocket hands in detail, their win rates under any conditions you set. Caro says this "hold'em software is the most powerful ever created." Great product!

2. TURBO SEVEN-CARD STUD FOR WINDOWS - $89.95 - Create any conditions of play; choose number of players (2-8), bet amounts, fixed or spread limit, bring-in method, tight/loose conditions, position, reaction to board, number of dead cards, stack deck to create special conditions, instant replay. Terrific stat reporting includes analysis of starting cards, 3-D bar charts, graphs. Play interactively, run high speed simulation to test strategies. Hand Analyzer analyzes starting hands in detail. Wow!

3. TURBO OMAHA HIGH-LOW SPLIT FOR WINDOWS - $89.95 -Specify any playing conditions; betting limits, number of raises, blind structures, button position, aggressiveness/passiveness of opponents, number of players (2-10), types of hands dealt, blinds, position, board reaction, specify flop, turn, river cards! Choose opponents, use provided point count or create your own. Statistical reporting, instant replay, pop-up odds, high speed simulation to test strategies, amazing Hand Analyzer, much more!

4. TURBO OMAHA HIGH FOR WINDOWS - $89.95 Same features as above, but tailored for Omaha High-only. Caro says program is "an electrifying research tool...it can clearly be worth thousands of dollars to any serious player. A must for Omaha High players.

5. TURBO 7 STUD 8 OR BETTER - $89.95 - Brand new with all the features you expect from the Wilson Turbo products: the latest artificial intelligence, instant advice and exact odds, play versus 2-7 opponents, enhanced data charts that can be exported or printed, the ability to fold out of turn and immediately go to the next hand, ability to peek at opponents hand, optional warning mode that warns you if a play disagrees with the advisor, and automatic testing mode that can run up to 50 tests unattended. Challenge tough computer players who vary their styles for a truly great poker game.

6. TOURNAMENT TEXAS HOLD'EM - $59.95
Set-up for tournament practice and play, this realistic simulation pits you against celebrity look-alikes. Tons of options let you control tournament size with 10 to 300 entrants, select limits, ante, rake, blind structures, freezeouts, number of rebuys and competition level of opponents - average, tough, or toughest. Pop-up status report shows how you're doing vs. the competition. Save tournaments in progress to play again later. Additional feature allows you to quickly finish a folded hand and go on to the next.

FROM CARDOZA'S EXCITING LIBRARY
ADD THESE TO YOUR COLLECTION - ORDER NOW!

POKER WISDOM OF A CHAMPION by Doyle Brunson. Learn what it takes to be a great poker player by climbing inside the mind of poker's most famous champion. Fascinating anecdotes and adventures from Doyle's early career playing poker in roadhouses and with other great champions are interspersed with important lessons you can learn from the champion who has made more money at poker than anyone else in the history of the game. You'll learn what makes a great player tick, how he approaches the game, and receive candid, powerful advice from the legend himself. The Mad Genius of poker, Mike Caro, says, "Brunson is the greatest poker player who ever lived. This book shows why." 192 pages. $14.95.

CARO'S BOOK OF POKER TELLS by Mike Caro. The classic book is now revised and back in print! This long-awaited brand new edition by the Mad Genius of Poker, takes a detailed look at the art and science of tells, the physical giveaways by players on their hands. Featuring photos of poker players in action along with Caro's explanations about when players are bluffing and when they're not. These powerful eye-opening ideas can give you the decisive edge at the table! This invaluable book should be in every player's library! 320 pages. $24.95.

KEN WARREN TEACHES TEXAS HOLD'EM by Ken Warren. This is a step-by-step comprehensive manual for making money at hold'em poker. 42 powerful chapters will teach you one lesson at a time. Great practical advice and concepts with examples from actual games and how to apply them to your own play. Lessons include: Starting Cards, Playing Position, Which Hands to Play, Raising, Check-raising, Tells, Game/Seat Selection, Dominated Hands, Odds, and much more. This book is already a huge fan favorite and best-seller! 416 pages. $26.95.

WINNERS GUIDE TO TEXAS HOLD'EM POKER by Ken Warren. The most powerful book on beating hold'em shows serious players how to play every hand from every position with every type of flop. Learn the 14 categories of starting hands, the 10 most common hold'em tells, how to evaluate a game for profit, value of deception, art of bluffing, eight secrets to winning, starting hand categories, position, and more! Bonus: Includes detailed analysis of the top 40 hands and the most complete chapter on hold'em odds in print. Over 500,000 copies in print. 224 pages. $16.95.

THE BIG BOOK OF POKER by Ken Warren. This easy-to-read and oversized guide teaches you everything you need to know to win money at home poker, in cardrooms, casinos and on the tournament circuit. Readers will learn how to bet, raise, and checkraise, bluff, semi-bluff, and how to take advantage of position and pot odds. Great sections on hold'em (plus, stud games, Omaha, draw games, and many more) and playing and winning poker on the internet. Packed with charts, diagrams, sidebars, and detailed, easy-to-read examples by best-selling poker expert Ken Warren, this wonderfully formatted book is one stop shopping for players ready to take on any form of poker for real money. Want to be a big player? Buy the *Big Book of Poker*! 320 oversized pages. $19.95.

HOW TO PLAY WINNING POKER by Avery Cardoza. New and expanded edition shows playing and winning strategies for all major games: 5 and 7-stud games, Omaha, draw poker, hold'em, and high-low, both for home and casino play. You'll learn 15 winning poker concepts, how to minimize losses and maximize profits, how to read opponents and gain the edge against their style, how to use use pot odds, tells, position, more. 160 pages. $12.95.

FROM CARDOZA'S EXCITING LIBRARY
ADD THESE TO YOUR COLLECTION - ORDER NOW!

COWBOYS, GAMBLERS & HUSTLERS: The True Adventures of a Rodeo Champion & Poker Legend by Byron "Cowboy" Wolford. Ride along with the road gamblers as they fade the white line from Dallas to Shreveport to Houston in the 1960s in search of a score. Feel the fear and frustration of being hijacked, getting arrested for playing poker, and having to outwit card sharps and scam artists. Wolford survived it all to win a WSOP gold bracelet playing with poker greats Amarillo Slim Preston, Johnny Moss and Bobby Baldwin (and 30 rodeo belt buckles). Read fascinating yarns about life on the rough and tumble, and colorful adventures as a road gambler and hustler gambling in smoky backrooms with legends Titanic Thompson, Jack Straus, Doyle Brunson and get a look at vintage Las Vegas when Cowboy's friend, Benny Binion ruled Glitter Gulch. Read about the most famous bluff in WSOP history. Endorsed by Jack Binion, Doyle Brunson and Bobby Baldwin, who says, Cowboy is probably the best gambling story teller in the world. 304 pages, $19.95.

SECRETS OF WINNING POKER by Tex Sheahan. This is a compilation of Sheahan's best articles from 15 years of writing for the major gaming magazines as his legacy to poker players. Sheahan gives you sound advice on winning poker strategies for hold'em and 7-card stud. Chapters on tournament play, psychology, personality profiles and some very funny stories from the greenfelt jungle. "Some of the best advice you'll ever read on how to win at poker" --Doyle Brunson. 200 pages, paperback. $19.95.

OMAHA HI-LO: Play to Win with the Odds by Bill Boston. Selecting the right hands to play is the most important decision you'll make in Omaha high-low poker. In this book you'll find the odds for every hand dealt in Omaha high-low—the chances that the hand has of winning the high end of the pot, the low end of it, and how often it is expected to scoop the whole pot. The results are based on 10,000 simulations for each one of the possible 5,211 Omaha high-low hands. Boston has organized the data into an easy-to-use format and added insights learned from years of experience. Learn the 5,211 Omaha high-low hands, the 49 best hands and their odds, the 49 worst hands, trap hands to avoid, and 30 Ace-less hands you can play for profit. A great tool for Omaha players! 156 pages, $19.95.

OMAHA HI-LO POKER (8 OR BETTER): How to win at the lower limits by Shane Smith. Since its first printing in 1991, this has become the classic in the field for low-limit players. Readers have lauded the author's clear and concise writing style. Smith shows you how to put players on hands, read the board for high and low, avoid dangerous draws, and use winning betting strategies. Chapters include starting hands, the flop, the turn, the river, and tournament strategy. Illustrated with pictorials of sample hands, an odds chart, and a starting hands chart. Lou Krieger, author of *Poker for Dummies*, says, Shane Smith's book is terrific! If you're new to Omaha high-low split or if you're a low-limit player who wants to improve your game, you ought to have this book in your poker library. Complex concepts are presented in an easy-to-understand format. It's a gem! 82 pages, spiralbound. $17.95.

THE WACKY SIDE OF POKER by Ralph E. Wheeler. Take a walk on the wacky side with 88 humorous poker cartoons! Also includes 220 wise and witty poker quotes. Lighten up from all the heavy reading and preparation of the games with a quick walk through this fun book. Perfect for a holiday gift. 176 pages filled with wit and wisdom will bring a smile to your face. At less than a ten-spot, you can't go wrong! 176 pages, $11.95.

THE CHAMPIONSHIP SERIES
POWERFUL BOOKS YOU MUST HAVE

CHAMPIONSHIP OMAHA (Omaha High-Low, Pot-limit Omaha, Limit High Omaha) by Tom McEvoy & T.J. Cloutier. Clearly-written strategies and powerful advice from Cloutier and McEvoy who have won four World Series of Poker titles in Omaha tournaments. Powerful advice shows you how to win at low-limit and high-stakes games, how to play against loose and tight opponents, and the differing strategies for rebuy and freezeout tournaments. Learn the best starting hands, when slowplaying a big hand is dangerous, what danglers are and why winners don't play them, why pot-limit Omaha is the only poker game where you sometimes fold the nuts on the flop and are correct in doing so and overall, and how you can win a lot of money at Omaha! 300 pages, photos, illustrations, $39.95. Now only $29.95!

CHAMPIONSHIP STUD (Seven-Card Stud, Stud 8/or Better and Razz) by Dr. Max Stern, Linda Johnson, and Tom McEvoy. The authors, who have earned millions of dollars in major tournaments and cash games, eight World Series of Poker bracelets and hundreds of other titles in competition against the best players in the world show you the winning strategies for medium-limit side games as well as poker tournaments and a general tournament strategy that is applicable to any form of poker. Includes give-and-take conversations between the authors to give you more than one point of view on how to play poker. 200 pages, hand pictorials, photos. $39.95.

CHAMPIONSHIP HOLD'EM by Tom McEvoy & T.J. Cloutier. Hard-hitting hold'em the way it's played today in both limit cash games and tournaments. Get killer advice on how to win more money in rammin'-jammin' games, kill-pot, jackpot, shorthanded, and other types of cash games. You'll learn the thinking process before the flop, on the flop, on the turn, and at the river with specific suggestions for what to do when good or bad things happen plus 20 illustrated hands with play-by-play analyses. Specific advice for rocks in tight games, weaklings in loose games, experts in solid games, how hand values change in jackpot games, when you should fold, check, raise, reraise, check-raise, slowplay, bluff, and tournament strategies for small buy-in, big buy-in, rebuy, incremental add-on, satellite and big-field major tournaments. Wow! Easy-to-read and conversational, if you want to become a lifelong winner at limit hold'em, you need this book! 388 Pages, Illustrated, Photos. $39.95. Now only $29.95!

CHAMPIONSHIP NO-LIMIT & POT-LIMIT HOLD'EM by T.J. Cloutier & Tom McEvoy. New Cardoza Edition! The definitive guide to winning at two of the world's most exciting poker games! Written by eight time World Champion players T.J. Cloutier (1998 and 2002 Player of the Year) and Tom McEvoy (the foremost author on tournament strategy) who have won millions of dollars each playing no-limit and pot-limit hold'em in cash games and major tournaments around the world. You'll get all the answers here—no holds barred—to your most important questions: How do you get inside your opponents' heads and learn how to beat them at their own game? How can you tell how much to bet, raise, and reraise in no-limit hold'em? When can you bluff? How do you set up your opponents in pot-limit hold'em so you can win a monster pot? What are the best strategies for winning no-limit and pot-limit tournaments, satellites, and supersatellites? You get rock-solid and inspired advice from two of the most recognizable figures in poker—advice that you can bank on. If you want to become a winning player, and a champion, you must have this book. 304 pages, paperback, illustrations, photos. $29.95

THE CHAMPIONSHIP SERIES
POWERFUL BOOKS YOU MUST HAVE

CHAMPIONSHIP TOURNAMENT POKER by Tom McEvoy. New Cardoza Edition! Rated by pros as best book on tournaments ever written and enthusiastically endorsed by more than five world champions, this is the definitive guide to winning tournaments and a must for every player's library. McEvoy lets you in on the secrets he has used to win millions of dollars in tournaments and the insights he has learned competing against the best players in the world. Packed solid with winning strategies for all 11 games in the World Series of Poker, with extensive discussions of 7-card stud, limit hold'em, pot and no-limit hold'em, Omaha high-low, re-buy, half-half tournaments, satellites, and strategies for each stage of tournaments. Tons of essential concepts and specific strategies jam-pack the book. Phil Hellmuth, 1989 WSOP champion says, "[this] is the world's most definitive guide to winning poker tournaments." 416 pages, paperback, $29.95.

CHAMPIONSHIP TABLE (at the World Series of Poker) by Dana Smith, Ralph Wheeler, and Tom McEvoy. New Cardoza Edition! From 1970 when the champion was presented a silver cup, to the present when the champion was awarded more than $2 million, *Championship Table* celebrates three decades of poker greats who have competed to win poker's most coveted title. This book gives you the names and photographs of all the players who made the final table, pictures of the last hand the champion played against the runner-up, how they played their cards, and how much they won. This book also features fascinating interviews and conversations with the champions and runners-up and interesting highlights from each Series. This is a fascinating and invaluable resource book for WSOP and gaming buffs. In some cases the champion himself wrote "how it happened," as did two-time champion Doyle Brunson when Stu Ungar caught a wheel in 1980 on the turn to deprive "Texas Dolly" of his third title. Includes tons of vintage photographs. 208 pages, paperback, $19.95.

CHAMPIONSHIP WIN YOUR WAY INTO BIG MONEY HOLD'EM by Brad Dougherty & Tom McEvoy. In 2002 and 2003, satellite players won their way into the $10,000 WSOP buy-in and emerged as champions, winning more than $2 million each. You can too! You'll learn specific, proven strategies for winning almost any satellite. Learn the ten ways to win a seat at the WSOP and other big tournaments, how to win limit hold'em and no-limit hold'em satellites, one-table satellites for big tournaments, and online satellites, plus how to play the final table of super satellites. McEvoy and Daugherty sincerely believe that if you practice these strategies, you can win your way into any tournament for a fraction of the buy-in. You'll learn how much to bet, how hard to pressure opponents, how to tell when an opponent is bluffing, how to play deceptively, and how to use your chips as weapons of destruction. Includes a special chapter on no-limit hold'em satellites! 256 pages. Illustrated hands, photos, glossary. $24.95.

CHAMPIONSHIP HOLD'EM TOURNAMENT HANDS by T.J. Cloutier & Tom McEvoy. Two tournament legends show you how to become a winning tournament player. Get inside their heads as they think their way through the correct strategy at 57 limit and no-limit practice hands. Cloutier and McEvoy show you how to use your skill and intuition to play strategic hands for maximum profit in real tournament scenarios and how 45 key hands were played by champions in turnaround situations at the WSOP. By sharing their analysis on how the winners and losers played key hands, you'll gain tremendous insights into how tournament poker is played at the highest levels. Learn how champions think and how they play major hands in strategic tournament situations, Cloutier and McEvoy believe that you will be able to win your share of the profits in today's tournaments—and join them at the championship table far sooner than you ever imagined. 368 pages, illustrated with card pictures, $29.95

DOYLE BRUNSON'S SUPER SYSTEM
A COURSE IN POKER POWER!
by World Champion Doyle Brunson

CONSIDERED BY PROS THE BEST POKER BOOK EVER WRITTEN
This is the **classic** book on every major no-limit game played today and is considered by the pros to be one of the **best books ever written** on poker! **Jam-packed** with **advanced strategies**, theories, tactics and money-making techniques—no serious poker player can afford to be without this **essential** book! Hardbound, and packed with 624 pages of hard-hitting information, this is truly a **must-buy** for aspiring pros. Includes 50 pages of the most precise poker statistics ever published!

CHAPTERS WRITTEN BY GAME'S SUPERSTARS
The best theorists and poker players in the world, Dave Sklansky, Mike Caro, Chip Reese, Bobby Baldwin and Doyle Brunson, a book by champions for aspiring pros—cover the **essential** strategies and **advanced play** in their respective specialties. Three world champions and two master theorists and players provide non-nonsense winning advice on making money at the tables.

LEARN WINNING STRATEGIES FOR THE MAJOR POKER GAMES
The important money games today are covered in depth by these **poker superstars**. You'll learn seven-card stud, draw poker, lowball, seven-card low stud (razz), high-low split (cards speak) and high-low declare; and the most popular game in the country today, hold'em (limit and no-limit). Each game is covered in detail with the **important winning concepts** and strategies clearly explained so that anyone can become a **bigger money** winner.

SERIOUS POKER PLAYERS MUST HAVE THIS BOOK
This is **mandatory reading** for aspiring poker pros, players planning to enter tournaments, players ready to play no-limit. Doyle Brunson's Super System is also ideal for average players seeking to move to higher stakes games for bigger wins and more challenges.

To order, send $29.95 by check or money order to Cardoza Publishing

DOYLE BRUNSON'S SUPER SYSTEM 2
A COURSE IN POKER POWER!
by World Champion Doyle Brunson

Super System 2 gathers together the greatest players, theorists, and world champions and expands upon the original with more games, new authors, and most importantly, more professional secrets from the best in the business.

POKER'S GREATEST PLAYERS SHARE THEIR SECRETS
This superstar lineup is led by Doyle Brunson, two-time World Series of Poker Champion, nine-time WSOP gold bracelet winner, and the greatest poker player of all time. His hand-picked roster of expert collaborators includes: Daniel Negreanu, winner of multiple WSOP gold bracelets and 2004 Poker Player of the Year; Lyle Berman, three-time WSOP gold bracelet winner, founder of the World Poker Tour, and super-high stakes cash player; Bobby Baldwin, 1978 World Poker Champion and president of Bellagio; Johnny Chan, two-time World Poker Champion and nine-time WSOP gold bracelet winner; Mike Caro, poker's greatest researcher, theorist, and instructor; Jennifer Harman, the best female player in the history of poker and one of the ten best overall; Todd Brunson, winner of more than twenty tournaments; and Crandell Addington, a no-limit hold'em legend.

THE COMPLETE MASTERPIECE OF POKER
Together with the original *Super System*, hailed by professionals as the most influential book on poker ever written, this two-volume set comprises a full library of the best poker advice, strategies, and professional concepts ever published.

SERIOUS POKER PLAYERS MUST HAVE THIS BOOK
This is **mandatory reading** for aspiring poker pros, players planning to enter tournaments, and players ready to play no-limit. Doyle Brunson's *Super System 2* is also ideal for average players seeking to move to higher stakes games for more challenges and bigger wins.